WHOLEFOOD *for* CHILDREN

Nourishing young children
with whole and organic foods

Jude Blereau

Introduction

WHEN MY BEAUTIFUL BABY GIRL was placed in my arms some 27 years ago, I knew beyond a shadow of a doubt that I wanted to nourish her in every possible way—with good food to build a strong and sound body, and with love, beauty, laughter and joy to feed her soul. This was my primary instinct and overwhelming desire. At that time I was living a very busy life as a fashion designer and was only at the beginning of my wholefoods journey, but I had grown up in a family with a strong culture of real food and it was natural for me to continue this practice with my daughter. I made simple food to feed a growing baby and used some pre-made commercial food for convenience—with Mum standing by to advise me.

But now things are shifting, and many of today's young adults have not had the benefit of a mother (or father) at home who understands what good food is, and how to prepare it. Traditionally, this is something that is passed on from parent to child, from generation to generation and constitutes part of one's food culture.

Over the past 40 to 50 years, quietly and almost imperceptibly, this essential wealth of knowledge of one's food culture has been all but lost.

As a true child of the 60s and 70s I find this disturbing. While you might see me looking quite conservative these days, in my soul I'm still wearing Indian cotton dresses and flowers in my hair, I have pretty beads on my ankle and love listening to Neil Young. As young women we burned our bras and fought to have it all.

Our children are a gift and a blessing.
Me with my daughter Nessie, circa 1986.

But now, at 55, I find myself wondering about the legacy of that fight. I'm seeing a whole generation of young women whose mothers were out having that brilliant career—I had that brilliant career back in my fashion days, and I can tell you it's hard to come home after a day at the office and organise dinner for yourself, let alone for your children, day after day, week after week, year after year. Something always gives. We are in great danger of losing our most essential of wisdoms about food—what makes it good, how we cook and eat it, and the importance of deliciousness.

This push to have it all and have it now has created a profound disconnection that often seduces us into accepting pre-prepared, processed foods that promise health and convenience in one easy package. But such foods cannot provide the nutrients and goodness required to build and run a human body and soul. Without a strong food culture, it's easy to be sidetracked by such things as hiding or disguising vegetables to make them seem palatable to young children, rather than providing good, solid food fundamentals. It is these fundamentals, more than anything else, that will nourish young children and enable them to grow and bloom to their full potential.

The food culture handed to me by my mother could best be summed up as 'all things in moderation'. It has since been shaped by many other influences: the work of people such as Annemarie Colbin, whose book *Food and Healing* made so much more sense to me than the fractionalised approach to food I came across when I was studying nutrition; my early macrobiotic days; the incredible legacy of knowledge left by dentist Dr Weston Price, who documented happy, healthy traditional cultures; the ancient Ayurveda, the 5000-year-old practice of natural healing. And I'm still learning— Holly Davis and Jessica Prentice have recently taught me what I now know about lacto-fermentation, for example.

My food culture has also been shaped by the many mistakes I've made. It would be fair to say that in my earlier days I was extreme—I felt the only path was to be vegetarian, and even a touch vegan. After World War II, food production began to become highly industrialised, and the societal food culture pendulum swung strongly in that direction. It's my belief that the vegetarian, vegan and macrobiotic movements were the only way we baby boomers and flower children knew how to voice our sense that all was not well. While these movements had and still have much to offer, I have found their viewpoints on what makes food 'healthy' or not to be somewhat restricted. I remember my daughter telling me some years ago on Mother's Day how much she loved going to her Nonna's because she could have meat! It was an important lesson. I love the understanding I've arrived at now—I feel much more centred and grounded in my views and I'm very grateful to all who have helped form them. I have found that there is no 'one size fits all' philosophy, and it's generally not what a food is that makes it bad, but how it's grown and what we do with it. My food culture could now be best summed up as 'all things real and as little refined as possible, that are compatible with you, in moderation and balance'.

This book is concerned with nutrient-dense and delicious food for developing happy, healthy and strong children. I am still deeply moved by a picture I saw in a magazine some years ago of an old lady with two young children, presumably her grandchildren. They were walking towards a house with baskets full of blueberries, and, in my imagination, were anticipating the blueberry pie, cake or crumble to be made, eaten and enjoyed. It is a tragedy that today, in all probability, that pie—if indeed there even was a pie—would be bought from a supermarket or at best a 'pâtisserie' where most of the ingredients would be fake copies of the real things: manipulated refined oils rather than butter; colour and flavour instead of true berries; bits of plastic or wood to imitate the decorative berry seeds; and not much else. It is this 'food' that is failing to nourish, in every sense of the word, our children, our teenagers and our community.

My hope is that this book, in its own humble, small way, might hold back the rising numbers of overweight, unhappy and poorly nourished children. I'm hoping that I, and all who reside in its pages and from whom I've learnt so much, can join you in the kitchen as mother and friend, passing on some of the knowledge and wisdom that are at risk of being lost.

I look forward to seeing you there.

Jude X

NOURISHING *the* WHOLE CHILD

*Welcome to the world little one.
Before we begin to consider the
quality and role of food in nourishing
our children, it's important to
understand that we nourish them in
so many other and equally
valuable ways.*

Building your food culture

A FOOD CULTURE IS HOW WE THINK ABOUT and relate to food. It is shaped largely by two influencing factors: the societal food culture, and the personal food culture we nurture within our home. Of the two, our personal food culture is more important, as it embodies our accumulated wisdoms about food and our experiences of food. Traditionally this knowledge has been held by society at large, and passed on within the home from generation to generation. But as society has changed, this link has become more and more tenuous.

We no longer trust or understand food
—sometime in the past 50 or so years,
we've handed over responsibility
for food matters to science and industry.

It has certainly been a good deal for the food companies—many are now richer and more powerful than governments and even some countries. But I don't think it's worked out all that well for us. We are sicker, more overweight and more unhappy than we ever were, and children are bearing the brunt of this.

I believe one of the most important things you can do for your child is to build a strong and delicious food culture within your home.

Nourishment is not just about providing nutrients to enable our children to grow physically strong and healthy. As a parent, we bear our child into life—and everything we do in the early years affects their ability to understand and experience that life. Over the past 20 or so years, I think life has become something of a struggle, and I believe this struggle is at the root of much of the unhappiness and disease within our society. These days, so much is required to be done, with so little time simply to be, and enjoy. Food has been reduced to fractionalised nutrients—joy and delight have little or no place.

It's critically important: our absolute needs are for food, love and joy, and these are deeply intertwined and equally important. This hierarchy of needs dictates that one cannot successfully grow or learn until such primary needs are met. It's incredibly important to understand the role of joy and, since food is one of life's greatest pleasures, the role of food in providing much joy. When babies are born they cry when hungry; once fed with milk (and held close), they begin to interact with you, gurgling and cooing before falling into a contented sleep. Much has happened here—the mechanical need for fuel has been met and crying stops. All is well, and as your baby begins to interact, practical and cognitive learning takes place. And on another and equally important level, the soul's need for love, touch, security and deliciousness are met. For the baby, having all physical and non-physical needs fulfilled has created joy.

This is the primary pattern for young children (and for young people well into late teenagehood) to thrive, learn, feel happy and become all they can be. The delivery will change: the breast or bottle-feeding is replaced by the smell and promise and satisfaction of delicious food. Being held is replaced by eating with the family around a shared table and eating with extended family and friends at celebrations. The child develops the knowing that they belong and are 'held' as a part of the family. This aspect of food culture is powerful stuff.

I also believe in giving thanks before you eat, or at least acknowledging where food comes from. This helps children to connect with the miracle that is food—remembering that a seed placed into the earth and tended with water and sunshine can become a tree, laden with sweet fruit, which in turn helps to build and operate their bodies.

Children learn about their family's food culture by being a part of it—growing food, seeing food being cooked, being involved in the cooking and sitting down at the table to eat it. I've always cooked, and my daughter also learned to cook at a young age and has cooked with me and at her Nonna's side since she was a baby. This aspect of children learning just by being around cooking within the home was brought sharply into focus for me a few years ago. I'd gone to dinner at my daughter's home—she was about 21—and she had cooked a shepherd's pie. Now, I couldn't remember teaching her that particular dish over the years and I asked her how she did it. 'Oh, I just remember what you used to do,' she replied. I can't tell you how proud of her I was.

As you learn more about what good food really is, you can begin to incorporate that knowledge into your own personal food culture and hence the food culture of your family. You are the most important person in your young child's life—and your attitude towards food will affect how they think about and relate to food. Children also learn about your food culture through the words you use when you talk to them about food. For example, your child may only want to eat pears, but these are not in season all the time. Food out of season is nowhere near as delicious, nor as nutrient-rich as fresh seasonal food. We can explain this to our children by reading stories about the seasons and how food grows. We can also back it up by saying, 'Look what's growing now—strawberries! Aren't we lucky.' When pears come back in, we can introduce them by saying, 'Isn't it lovely to have pears back again.' This is how we teach our children about the seasons and begin to wind back the damage caused to the environment by unsustainable farming practices and an over-reliance on transportation systems, which result when all foods are demanded all year round.

I happened to be in a daycare centre recently, and was shocked to see that when it came time to feed the children—from the very little ones in high chairs to the older ones sitting at a table—the adults all wore plastic gloves. The message being sent to the children was that food and eating is unclean and unsafe—this is the kind of message that sets up nutritional and eating problems in later years.

If you want your children to be happy and healthy eaters, it's important to develop a wholesome family food culture by providing an abundance of organic, real, delicious foods and connecting the children with the source of those foods. This is a far better approach than telling them to eat something because it is 'healthy'. *All* the food that comes into your home should be wholesome and delicious.

Fussy eaters

THERE ARE MANY ASPECTS TO THIS ISSUE, but without doubt one of the biggest influencing factors is the food the parent eats, and the attitude you, the parent, have towards food. I see many children who eat a broad range of wholefoods all the time without fuss; invariably, what they have in common is that wholefood is what their parents eat and it's what they know as food. Brown rice? No problems. Taste develops according to what is experienced, and an important part of a child's learning in the very early years is what food tastes like. When a child is very little—*especially* between the ages of six months and three years—it's important to offer them the opportunity to taste each type of food at least 15 times. They may make faces which don't necessarily mean 'yuck', but rather, might mean: 'Oh, what's this? Do I like it? How do I eat it? Do I like this texture?' At this stage, much is still being worked out and this can often be mistaken for fussy eating.

It's also vital that children are allowed to respond to their feelings of hunger and fullness. It can be very healthy to let children say 'I've had enough' when they feel full. Especially between the ages of one and three years, children eat differently to adults, and this is often mistaken for fussy eating. The reality is that young children have small stomachs, and prefer to eat smaller amounts at more frequent intervals (see *Managing meals and snacks*, page 30).

Invariably though, as children move beyond the age of two years, they will use food as a way of asserting their individuality—food is one of the things they have most control over and it is often used in subtle games of blackmail. Within reason, try not to fall prey to the idea that they will starve to death if you don't give them the food they want. You are the parent, and you set the boundaries—this is the way we teach our children. What I mean by 'within reason' is that you also need to respect your child. Asking a child to eat when they are tired is never a good or fair thing. As children get older, avoid being fanatical and restrictive—draw your line and choose your battles wisely.

Accept, also, that we are all unique and will prefer some foods to others. Furthermore, certain foods are better suited to different body types and we are naturally drawn to the foods that suit us best. For example, I've never been a huge fan of raw vegetables, and from an Ayurvedic viewpoint this correlates with my body type. (Ayurveda is the collection of ancient Indian wisdoms which holds that humans, as a part of nature, are governed by particular environments—including food—both inside and outside the body.) My daughter, however, loves raw vegetables and did even when she was little—again, that correlates with her Ayurvedic body type.

Learn how your child primarily likes their food—and by this I certainly don't mean you should be making two or three separate meals to accommodate different family members. Rather, take notice of whether each child prefers their food wet or dry, ground up or in small pieces, and work these preferences into the daily meal planning and cooking.

Finally, don't forget that when dinnertime is joyful and food is a delicious experience, fussiness tends to leave the table (see *Vegetables and fruit*, page 45.)

Weight issues

THERE ARE TWO ASPECTS TO THIS ISSUE—the physical and the psychological. In physical terms, it is possible for a child to be carrying either too much or too little weight. Some children are naturally inclined to carry a little more, or a little less weight— this is not what I am talking about. Problems occur when there is far too much (overweight, leading into obesity) and far too little (underweight, leading into eating disorders such as anorexia and bulimia). Both these extremes are on the increase in young children and adolescents. Problems with body weight revolve around many factors, but mainly stem from the food we eat, and the attitudes we hold to that food. Whether you feel your child is overweight or underweight, you don't need to be afraid of giving her whole, real foods—these include quality fats (especially saturated fats).

If your child is overweight, it is vitally important to understand that eating fat does not necessarily equate to putting on weight, although vegetable oils are more prone to contribute to weight gain than saturated animal and coconut fats. Rather, I believe the high dependence on grains and flours (especially refined ones) and refined sugars (including large amounts of fructose) is the main contributing factor in the overweight and obesity issues we now face. Interestingly, it's these refined foods that form the basis of most 'snack' foods, including many cereals.

If your child is overweight, go easy on grains and flours. Unrefined, they form a wonderful part of any diet, but when they become the main or only component of every meal, body systems will get out of balance very quickly. Remember that fat is important to sate a healthy appetite, and look to protein and fat to anchor and provide density to a meal or snack. Children who eat nutrient-dense foods, in a wholesome and balanced way, and who don't rely on carbohydrate and sugar to fill their needs, are not going to get fat.

Before you become concerned your child might be underweight, remember that all children have growth spurts—as they suddenly become taller, they thin out. When children are consistently underweight, however, they are generally eating in an unbalanced way. We have some very skewed ideas today about what constitutes 'healthy' food; cold and raw fruits and vegetables with little fat, or puffed rice cakes with hummus—which are invariably considered to be 'healthy' food for children—are difficult to digest, and offer minimal nourishment for many children, especially in cold weather. Again, protein and quality fats are often overlooked. For many underweight children, warm and cooked foods based on good bone stock and fat and served as a meal, rather than as a snack, will deliver the nourishment their bodies need to grow and thrive.

It is important to remember that up until at least 16 to 20 years of age, children are still growing. Energy will go first to the daily running of the body, and second to growth and function of bone, muscle, hormones and so on. If their diet does not supply enough quality nutrients (including protein and, especially, saturated fats) there will be no energy left for padding and warmth. When there is an absolute deficiency of quality nutrients, even the basic functions of running a body and growth are compromised.

Remember, the psychology of food is very relevant too. It is important that you, as a parent, develop your own healthy attitude to food, because your child will pick up any fears or issues you have. Instilling a healthy attitude comes from valuing real food for all it is—a deeply delicious and joyous source of life. Food should never be about deprivation. Classing food as 'bad' sets up enormous problems and inner conflicts for young children—'I like that sweet taste but it's bad'—

My experience has been that when a child's needs are met within the home with delicious and nutrient-dense foods, the lure of chips and lollies is vastly diminished as the child's palate becomes attuned to real food.

and creates a desire for illicit foods. As much as I hate to say it, there is even a role for some junk foods—for example, eating chips at a family get-together—although this is very different from considering them a viable alternative to everyday wholesome food.

Birthday parties

MOST BIRTHDAY PARTY FOOD CONSISTS OF REFINED sugar- and additive-laden non-foods—all likely to send your child into a hyper spin. The best advice I can offer is to feed children well with nutrient-dense foods before they go to the party. Protein and fat, with or without a little complex carbohydrate, will fill and satiate them and reduce their desire in the following few hours to fill up on shallow 'pretend' food.

On the other hand, as we have already discussed, it is equally important to guard against children becoming apprehensive of 'bad food'. As well as setting them apart within a social gathering, it can be deeply conflicting for a child to be at a birthday party, but know they are not allowed to eat 'bad food'. By establishing a culture of wholesome, real food within your home, you will have educated their taste buds. It's amazing how many children taste the food (as they are naturally curious) and find out, all by themselves, that they don't like or want much of what's on offer.

On the home front, the birthday parties you create for your child need not be boring. With some imagination, many wholesome recipes can be turned into delicious offerings (see *Celebrations*, page 290).

The world outside the home

AS YOUR CHILD GETS OLDER AND IS EXPOSED to both societal and peer pressure, you will lose a good deal of control over their eating. This is natural and normal. Again, it pays to not be too fanatical or restrictive, and, as I said earlier, you need to choose your battles. There are two main ways to lessen the impact of the outside world's processed foods:

- Establishing and maintaining a strong, wholesome food culture within your home is critical and will help children to make healthy choices.
- If your child eats nutrient-dense breakfast, lunch, dinner and snacks, they will be less attracted to junk and other non-foods. When the body's need for fuel and nourishment is met with good, wholesome food, there will be less desire to search outside the home for sustenance.

BUILDING BLOCKS *for* BODY *and* SOUL

*I believe that good health is not simply
a result of the food we eat, but that it is
also a reflection of a contented soul
and a peaceful, happy mind.
In essence, the body, mind and soul
connection. It is my belief that we are
a spiritual being housed in a human
body, and when all are in balance
and nourished, good health
and happiness result.*

Building the body

A HUMAN BABY COMES INTO THE WORLD incomplete and unfinished. The growth, development and healthy functioning of bones, skin, organs, nerves and brain, for example, will require building materials, and those materials are called nutrients.

It would be an understatement
to say that children
have a high requirement for
nutrient-dense food.

Food is how we take in the nutrients we require—we are very much a product of the food we eat, and the body a child builds will depend to a large extent on the building materials supplied.

Nutrients are categorised into two main groups: *macronutrients*, which are proteins, fats and carbohydrates; and *micronutrients*, which are vitamins, minerals, enzymes, phytonutrients and water.

PROTEINS

Proteins are the building blocks of life, and are used to build and repair cells of all descriptions—really, there is little going on in the body that does not require a protein. They are made from varying combinations of 22 amino acids, eight of which are essential. They are involved in the making of muscles, nerves and organs, and are essential for the formulation of hormones. Antibodies and enzymes are examples of specialised proteins.

Animal products such as meat, fish, full-cream (whole) milk, cheese and eggs are the best sources of protein. While nuts, most whole grains (excluding amaranth and quinoa, which are considered to be complete), legumes and sea vegetables also contain protein, they do not carry the full range of amino acids, and so the protein they provide is incomplete. Therefore, one cannot thrive on either legumes or whole grains alone; however, when they are paired together, they complement each other, creating a balance of amino acids essential for growth.

FATS

A commonly accepted belief is that fat—particularly saturated animal fat—is dangerous, as well as being directly responsible for obesity. However, many scientists and doctors disagree, and history also points to previous generations and traditional cultures that have thrived and remained healthy eating such fats.

Saturated animal fats (so-called, although these are really a blend of saturated, monounsaturated and polyunsaturated fatty acids) are responsible for many critical functions in the body and are especially important for growing children.

Healthy fats occur in a wide range of foods: all animals (internal fat, organs and skin), fish, eggs, milk, whole grains, seeds, nuts, coconuts, legumes and sea vegetables (see *The Wholefood Kitchen*, page 32).

Here are some points to consider about fats:

- The brain and nervous system are built on fat (especially cholesterol) and continue to require large amounts of fat—in particular, the essential fatty acid, the omega-3 family, found in fish—to function. A brain is highly dependent on cholesterol.
- Saturated and unsaturated fats are prime sources of the critical fat-soluble vitamins A, D, E and K. In turn, many minerals, such as calcium, can only be properly absorbed and utilised by the body if there is enough vitamin A and D. Ancient Ayurvedic teachings considered the saturated fat ghee (see page 107) to be the most sacred of foods as it enabled all other 'goodness' to be delivered to the cells and absorbed. Ghee is rich in vitamins A and D.
- Saturated fats fight infection and provide immunity and protection against microorganisms. They include glycosphingolipids—special milk fats that protect against gastrointestinal infections. Poultry fat also contains palmitoleic acid—an antimicrobial monounsaturated fat involved in fighting infections.
- Fats protect and pad the organs.

Based in San Francisco, Dr Thomas Cowan is Western-trained with an anthroposophic slant, and one of my favourite doctors. He goes so far as to say that fat is the most important nutrient for children—especially saturated animal fat, and also the saturated non-animal fat, coconut. He notes that children need saturated fats in their very early years for the development of the nervous system, in the school years for a healthy immune system, and in the teenage years for hormonal and sexual development.

- Animal fats contain conjugated linoleic acid (CLA), a polyunsaturated omega-6 fatty acid. This is proving to reduce heart disease and to be a potent tool in fighting cancer.
- Saturated fats are essential for digestion (especially of protein).
- Saturated fats extend the usefulness of omega-3 essential fatty acids.
- Saturated fats are essential for hormonal development.

COMPLEX CARBOHYDRATE

Carbohydrate ultimately breaks down to the body's most basic fuel—sugar. Carbohydrate should always be complex—meaning whole, and not refined.

Whole grains are not only a good source of complex carbohydrate; they are also a rich source of unsaturated fats, protein, fibre, vitamins and minerals. Most of these nutrients are lost when the grain is refined. There are a large variety of whole grains and flours available, including products, such as bread and pasta, made from them (see *Whole grains*, page 51).

Some vegetables such as potato and sweet potato are also a source of complex carbohydrate.

VITAMINS, MINERALS, ENZYMES AND PHYTONUTRIENTS

These are nature's pharmacy, all found in the diverse, wide variety of foods that make up a healthy balanced diet.

Vitamins and minerals are found in virtually all fruits and vegetables, but you will also find them in animal products such as meat, meat fat, milk, cheese, eggs, fish and non-animal foods such as legumes, whole grains, nuts, seeds and sea vegetables. *Minerals* are also found in animal-bone stocks.

All foods lacto-fermented (see page 98) and raw foods provide a wealth of *enzymes*. These foods include yoghurt, kefir milk, lacto-fermented pickled vegetables and meats, raw milk and raw milk cheeses, and fresh raw fruit and vegetables.

Phytonutrients are primarily found in colour-rich vegetables and fruits, and cover an enormous range of compounds, all of which contribute to good health. Some examples are the carotenoids (for example, beta-carotene, lutein and lycopene—yellow/orange, green and red respectively) and anthocyanins, which are powerful antioxidants (deep- and brightly coloured berries are some of the best examples of anthocyanins). An easy way to include a good dose of carotenoids and anthocyanins in the diet is to eat a wide colour range of fruit and vegetables.

WATER

Water makes up a large part of the human body and is critical for many bodily functions, including maintaining blood pressure and a healthy nervous system. There is an amazing amount of heavy metals, herbicides, pesticides, chlorine and bacteria in most water supplies, and I believe that filtered water is essential. Rather than reverse osmosis, I prefer to use a system that removes most of the contaminants, but retains the naturally occurring trace elements and minerals.

Nurturing the soul

THERE ARE MANY CONFUSING IDEAS ABOUT what healthy and wholesome food actually is. Really though, it's simple; the following fundamental truths form the basis for healthy and wholesome eating for the entire family, including babies and young children.

ORGANIC IS IDEAL

Choosing organic foods when possible will increase the nutrient density of the foods you eat and reduce the pesticide load. This is critically important for babies and growing children. The term 'pesticide' covers a broad range of chemicals (fungicides, insecticides, rodenticides and herbicides) and these are designed to kill or corrupt the systems of living things—and humans are also living things. With a smaller body mass, underdeveloped organs and body systems, babies and children are especially vulnerable to side effects. It is particularly important to consider this issue when buying fats, or fat products (butter, eggs, cream and meat) as pesticides and chemicals store well in fat.

REAL INGREDIENTS MEAN REAL FOOD

Food should be made with real ingredients, rather than chemicals that mimic them. Many toxic and poisonous chemicals are used in the commercial production of food, especially in the roles of additives, flavours, colours, emulsifiers and preservatives. It would be an understatement to say that these ingredients are not body compatible. There is evidence to indicate that many are carcinogenic (cancer causing), mutagenic (agents that damage DNA) and teratogenic (agents that cause birth defects), not to mention the range of toxins that disrupt the intelligent operation of cells. Again, with a smaller body mass, children are especially vulnerable.

REAL FOOD IS NATURAL AND UNREFINED

Food should be as close as possible to its natural state and as little refined as possible. When food is refined, there are nutrient losses and no amount of 'enriching' or adding back will make it whole again. But more importantly, when a food is whole, with all the 'parts'—vitamins, minerals, fat, fibre, protein, carbohydrate, the known and unknown—that nature has put there intact and in their original ratios, optimum effectiveness is ensured. Milk is a good example—fat is a core component of milk, containing the fat-soluble vitamins A and D, which are essential for the assimilation of calcium and protein. Real milk has its fat for a reason, and real milk has its fat intact. Processed 'milk', however, no longer contains its original fat content (see *Dairy*, page 34).

REAL FOOD IS FAR MORE THAN ITS PHYSICAL COMPONENTS

Fractionalising food into its components and eating what may be considered the 'healthiest' meal on the planet can *never* satisfy, fulfil and truly nourish, if the food is not enjoyed. In ways I can not understand, but know exist, deliciousness and joy invite food into the body and enable it to be understood and fully utilised. Equally though, the most delicious and enjoyable meal cannot nourish if there are no nutrients present. Both aspects make up what I consider to be healthy, wholesome food.

Wholesome, balanced eating

A WHOLESOME, BALANCED DIET PROVIDES young and growing children with a broad range of whole and real foods, rich in nutrients. When it comes to feeding your child, I believe that young children are just like you and me—albeit in a smaller body that needs to grow, and with systems that are not yet fully developed. Even when they are little, it's good to offer them the same food the whole family eats, simply leaving out unsuitable foods or puréeing. I do believe, however, children's needs influence and affect the food choices we make, and how, in turn, we choose to prepare these foods.

THE DIGESTIVE SYSTEM

Good health relies on a healthy digestive system. And it can take up to several years for a child's digestive enzymes to fully develop; this can and does vary from child to child. In the child's very early years—up until two years old—we need to be particularly careful how digestible their food is, especially with regard to carbohydrate. One of the most important aspects of a healthy digestive system is developing a rich ecosystem within the stomach, with an abundant range of friendly microorganisms. These help digest our food, move food through the digestive system (even more than fibre does), help protect us from infection and parasites, manufacture vitamins and form a protective barrier between the stomach and the rest of the body.

Taking this into account, there are some things we can do that will promote better digestion:

- *Use whole, real, unprocessed foods* This is what the body understands, smells and responds to. For example, raw or full-cream (whole) milk and whole grains are easier to digest than processed and fractionalised foods. Refined foods—especially white flour and white sugar—actually remove valuable nutrients from the body in the process of being digested.

● *Introduce and use lacto-fermented foods* You're probably hearing a lot about probiotics these days and how good they are for you—and for your children. Well, lacto-fermented or cultured foods are the original probiotics, providing an abundance of beneficial bacteria that help maintain a healthy digestive system. Some examples of lacto-fermented foods include yoghurt, kefir (fermented 'grains' or good bacteria and yeast), cheese, kombucha (a colony of friendly bacteria and yeasts) and pickled vegetables, such as sauerkraut and kimchee. When we culture food, good bacteria proliferate and produce lactic acid, which also preserves the food. A little sour cream, yoghurt or pickled vegetables with a meal goes a long way towards helping digest heavier foods, such as meats, legumes and whole grains.

● *Respect grain* Whole grains can be difficult to digest and this is one of the reasons some children have problems with them. While I absolutely believe whole grains are wonderful, reducing the amount used in the very early foods served to young children does no harm and can help protect against allergies. (See *Raising a wheat-free or gluten-free child*, page 78.)

● *Use the 'softer', easier-to-digest grains* Use grains such as hulled millet, oats, rice and my particular favourites, quinoa and amaranth. Other than oats, all of these are gluten free, although very often you can also obtain gluten-free oats. Barley, kamut, rye, wheat and spelt—all gluten grains— are much more difficult to digest, although spelt is one of the easiest of this group, as it is more water-soluble than the others.

● *When possible, soak grains before use* Most traditional food cultures and virtually all pre-industrialised peoples soaked or fermented their grains. Soaking delivers huge benefits. All grains contain phytic acid in the outer layer or bran, as well as enzymes that inhibit digestion. Phytic acid is well known to bind calcium, magnesium, phosphorus and especially zinc in the intestinal tract and block their absorption. As little as seven hours of soaking in water with an acid (lemon juice, vinegar, whey, buttermilk, yoghurt or kefir) encourages lactobacilli and other helpful organisms to break down phytic acid and enzyme inhibitors. Another benefit of soaking grains is that lactobacilli break down gluten and other difficult-to-digest proteins and, in effect, pre-digest the protein (see *Grains*, page 88).

- *Choose sourdough breads* Sourdough leavening (rising) is ultimately a process of lacto-fermentation, and will provide similar benefits to those described in relation to using lacto-fermented foods (see opposite). Yeast (as opposed to sourdough) can be a problematic leavening agent for some people, and is best avoided when possible.
- *Include liberal amounts of coconut oil, cream and milk* Coconut is one of the gut's best friends as its short- and medium-chain fatty acids can help promote beneficial bacteria.
- *Limit the use of soy products* Soy products can be very difficult to digest (see page 50).
- *Support the digestive process with bone stocks* Bone stocks are full of gelatine which aids digestion—it is a good idea, for example, to cook grains in stock.
- *Use real (unrefined) salt* Real salt aids digestion (see page 66).

THE IMMUNE SYSTEM

The other key consideration when choosing foods for children is the immune system. Because a young child has so much growing to do—including building a fully developed immune system—they also has some differing nutrient needs to an adult, especially in regards to fat. Please don't be afraid of fat. It is the primary tool for boosting immunity and, in fact, most traditional and healthy cultures provide a large amount of fat from a broad range of foods for growing children. Good stable saturated fats include milk (preferably raw), butter, cream, eggs, the fats on meat and coconut. Monounsaturated and unsaturated fats can include unrefined nut and seed oils, such as olive, macadamia and sesame oils, avocado, nuts and seeds, and long-chain essential fatty acids from fish. It is because of this need that you will see a large number of recipes with these kinds of fats included (see *Fats and oils*, page 57).

MANAGING MEALS AND SNACKS

Optimally, the structure of a daily diet should be based around breakfast, lunch and dinner, plus quality snacks when required, all of which supply a range of nutrients found in wholesome healthy foods. Unfortunately, what happens for many children is that the good, nutrient-dense meals rarely eventuate, leaving a high reliance on snacks, which is very different from having frequent small meals. The body has a vast daily requirement for nutrients (not necessarily food, but nutrients). It works along the lines of Maslow's Hierarchy of Needs— in order to perform tasks, such as focusing, thinking, walking or any other function, first, it needs nutrients.

Our most basic fuel requirement is for sugar and the prime source for this is carbohydrate, but fat and protein are also excellent sources of energy, although the body takes a little longer to turn them into fuel. So critical is sugar to the body that many mechanisms are in place to make sure blood sugar levels don't drop.

The following suggestions are some simple ways to ensure that your child eats healthily most of the time; it just takes a little thought and planning.

⊛ *Establish your child's optimal eating times* They will differ from those of an adult, especially as the child reaches school age. Traditionally, afternoon tea is a child's natural and best time to eat dinner (remember the nursery meal and high tea?) or at least something very substantial. It's best to think of afternoon tea as a mini-meal, rather than a snack— this will often settle children down (hunger needs have been met) and they will be less tired and scattered at dinner. I'm not at all suggesting that you don't eat together as a family, but making children (generally up to 10 years) wait to eat their main meal until later in the evening is far too difficult. They are tired, and if they have had to snack on food with little nutrient density (even though it might be healthy food, such as fruit), their body and biochemistry will be stressed to the max, and they will merely pick at their dinner. These children find it difficult to settle, their cells are starving for nutrients, and this continues into the evening bed routine. Try to have your family dinner as early as possible and also think of afternoon tea as a small meal—enough to sustain, but not so much as to fill them up.

Snacks are a time-honoured and valuable way to top up fuel requirements— especially with young children, who eat smaller meals— but they should never, ever replace the meal itself.

- *Plan your child's main meals for the day* This is where they will (and should) get the bulk of their nutrients and fuel. Immediately, the reliance on snacks will lessen (and with it, the never-ending search for 'healthy' snacks). You will also need to consider the nutrient density and fuel density of their breakfast, lunch and dinner. For example, protein and fat (such as eggs) will always be the more sustaining breakfast over a carbohydrate meal (such as rolled oats). Then again, the more complex and closer to its natural state the carbohydrate is, the more sustaining it will be.

  As children also have smaller stomachs and different times and patterns of eating, you may like to try breaking their main meals into smaller parts—a bit now, a bit later. They can graze on their breakfast, lunch and dinner rations at the pace that works for them. For example, if they were fussy in the morning and didn't eat their scrambled egg, the leftovers could be put into a wrap or sandwich for morning tea, rather than being discarded and replaced by something like a biscuit. This is most relevant for the very young and toddlers, but also works for children at kindergarten and primary school.

- *Understand your child's body* They may have a slower digestive process and not require a snack at all, or prefer warmer and wetter foods— we are all individuals.

- *Prepare healthy, delicious snacks* When your child does eat snacks they should be of the very best quality, rich and dense with nutrients, made with real ingredients and as whole as possible (see *Lunchboxes*, page 243). There is absolutely no role for most of the so-called snack foods available today—commonly bread, crisps, chips or other highly refined carbohydrate foods. So many commercial snack foods are gaining acceptance because they are viewed simply as a snack rather than a meal, and thus considered okay. The problem with this is that for many children, there is no meal, or perhaps only one good meal a day, which is generally dinner.

The WHOLEFOOD KITCHEN

*So what is this good, wholesome food
and what does it look like?
Nature, rather than a food company or
science, has provided us with a wealth of
delicious real food, rich in nutrients.
Come into the kitchen with me, and
we'll take a look at the contents
of my fridge and pantry.*

Dairy

I'M USING THE TERM 'DAIRY' TO ENCOMPASS ALL animal-based milks, and all products derived from them. While I only mention two milks—cow's and goat's—in detail, you might also find the milk from sheep, buffalos, yaks (or some other animal) is suitable for your child. All full-cream (whole) animal milks are deeply nourishing and nutrient-dense foods.

Low-fat and skim milk are highly refined and processed products. Not only does low-fat and skim milk offer very little nourishment, if any, it is also extremely difficult to digest because fat is needed for the digestion of protein. As I say to my students, 'Nature didn't make a mistake by putting fat in milk, it's an essential part of a child's diet, treasured by traditional, healthy cultures.' Nature put fat in milk to carry the fat-soluble vitamins which are critical for good health, and to help absorb and utilise the minerals in milk (especially calcium) and the protein.

Most commercial low-fat and skim milk products contain a large amount of milk solids to give them body. These milk solids are highly processed, extremely difficult to digest, and generally oxidised (meaning they are rancid and dangerous).

If you truly prefer to use a lower-fat dairy product in your child's diet, you are better off using a lower full-cream product than a low-fat or skim version.

COW'S MILK

When cows graze naturally on grass—particularly grass grown in nutrient-rich soil—they take in what is essentially sunshine, and turn it into a profound and complete food that contains protein and a broad range of vitamins and minerals used for growth and repair of the many operating systems within the body. Milk fat is especially rich in the fat-soluble vitamins A, D and something known as the X factor (now thought to be vitamin K2), all of which are critical for the absorption and utilisation of minerals in the body, and for immune function. Cream and butter (see page 37) are extremely nutrient-dense foods. The fact that so many people are now allergic to milk is more a reflection on current farming and processing practices than the food itself.

When people are told to avoid cow's milk, it is generally because of a problem either with the milk sugar known as lactose or the protein known as casein. Depending on their genetic background, some people do not produce the enzyme lactase, which is required for the digestion of lactose. This condition is known as lactose intolerance. And for some, especially those with a delicate digestive system, casein can also be difficult to digest. There are two predominant types of casein in milk—A1 beta casein and A2 beta casein. A long time ago, most milk contained the more easily digested A2 casein, whereas today most cows produce A1. There is currently a significant trend to favour cows that produce A2 casein, but while it may be promoted as the healthier (and easier-to-digest) option, A2 milk might not always solve the problem—especially for a child with an immature digestive system.

When milk (whether it be A1 or A2) is pasteurised, it becomes even more problematic. Milk that has not been pasteurised (or heated at a specific temperature to kill off any dangerous bacteria) is known as *raw milk* and is a rich source of enzymes that actually aid digestion, including the enzyme lactase to digest lactose. When milk is heated for pasteurisation, any bad bacteria is destroyed along with the good enzymes, and the protein structure is altered. It is thought the body can no longer recognise the protein, but rather sees it as a foreign substance and so mounts an immune response. Pasteurised milk—even if it is organic and full-cream (whole)—is an exceptionally difficult food for adults to digest. It's even harder for young children with immature digestive systems.

Pasteurisation has developed within our industrialised food system where cost efficiency is the main goal. The heating process eliminates the presence of potentially life-threatening bacteria such as salmonella, *E. coli* and listeria (the kinds of contamination that can occur if there is poor hygiene on the farm or unhygienic conditions in the dairy). Pasteurisation also gives milk a longer shelf life. However, it means that cows can be farmed more cheaply in unsatisfactory conditions, using grain as the main (and sometimes total) feed—ironically, the kind of poor farm conditions that allow problems with disease and bad bacteria to develop. The product in the shop might look like milk, but looking like and being milk are very different things—the human body is infinitely wise, and it knows the difference.

Over many years, and throughout many traditional cultures, raw milk and dairy products have been considered sacred, nourishing and healing foods.

It's worth remembering here that it's not what a food is that makes it good or bad, but how we grow and process it.

I am a big fan of raw milk, but currently it is illegal in many countries throughout the world. This does not seem to stop increasing numbers of consumers looking for and using it. My personal experience, and that of my clients, has been that the benefits are so noticeable, it's incredibly hard to continue believing that pasteurised milk is a better product. *In Australia, raw milk is legally sold as 'bath', 'beauty' or 'pet' milk and can be sourced from cosmetic and natural food shops, but according to the Food Standards Australia and New Zealand (FSANZ) regulations, these milks must also be labelled 'not for human consumption'.*

A word of caution—if you choose to use raw milk, you must always look into its source and the practices of the farmer. I prefer my raw milk to be from a certified organic or biodynamic farmer. I also want to know that the cows eat their natural food (grass), are farmed with respect for their natural instincts, and are husbanded by a good farmer. If the farmer is not certified, I want to know the frequency and results of their testing—any presence of salmonella, *E. coli* and/or listeria would tell me those animals are not being farmed well.

I often find people are confused about the difference between pasteurised and homogenised milk. Homogenisation is a process by which the fat molecules are broken down under pressure so that they disperse through the milk. This in itself is a problem as it can oxidise the fat, and change the way it behaves in the body. You always want to see the fat *separated* and sitting on top of the milk. Therefore the best milk is non-homogenised, full-cream (whole), raw milk.

If you cannot find raw milk from a source you trust, you would be better off to prepare pasteurised, non-homogenised, full-cream (whole) milk in the Ayurvedic manner. This involves putting it in a saucepan with a pinch of ground ginger and cardamom, and bringing it to the boil. When you see the milk begin to rise, just as it begins to boil in the pan, take it off the heat and allow it to settle for a minute, before repeating this step twice more. Whereas pasteurisation just begins to damage the milk protein, this Ayurvedic process finishes the job, leaving the protein completely broken down so that it does not pose problems for digestion.

GOAT'S MILK

Even when pasteurised, goat's milk is far easier for humans to digest than cow's milk and, like cow's milk, is always better raw. It's an excellent alternative. While it's legal to sell raw goat's milk, when buying it, make sure you know and trust its source.

CULTURED MILKS

Next to raw, the best way to have your milk is cultured, or both raw and cultured. In lacto-fermentation, lactic acid-producing bacteria consume the lactose and casein, proliferate and in so doing produce lactic acid, and create enzymes which aid digestion (see more page 98). Most traditional communites practise culturing or lacto-fermenting their milk products, such as soured (clabbered) milk, buttermilk, kefir milk and labne (see pages 100 and 99), yoghurt (see page 100), crème fraîche and sour cream. Comparing yoghurt and kefir products, the latter offers a broader range of beneficial bacteria.

YOGHURT

Yoghurt is a great food, as discussed above, but for it to be good, it needs to be real. Made simply from full-cream (whole) milk and cultures, good yoghurt will invariably also be fairly runny, as it is not thickened with milk solids. Most commercial (even organic) yoghurts are highly sweetened and thickened with gums and milk solids. I would rather you flavour a plain yoghurt (made simply from full-cream milk and cultures) yourself with the natural sweetness of ripe fruit, than buy from a producer who will use sugar and flavouring agents. It's also very easy—and cheap—to make yoghurt yourself (see page 98).

CREAM, BUTTER AND GHEE

Cream and especially butter are rich sources of the fat-soluble vitamins A, D and E, as well as conjugated linoleic acid (CLA). You could view the cost of organic butter (as I do) as a wise investment—a small amount delivers great benefits. A portion on steamed vegetables or wholegrain porridge not only makes them taste delicious, but ensures optimum absorption of vitamins and minerals. Butter is a medium-chain fatty acid, and does not contribute to weight gain.

Cream and butter contain few milk solids, are always more easily digested than milk, especially when the cream is cultured for eating and making butter (you can even make kefir cream, see page 102). Butter is approximately 20 per cent milk solids and water; when these are removed you have ghee, the pure butterfat. As it contains no milk solids (and thus no protein casein), it is generally well tolerated by the digestive system.

CHEESE

Because cheese retains a large part of the milk solids, it contains the protein casein and can be problematic for many children. When made from raw milk, cheese will always be more digestible, but this kind of cheese is not easily obtainable due to the many legal restrictions. Our current political food systems are besotted with pasteurisation, and cheese is no exception. Cheese made from goat's milk will always be far more digestible than cheese made from cow's milk, even more so when it is made from raw goat's milk. Soft cheeses made from cultured cow's or goat's milk products, such as labne (see page 99), are much easier for a young tummy to digest.

IN SUMMARY

- Cow's milk is more digestible raw.
- Goat's milk is easier to digest than cow's—again, raw is best.
- If you cannot find either of the above, treat your pasteurised, non-homogenised, full-cream (whole) milk in the Ayurvedic manner (see page 36) or consider culturing it (see page 100).
- Culturing milk increases its digestibility, as the culture consumes much of the lactose and casein.
- The fewer milk solids a cow's milk product contains, the easier it will be to digest—consider cream, butter and ghee.
- For some children, however, cow's milk and its products may not be compatible in any form—we are all individuals and this needs to be taken into account (see *Raising a dairy-free child*, page 75).

Eggs

SUCH IS THE VALUE OF EGGS THAT THEY deserve a section all to themselves. Throughout the ages, in many cultures, eggs—and particularly the fat-containing yolks—have been considered to be a primary food for young children. With regard to the egg white, it's best to leave this until after 12 months, when the baby's more mature digestive system will be able to handle the proteins it contains.

The humble egg yolk is a gold mine of critical nutrients:

- *Choline and cholesterol* Both are critical for brain development; in particular, choline provides insulation for the nerves in the brain.
- *Biotin* This is a B vitamin beneficial for skin and nerves.
- *Essential fatty acids* These include the long-chain omega-3 essential fatty acid and the very long-chain essential fatty acids docosahexaenoic (DHA) and eicosapentaenoic (EPA)—all critical for development and continued function of the brain and nervous system.
- *Vitamins A and D* Fat-soluble vitamins essential for immune function and for the absorption and utilisation of minerals in the body.

Good eggs come from chickens that range on lush grass, eat scraps and some organic grain, and peck for insects as they roam. Unfortunately, the term 'free range' means very little these days. An optimal egg would have an organic certification and be labelled pasture or grass fed and free ranging. These eggs are a far richer source of omega-3 essential fatty acids and fat-soluble vitamins than eggs that are barn-laid or produced by caged hens. They are also one of the cheapest ways to obtain nutrient density.

Red meat and poultry

RED MEAT AND POULTRY ARE DEEPLY NOURISHING foods for growing children, providing valuable protein and fats, saturated and unsaturated. Along with eggs and fish, they are the prime and most complete protein sources. Red meat is also a rich source of magnesium, iron and zinc, and B vitamins including vitamin B12—essential for utilising iron. In fact, all animal products are rich in B12.

CHOOSING GOOD MEAT

Knowing who raises and farms the meat and meat fats you eat is very valuable and I encourage you to develop these relationships—your local farmers' market is a great place to start.

I believe you need to be very careful about the meat you choose—especially for growing children. Good meat comes from animals that eat their natural foods and that have not been given antibiotics or hormones. Chickens should be free to forage on grass, eating scraps supplemented with some grain, and scratching for insects (their protein source). Cows should eat grass, not grain. Animals should all be allowed to express their natural instincts and indeed, this aspect is an important foundation of organic or biodynamic certification.

It can be very confusing working out what meat to buy. Without a doubt, overall, I would say: buy organic. But even this can have its pitfalls and problems. I would choose a non-certified, free-ranging chicken that has been eating its natural foods and living its natural life, raised by a farmer I know, rather than an organic one where the chicken only eats grain—albeit organic grain.

OFFAL AND BONE MARROW

The organs and bone marrow of animals deserve special mention here as prime, nutrient-dense foods for children. They are an especially rich source of the fat-soluble vitamins A and D and many other very long-chain essential fatty acids. Brain and liver have been considered some of the most important foods for young children in traditional cultures. Pesticides and hormones accumulate in fat, so it is particularly important that any *offal or marrow you or your children eat is organic.*

Fish

FISH IS A SUPERB SOURCE OF PROTEIN AND MOST CRITICALLY, our key source of the long-chain omega-3 essential fatty acids docosahexaenoic acid (DHA) and eicosapentaenoic acid (EPA). Fish is by far the best dietary source of EPA and DHA, although there is a small amount of both in properly raised chicken and eggs (see pages 39 and 40). Some plants do contain omega-3 essential fatty acids (walnuts, flax [linseed] and hemp being the richest) but in the form of alpha linolenic acid (ALA) which, in theory, can be converted to EPA and DHA. However, it's not always a sure thing and can be a tricky conversion at the best of times, requiring a specific range of nutrients, especially for children.

EPA and DHA are both essential for building the brain (especially DHA) and then for running it.

Fish is also a rich source of the fat-soluble vitamins A and D—remember cod liver oil (see page 44)? This was a traditional supplement for vitamins A and D, critical for immune function and the absorption and assimilation of so many nutrients within the body.

CHOOSING GOOD FISH

It sounds like such a great piece of advice—eat more fish; but unfortunately, it isn't that easy. There are many problems associated with fish these days, and you need to be able to navigate your way around them.

The best way to work out what fish are sustainable, unfarmed and low in mercury and polychlorinated biphenyls (PCBs) is to connect with your regional Marine Conservation Society. Local fish types vary, and a group like this will be able to give you a list of sustainable fish in your country or state. Furthermore, a good fishmonger should be able to tell you whether a particular kind of fish is sustainable or not.

SUSTAINABILITY AND FISH FARMING

As a result of overfishing and exploitation, fish stocks are in decline all over the world. Many fish are in danger of extinction—it's incredibly important that the fish you choose be sustainable, local (not imported) and seasonal (not all fish are available all the time).

With the decline in fish populations, farming has proliferated, and I know there are many who feel fish farming is the way of the future. I cannot agree. There are many, many issues in regard to farmed fish, including the high level of environmental destruction that results from pollution associated with fish waste. Other issues include a weakening of the DNA of wild fish when farmed fish escape and infiltrate wild fish populations, as well as disease, infection and parasites that can transfer from caged fish to wild fish stocks. Ethically, I feel fish farming also disconnects us from the consequences of our actions. We simply cannot overfish the ocean, and when it can no longer give us the fish we demand (or desire), turn to other ways of raising fish that, in so many ways, are just as destructive as the original overfishing.

What farmed fish actually eat is also an issue. Carnivorous fish (salmon and tuna, for example) need to eat other fish in order to grow and live. In the manufacture of feed for farmed fish, smaller fish are ground into meal which is supplemented with fish oils, soy protein and grains. This practice is causing an enormous load on smaller fish globally, especially when you consider that it takes about 4 kilograms of wild-caught fish to produce 1 kilogram of saleable farmed salmon, and about 12 kilograms of wild-caught fish to produce 1 kilogram of saleable farmed tuna. As well, these farmed carnivorous fish are generally far higher in PCBs than wild-caught fish because, from the beginning, they eat larger amounts of fish meal and oils derived from fully grown fish—they don't begin their lives by eating baby fish. Another thing to consider is that many people, especially children, can be extremely allergic to soya beans and soy products (see page 50) and these are a large component of almost all feed used in fish farming.

When farmed, herbivorous fish have their problems too, as they are commonly fed pellets to hasten and encourage consistent growth; while the pellets don't contain fish meal, they do contain soy and grain.

For all these reasons, it is especially important for children, with their smaller body mass, to avoid farmed fish. They are also the reasons you won't see recipes for salmon in this book. I live in Australia, and Atlantic salmon is not a native fish here. While there are some better farming practices being developed—salmon are farmed in freer flowing water, and at lower stock densities than in the past—I am still not a fan. There are a lot of delicious, high omega-3 fish available that are sustainable (not overfished), local (not imported) and wild (not farmed). If you live in the northern hemisphere where salmon are native, please enjoy them, but choose wild salmon in season.

If you need any further convincing, farmed fish are likely to contain large amounts of antibiotics and in some cases, colours and other chemicals. Like any animal, fish can get pretty sick when they are living in industrialised systems designed for efficiency and profit.

CONTAMINATION WITH MERCURY AND PCBS Our rivers and coastal waters are awash with toxic chemicals that leach from agricultural runoff and industrial waste. These include mercury, which once in water becomes methylmercury, easily absorbed by humans, and PCBs. Both will cause a lot of problems for a human, but a young child is especially vulnerable as they have less-developed systems to help filter the toxins and, most importantly, they have a lower body mass. Methylmercury is stored in fish muscle and will bioaccumulate—big fish eat smaller fish, and as the largest fish at the top of the food chain eat lots of tiny fish, they tend to accumulate a higher load of methylmercury. This includes shark, swordfish and tuna. I don't eat these fish and certainly don't recommend tinned tuna. Even though PCBs have been banned for some time now, they persist in our oceans and river systems and contaminate a wide range of fish. Like most chemicals, PCBs accumulate in fatty tissue, and will also bioaccumulate as they move up the food chain. And it's not quite as simple as avoiding larger fish, as it also depends on where they come from. Fish found closer to industrial centres, or rivers close to farmland, will generally carry a higher level of these toxins. Farmed fish fed protein and oil from smaller fish will also carry a greater load.

COD LIVER OIL

One of the richest sources of vitamin A and D, cod liver oil has been a traditional protective supplement for young children for a very long time and I'm a big fan of it—especially for children who are dairy free and/or vegetarian. With regard to the oil itself and contamination, most cod liver oils are filtered of PCBs via high-grade distillation techniques. Mercury is not an issue here as it only accumulates in the muscle, and not in the liver. However, I recommend being very fussy about the cod liver oil you choose—it should have a ratio of vitamin A to D of at least 10:1 and be pristine. There are many excellent sources on the Internet for quality cod liver oil including www.nordicnaturals.com and www.greenpastures.com.au.

IODINE

Iodine is critical for mental development in the young child and for maintaining healthy thyroid function. Recent studies have shown many children to be deficient in iodine, with a corresponding push to legislate for the mandatory fortification of all edible salt (iodised salt) as well as other staple foods like bread. As we eat less and less real food, we forget that iodine does exist outside of iodised salt—anything from the sea is a rich source—real fish, real (unrefined) salt (see page 66) and sea vegetables (see page 64). If you are raising a vegetarian child (see page 74), do make sure to include good salt and sea vegetables in their diet.

IN SUMMARY

- *Avoid all farmed fish* If you do decide to eat organic or herbivorous farmed fish, you may want to track down the farmer to find out exactly what the fish are eating (especially if you want to avoid soy).
- *Avoid tinned tuna wherever possible* Wild-caught and sustainable salmon is available in tins (imported into Australia) and can occasionally be useful in an emergency.
- *Avoid the larger predatory fish* In particular avoid shark, tuna and swordfish.
- Where possible, ask your fishmonger where the fish comes from— if they can't tell you or do not respect your question, look elsewhere.

Vegetables and fruit

VEGETABLES AND FRUIT GROWN IN NUTRIENT-RICH soils are nature's pharmacy. They are full of vitamins and minerals, fibre and an abundance of antioxidants—including carotenoids and flavonoids. They come in oranges and yellows, reds and pinks, blues and purples and greens of all shades—a rainbow of goodness. We are told again and again to include lots of vegetables in a child's diet—indeed, they have become a holy grail of good eating. I agree that they are incredibly important (and delicious) but I know a lot of children refuse to eat them.

I encourage you to think about the vegetables you offer your children—have you tasted them lately? Even when vegetables are organic they may have lived in a coolroom for some weeks, or may have been unripe when picked—they really might taste awful. If they are not organic, they would have even less flavour and could taste even worse. Quite frankly, I think children are often using their natural instincts to discern quality food when they refuse to eat what frequently poses as fruit and vegetables these days. Fruit or vegetables will taste better—and be better for you—when they have been grown in a mineral- and nutrient-rich soil, and are eaten as close as possible to harvesting.

My favourite doctor, Thomas Cowan, in San Francisco has some interesting thoughts on the subject of children and vegetables. He notes that children under the age of five years generally don't do well with vegetables, as they lack the enzymes that convert plant nutrients into vitamins. He suggests it is probably better left to the cow to do the conversion and for young children to eat butter and cream.

While hiding vegetables in all sorts of foods has its place, it is not and should not be the beginning and end of it all.

CELEBRATE THE SEASONS

Seasonal fruit and vegetables will always be fresher and better tasting than those which have been kept in storage. We are not just physical beings, and the nutrients we require are not just physical. Eating food within its season provides us with nutrients that feed the soul—the concentrated and grounded forces from root vegetables, nuts and seeds nurture and comfort us when the weather is cold, for example. As the sap and temperature rises, the energy expands upwards and outwards above the ground, giving us the flowers that form into fruit and vegetables. When we eat food out of season, we are easily disconnected from the subtle, non-physical nutrients and life forces in our food. If you are eating mostly conventional food, there would be none of either, and this is another fundamental reason for eating organic and biodynamic food. It tastes amazing (especially when eaten soon after picking) as life force often translates into great deliciousness.

VEGETABLES—COOKED OR RAW?

It helps to understand how to cook vegetables properly—I think there's too much emphasis on serving them raw. Vegetables are still healthy when they are cooked. Indeed, some are at their best cooked—raw broccoli and cabbage, for example, contain goitrogens, which suppress the function of the thyroid, and raw silverbeet contains oxalic acid which blocks the body's ability to absorb iron and calcium, but cooking breaks down these goitrogens and oxalic acid.

Many vegetables also taste so much better with some fat on them—especially butter, which can be added during or after cooking. This not only tastes delicious but enables the vitamins and minerals to be used by the body.

Remember: a child's digestive system is delicate and not fully developed, and cooking helps to make many vegetables and even some fruits more digestible. High-pectin fruits, such as apple, are often more digestible when cooked, and cooking can even make some nutrients more bioavailable—the bright red antioxidant lycopene in tomatoes, for example. Yes, you can lose some goodness to heat, but there's an awful lot left. Please don't cook vegetables in a microwave, which destroys far more goodness than traditional cooking methods, such as steaming (my favourite), blanching, boiling, frying or roasting.

Ayurvedic teachings also hold that some body types do not have a sufficiently robust digestive system for a large amount of raw vegetables. We are all individuals, and children are no exception. Raw vegetables and salads have their place for young children, but should be served with delicious, fat-based dressings, and mainly in warmer weather.

CHOOSE ORGANIC FRUIT AND VEGETABLES

Vegetables and fruits come in for a large amount of spraying at all stages of growth. While we are told there are many safeguards and protections in place, I am not convinced that this is true and it's certainly not what I see. Research shows that many fruits have one to three types of pesticide residues, and often more. Because of children's small body mass and undeveloped protective and filtering systems, these toxins will have a far greater impact on a child than an adult. Where possible, use organic fruit and vegetables.

CHOOSING DRIED FRUITS

When buying dried fruits, look for unsulphured—they may appear less attractive and darker in colour, but won't cause problems, such as allergic reactions. Also try and find dried fruit that is not packed in vegetable oil (to stop it sticking) or sweetened.

GROW YOUR OWN

A final word on the subject of children eating vegetables: I've rarely met a child who was involved in the growing of vegetables and who will not eat them. Growing your own vegetables (and fruits) teaches children about the wholeness and interconnectedness of life, while giving you the added bonus of organic and nutrient-dense fresh foods, more cheaply.

Nuts and seeds

NUTS AND SEEDS ARE WONDERFUL FOODS—excellent sources of protein, unsaturated fats, calcium, zinc and iron. Adding them to meals with whole grains and legumes will increase the complete protein available. As nuts and seeds, especially flax (linseed), are such a rich source of quality unsaturated fats they are extremely prone to rancidity—it's incredibly important to buy only the freshest, best quality nuts and seeds. Rancid fats can damage the body, setting up all sorts of problems. Good nuts and seeds should smell fragrant and full, not at all bitter—if your nose wrinkles a little, it's generally detecting some rancidity.

Like whole grains, nuts and seeds contain phytic acid and enzyme inhibitors. To neutralise these, traditional cultures generally soaked the nuts or seeds overnight in water with a little salt, then dried them in an oven at low temperature or in the hot sun (see pages 103–106). I don't always do this, and the world won't fall apart if you don't, but it does make them easier for little tummies to digest.

Nuts are a high-allergy food and they are banned from most schools because of this. I believe the way we farm and store our nuts is a major factor in the increased levels of allergic reaction to nuts, along with the weakened digestive and immune systems we see in many children and adults today. Respecting the development of your baby's digestive and immune systems is a critically important part of avoiding allergies (see *Wholesome, balanced eating*, page 27). If your child has problems with digesting food, and has a poor immune system, I highly recommend you hold back from using nuts. Introduce nuts slowly, and in very small amounts, and certainly not until after your baby is 12 months of age—preferably not until two years. Peanuts are one of the high-allergy nuts, and should be left until your little one is at least three, if not five, years; peanuts should always be organic.

Because they are fat sources, nuts and seeds are best grown organically, but this doesn't necessarily mean they are fresh. Always make sure your nuts and seeds are pristine and store them in the fridge.

Legumes

BEANS, LENTILS AND PEAS (INCLUDING SPLIT PEAS) are all legumes and provide a rich source of protein and complex carbohydrate. Unlike meat, poultry, fish and eggs, they are not a complete protein—they are generally lacking in the amino acid methionine, although they do have plenty of lysine (which aids calcium absorption and bone development as well as helping to build hormones and antibodies). Grains, on the other hand, have plenty of methionine, and no lysine; hence the idea of complementation—eating beans with whole grains. The one exception is soya beans, but these presents problems which need to be considered before you use them (see *Soya beans and soy products*, page 50).

Legumes can also be a rich source of B complex vitamins and minerals, including iron, calcium, phosphorus and potassium. Take note that this iron (as in all vegetable foods) is of the non-haem variety. This means it's not absorbed into the body as readily as the iron in meat. You can help its absorption by eating with foods rich in vitamin C, such as leafy green vegetables, berries, tomato and capsicum (pepper). If you are in a vegetarian family, you need to take this into account, as iron is important for brain development and therefore critical for young children.

Beans are different in their structure from lentils and the pea family. They contain long-chain sugars called oligosaccharides, which the human stomach is not able to break down—these ferment in the stomach and cause gas. To make digestion easier, beans must always be properly prepared and well cooked. A robust digestive system is also required, so they are not suitable until a child is at least 12 months old. As a child gets older though, they are a wonderful food to include. Young fresh beans still in the pod, as opposed to dried beans, have not developed oligosaccharides and, if available, are a better choice for very young children. However, the best dried bean to start with would be the adzuki, as it's very easy to digest (see *How to cook beans*, page 84).

Lentils and the large family of dried peas are a far better option than beans for the very young. Mung dhal and split red lentils are a great place to start (see *How to cook lentils and peas*, page 86).

Soya beans and soy products

BECAUSE SOYA BEANS ARE CONSIDERED TO BE HIGH in amino acids, soy products are a popular protein addition to many vegetarian diets. It is essential, however, that you understand the pros and cons, and choose wisely—especially for young and growing children.

There are many problems with soy: it is very high in phytates, which bind with minerals and reduce their availability to the body; it is high in enzyme inhibitors, including one that inhibits trypsin (which is essential for digestion); it depresses thyroid function; it is an endocrine disrupter; and it is very high in phytoestrogens. All these factors make it tricky for a young child with an immature digestive system to process soya beans and soy products.

I do think soy has a great role to play in a plant-based, vegetarian and/or dairy-free diet, especially for adults, but I believe it should be used with respect and sparingly for young children. Fermented soy products such as tempeh, natto, miso, tamari and shoyu are preferred over 'raw' soy in the form of soy milk and tofu, as fermenting breaks down phytates and some of the enzyme disrupters. Raw soy (tofu and soy milk) is exceptionally difficult to digest, and because of the high levels of phytoestrogens (female hormones), any soy should be used with caution for the developing child, especially boys. It's also important to remember that in the teenage years, the body and its systems (particularly the hormonal and reproductive systems) are still maturing; large amounts of soy milk are not a great idea for teenagers, especially boys.

Any soy product you use should be made from whole, organic soya beans and never from soy protein isolate (SPI) or protein extract. Soy products should always be *first generation*—that is, tempeh, natto, miso, tamari, shoyu, tofu or soy milk. Many soy cheeses, margarines and soy 'meats' are highly processed and refined foods based on SPI, refined with oils, colours, flavours and gums, and have no place in a wholesome diet (see *Raising a dairy-free child*, page 75).

Whole grains

WHOLE GRAINS ARE A RICH STORE OF PROTEIN, numerous vitamins and minerals, quality fats, fibre and complex carbohydrate, which is the source of our most basic fuel, sugar.

Once the inedible husk is removed, a grain is made up of three parts:

- *Bran* This is the outer layer—the skin, so to speak—of the seed. It protects the valuable fat stored in the germ and endosperm from light and insect damage. It is rich in B vitamins, antioxidants and fibre.
- *Germ* Rich in B vitamins and fat, this layer is underneath the bran and it also contains some protein and minerals.
- *Endosperm* At the very core of the kernel lies the starch, with some protein and small amounts of vitamins and minerals.

One of the biggest nutritional problems today is the refining of whole grains—the removal of the bran and germ, leaving nothing but the starchy endosperm. The carbohydrate in grain is described as complex because it takes longer to convert to sugar in the body than a simple carbohydrate (like the sugar in milk or fruit). Nature goes to a lot of trouble to provide fibre and fat in the grain's bran and germ, to slow down the conversion of carbohydrate to sugar. Pure white flour, on the other hand, is like high-octane fuel—it converts to sugar in the body very quickly.

Just as important for good health are the abundant B vitamins found in whole grains—you need them to digest carbohydrate. When you eat a large amount of white refined flour (which is lacking in B vitamins), your system has to source these vitamins from reserves within the body. Current law stipulates that refined flours (and thus breads) must be fortified with thiamine, niacin, iron and calcium. But just like the starchy carbohydrate, vitamins and minerals need other components (like fats) to enable them to be digested and used. It's simple really—any nutrient is always best absorbed from the whole food rather than from food that has been refined and then had bits and pieces added back into it.

Whole is the best possible way to eat grain—for example a bowl of brown rice—but you can also break the whole grain up (in a food processor or blender);

Excluding amaranth and quinoa, whole grains are not a source of complete protein, meaning they don't contain all essential amino acids, and are generally served with legumes for this reason.

or roll and flatten it out, to make it quicker to cook; or grind it into flour. A porridge made from any whole, rolled or ground grain is better than a breakfast of puffed or flaked cereals, and a muffin made with wholemeal flour is better than one made with a refined, white flour. I don't use or recommend any puffed or flaked grains, especially for children (this includes puffed rice cakes and crackers). It's not just because many are loaded with sugar, but also because they are processed at such extremes of temperature and pressure. (Although many of the organic puffed and crispy flaked products—breakfast cereals, puffed grain crackers and cakes, for example—stocked in health food stores aren't high in sugar, they are nonetheless still processed at extremes of temperature and pressure.) It's thought that under the extreme pressure and high temperatures used during processing, the chemical structure of protein can change, creating toxins. I would encourage you to avoid these kinds of products altogether.

INTRODUCING GRAINS AND FLOURS TO CHILDREN

Avoid feeding babies under the age of 12 months too much grain and flour—babies are not geared for carbohydrate, but rather for protein and fat (see *Nutrient-dense first foods*, page 112). Also, a very young child's digestive system cannot cope well with large amounts of bran and fibre.

When you decide to feed grain to your baby (see page 124), start with the gluten-free, easy-to-digest, high-protein amaranth, quinoa, hulled millet and brown rice. Once your baby has reached 12 months, you can begin to include gluten grains, start with oats and spelt. Both are more water-soluble than the other gluten grains, and easier to digest.

FLOURS

A flour ground from a whole grain (generally referred to as 'wholemeal' in Australia and 'whole wheat' in the United States) will always be more nutritious than refined flour, but with a high content of bran and germ, these flours can be difficult to use; and in any case, too much fibre for the very young is not always a good thing. Using white (unbleached) grain flours will provide less bran (and thus less fibre) and deliver a better end result, yet still provide a large amount of wholesome goodness.

Wheat and spelt both offer excellent white (unbleached) flours. They are made by grinding the whole grain, then sifting it to remove the bran and germ—some types remove a lot, giving you a whiter flour that is mostly endosperm, and some remove only a little, leaving you with white flour lightly speckled with bran and germ—a light wholemeal, so to speak. Optimally, stoneground flour is better than flour that has been ground on a steel mill, as the heat from the steel oxidises the highly desirable fats. Here are some flours I keep in my pantry:

SPELT This is my preferred flour for general baking. A relative of modern wheat, it behaves much the same as wheat flour, except that it has a far lower gluten content and is more water-soluble. It has a darker colour than wheat and produces a darker crumb. Because it's far easier to digest, I've used spelt rather than wheat for many of the recipes in this book. These recipes will be wheat free, but not gluten free.

I keep two spelt flours—wholemeal and white (unbleached). I like to use a 50:50 ratio for most baking—this way, I end up with a 'light' wholemeal. When I want a light end result, I use 100 per cent white. Because of spelt's unique characteristics, even a white spelt will have a good dose of nutrients. But in the world of spelt, a white spelt can vary enormously. Some are simply endosperm—fine and white—with all the bran and germ sifted out (my preference); some have a little germ or fibre; and some are similar to light wholemeal—the bran and germ are quite obvious. This matters, because the more 'wholemeal' your white spelt is, the more liquid it will absorb, and the heavier your end result will be.

When cooking with spelt flour, you may also notice that cup weights can vary considerably. While we specify 130 grams (4¾ oz) for 1 cup of white spelt, I have found that this can vary by up to 10 grams (¼ oz), less or more, for differing brands and in different seasons. This is not too much of a problem with everyday cooking, but when making a cake with a delicate crumb—genoise sponge cake or vanilla and coconut cupcakes (see pages 294 and 298), for example—I would suggest you weigh your white spelt flour, rather than relying on the cup measure.

If you find you have a heavier white spelt flour that looks more like a 'light' wholemeal, you have a couple of options:
- Sift the flour, using a fine sieve, catching the bran and germ before using. Discard the bran and germ, and measure your quantity from the fine, sifted flour.

⬤ Where the recipe calls for 50 per cent white and 50 per cent wholemeal (130 g/4¾ oz/1 cup white spelt flour and 165 g/5¾ oz/1 cup wholemeal spelt flour), I suggest simply using 295 g (10½ oz/2 cups) of the heavier 'white' spelt. The end result will be exactly the same—a 'light' wholemeal.

WHEAT Bear in mind that the gluten in wheat is more difficult to digest than the gluten in other grains, and some wheat flours can be very 'hard' (high in protein)—great for pizza, but bad for cakes and pastry. In some places you can buy 'cake' or 'pastry' wheat flour—this indicates it is a low-protein flour, and will give softer results. Other wheat flours include atta—a wholemeal wheat flour that has been sifted to remove some of the heavier bran—to create a light wholemeal.

Coming onto the market is a product called 'whole white wheat flour'. Made from a variety of white wheat, it has no colour and is mild in flavour, making it a good option for children who only like white flour. It's a light-coloured, light-tasting wholemeal flour. You can replace the spelt flour in any of the recipes with this kind of wheat flour, and you will get similar results.

WHEAT-FREE AND SPELT-FREE FLOURS Oat flour and barley flour are the best options for baking if you want to avoid wheat and spelt, but it's important to note that they are almost always wholemeal.

Oat flour and *oatmeal* will give a chewy consistency to the crumb and generally don't require as much added moisture as other wholemeal flours. Oat flour and oatmeal are made from finely ground, stabilised (steamed) rolled oats, and of the two, oatmeal has more bran and germ. Once the rolled oats have been ground into oatmeal, it is then sifted to remove some of the bran and germ, leaving you with oat flour.

Barley flour is generally ground from pearled barley or whole barley (minus the inedible husk). In Australia, most barley flour is ground from pearled barley, which I prefer, as it's a little lighter. Because barley flour has a very low gluten level, it is best mixed with a flour with a higher-gluten content when baking.

GLUTEN-FREE FLOURS I never use commercial gluten-free baking flours. They are generally highly refined starches, such as potato, tapioca or corn. When mixed with liquid they resemble glue—they will react the same way in the stomach. Here is a list of gluten-free flours I enjoy working with.

- *Rice flour* The best option here is brown or white rice flour, which is very dense and should always be 'softened' by mixing in some desiccated coconut or ground nuts. Small amounts of other gluten-free flours, such as buckwheat, amaranth or quinoa, can be included.
- *Buckwheat flour* This makes a beautiful tasting flour, but is always best used in combination with brown rice flour. It absorbs large quantities of liquid and becomes quite viscous when left to sit.
- *Amaranth and quinoa flours* These are both very assertive in flavour, and again are best used in small amounts with brown rice flour.
- *Millet flour* This has a strongly astringent taste, and is also best used in partnership; brown rice flour works well.
- *Coconut flour* While not a grain flour, coconut flour is being sold and used as a baking flour. Coconut flour is actually what is left when the oil has been extracted from the coconut meal. It is extremely high in fibre, high in protein and gluten free. Because it contains so much fibre, you need to be careful about using too much of it with very young children, and too much of it in a recipe will give you a brick-like result. Used in small amounts, though, it's delicious.
- *Maize flour (golden cornflour)* This is another flour I love to use. Made from 'flour corn', this gluten-free flour is a beautiful pale yellow, wholemeal cornflour. It's a great choice for dredging foods before pan-frying. The cornflour (cornstarch) commonly sold as a thickener for sauces is actually the white starch inside the grain.
- *Masa (maseca)* This is a cornflour treated with lime (an alkaline, not the citrus), and is used for making authentic corn tortillas. When dried it is called masa harina.
- Some thickening agents (see page 61) can also have a valuable role in gluten-free baking.

RAISING AGENTS

The common ratio is 2½ teaspoons of baking powder to 1 cup of flour. I prefer to halve that amount; I use 1¼ teaspoons of baking powder per cup of flour and find it is more than adequate.

Baking powder is a blend of acid and alkaline powders, which react when mixed with moisture and heat, creating carbon dioxide to lift and thus lighten baked foods. Most commercial brands use acids that are aluminium-based (sodium aluminium sulphate, phosphate aerator, sodium aluminium phosphate)—these are best avoided. Natural food stores stock brands that use the healthier acid calcium phosphate, and are often labelled aluminium free. They also commonly use potassium bicarbonate for the alkaline (though sodium bicarbonate is fine).

You can create your own healthful raising reactions using bicarbonate of (baking) soda (as the alkaline) and choosing from a range of everyday acids, such as apple cider vinegar, yoghurt, buttermilk or kefir milk (see page 100).

BREAD

The most nutritious and delicious bread is made from freshly ground whole grains and will be rich in vitamins, minerals, proteins, complex carbohydrate and good fats. Optimally, stoneground grain is better than grain that has been ground on a steel mill, as the heat from the steel oxidises the highly desirable fats.

Bread should not be introduced too early to baby's diet, and preferably not until after 12 months. Then, only ever use sourdough, sprouted grain, or sprouted grain flour breads, and avoid wheat, if possible.

Good bread is leavened with a sourdough culture rather than commercial bakers' yeast. Sourdough breaks down the grain's phytic acid (which combines with iron, calcium, zinc and phosphorus and blocks their absorption) and 'pre-digests' the grain's protein, making it easier for humans to digest, especially young children who have an immature digestive system. Given a nice slow ferment and rise, sourdough also helps break down some of the gluten, making wheat bread more digestible.

Breads made from sprouted grains follow the same principle and are easier for young children to digest. Some are heavy and moist, such as Essene breads, which are made from grains that have either been sprouted, then 'baked' in the sun or a warm spot *or* made from grains that have been sprouted, then dried and ground into flour before baking. These make nice soft breads, great for school lunches.

If you are using wheat bread, it absolutely must be a quality sourdough, where the grain has been given enough time to rise slowly and optimum opportunity for the protein to be broken down prior to baking. A spelt sourdough would be a better option as the protein is more water-soluble and more easily tolerated (see *Raising a wheat-free or gluten-free child*, page 78).

PASTA AND NOODLES

There is a broad range of pasta and noodles made from whole grains and lightly refined flours on the market. I generally prefer spelt, as it's a far more easily digested option than wheat. The star-shaped stelline (also available in spelt) is a great pasta option for young children because of its small size.

With regard to gluten-free pasta and noodles, avoid those made from highly refined tapioca, potato and rice starches, and vegetable gums and choose naturally gluten-free whole grains, if possible. My favourites include those made from 100 per cent buckwheat (soba noodles), quinoa, amaranth and rice.

Fats and oils

FAT IS AN ESSENTIAL MACRONUTRIENT, and is especially important for a young and growing child. Fats damage easily (heat, light and oxygen are the culprits) and damaged (rancid) fat is extremely dangerous to the body (that's why antioxidants are so important). The less saturated fats are, the more fragile they are.

Fat stores any chemical or pesticide, so it is especially important your fats and oils are organic. Fat also stores xenoestrogens, industrially made compounds which are found in plastic, and for this reason fat is always best stored in glass rather than plastic.

Let's look at the fats and oils I prefer to use, and which have nourished traditional peoples for hundreds of years.

It is of critical importance that the fats you eat are of the highest quality (they will have more nutrients this way), and that they are undamaged.

SATURATED ANIMAL FATS

All animal fats are highly stable to light, heat and oxygen. Though termed saturated, they are in fact a mix of saturated, monounsaturated and polyunsaturated fatty acids. All animal fats contain cholesterol. The fats (and all the other animal products) from grass-fed animals will be more potent than those from their grain-fed counterparts and are well worth sourcing and paying for.

BUTTER AND GHEE Butter is one of the best mediums for baking, giving beautiful flavour and a soft crumb. It's a little difficult for frying however, because the milk solids brown and burn as the heat increases. If you remove the milk solids and water from butter, you will end up with ghee and this is an excellent choice for frying and also for baking. Because the milk solids are removed, people on a casein-free diet can readily include ghee. If using ghee instead of butter to bake, remember it is pure butterfat. You might choose to (but don't have to) reduce the amount of ghee used by about 20 per cent.

DRIPPINGS AND RENDERED FATS Drippings are left-over fat from a roast or other cooked meats, poured while still hot into a small dish to set, and kept for cooking. These can be from all kinds of animals: beef and sheep fat is known as tallow; suet is the fat that protects the kidneys of cows and sheep; pork fat is generally known as lard; and some of the most delicious fats come from poultry. All are deeply nourishing, will give depth of flavour to the meal and leave the consumer feeling sated. These will keep for 4–6 weeks in the fridge.

COCONUT OIL

I cannot praise too highly the benefits of unrefined coconut oil, a non-animal saturated fat. This short-chain fatty acid is deeply nourishing and, other than mother's milk, is one of the richest sources of lauric acid—a known antiviral, antifungal and antimicrobial. It does not contribute to weight gain because there is no need for it to be emulsified with bile acids from the liver; rather, it is digested in the gut and provides energy. For all of these reasons, coconut oil is a brilliant fat to use for young children. With a high smoke point of approximately 170°C (325°F), it is also an excellent choice for frying (especially stir-frying).

Baking with coconut oil has its limitations, though. When the cookie or cake comes out of the oven, the crumb will be soft and moist, as if made with butter, but as it cools the crumb will toughen and constrict, and it will be slightly crumbly. Nothing will change this once the product has cooled. Having said that, coconut oil can be fabulous in some baked goods—it's an especially good choice for muesli bars. Served warm from the oven, cookies, cakes, pastry and puddings will all be delicious.

For those with a highly limited diet (no animal fats, no dairy, no nut oils) coconut oil is a godsend; in a piece of cake or a cookie, although crumbly and slightly more chewy, they are a welcome and delicious food.

I use three kinds of coconut oil:

- *Extra virgin (unrefined, full flavour)* This will be labelled different things by different brands, but has the full fragrance of coconut and has more nutrients than the flavourless ones. When cooked into a cake, it can have a strong aftertaste and not everyone likes this.

- *Virgin (less flavour)* This is also called refined or flavourless, but again, will be given different names by different brands. This oil has been deodorised (generally by running through clay) to remove the strong coconut fragrance, although with some nutrient loss. This is a good choice when you don't want that cooked coconut aftertaste (in biscuits, pastry, cakes and so on).

- *Coconut butter (spread)* This is coconut flesh ground into a paste —so delicious. Because it's the whole coconut, it retains all the protein, fibre, vitamins and minerals as well as the fat. This is a great choice to use in dried fruit and/nut and seed balls and energy bars (see dried apricot, date and coconut balls, page 278).

MONOUNSATURATED
AND POLYUNSATURATED FATS

Monounsaturated and polyunsaturated fats are called oils, and are liquid at room temperature. The more unsaturated they are, the more unstable they are when exposed to heat, light and oxygen. Most commercially available oils are highly refined, using chemical solvents and high heat. Because of this, they are highly damaged (rancid/oxidised) and procedures such as bleaching, steaming and deodorising help to clean them up and mask the damage. What is left is a nutrient-deficient oil, rich in free radicals—known to cause numerous problems for the human body. The oil you buy should be as unrefined as possible, and pressed with as little heat as possible, as heating damages the oil and encourages the production of free radicals (which is why these oils are unsuitable for stir-frying, which requires a very high heat). They should always come in a dark, glass bottle.

These are the oils I keep and feel comfortable using:

EXTRA VIRGIN, COLD-PRESSED OLIVE OIL This healthful oil is high in vitamin E and antioxidants. More importantly, because it has a high amount of oleic acid (approximately 71 per cent), it is relatively stable to heat, light and oxygen. I buy an expensive, unfiltered, organic extra virgin olive oil for cold work (salads and dressings) and a cheaper non-organic, extra virgin, cold-pressed olive oil for heating (including gentle frying—not stir-frying, though). If I come across a good deal and can justify bulk-buying, I use the organic one even for hot work.

MACADAMIA OIL A richly flavoured oil that will tolerate heat well. Great for baking and gentle frying.

UNREFINED SESAME OIL Not as stable as olive oil, but because it has its own antioxidant (sesamin) it can withstand gentle heating (although not stir-frying as is often recommended). It's also great in salad dressings.

ALMOND OIL With a high (about 61 per cent) level of oleic acid and a light flavour and colour, this has been a favourite of mine for baking when I can't use butter or coconut. However, because it's getting expensive, I use macadamia oil more often.

WALNUT OIL If you can find this oil *fresh* and in a tin or dark glass bottle from a fridge—buy it. It is highly unsaturated, has a good amount of omega-3 essential fatty acids and is utterly delicious as a dressing. Always store this oil in the fridge and never heat it in any way—it should only ever be used cold—straight from the fridge into a dressing or drizzled straight from the bottle over some steamed vegies, but never put in a pot or frying pan.

FLAX (LINSEED) OIL This is one of the richest land sources of omega-3 essential fatty acids. It should always come in a tin or a dark glass bottle, and should be stored in the fridge. Like walnut oil, flax oil is highly unstable and should only ever be used cold.

OTHER NUT AND SEED OILS If they are *unrefined* and I can find them, I may use pumpkin, hazelnut or peanut oils from time to time. Again, they are to be used cold and should never be heated.

MARGARINE

Margarine is made from the highly refined and damaged oils described on page 59. It is then mixed with nickel oxide and pumped with hydrogen atoms that create very dangerous trans fatty acids. It is worth noting that this hydrogenated oil (margarine/ shortening) is used in pretty much every commercial cake, pastry, croissant, Danish and biscuit. For young and growing children, it's not only *extremely* damaging to cells, but denies them the critical nutrients found in real fats—especially butter. There are also some non-hydrogenated oil spreads on the market—generally high in omega-3 fatty acids, produced by a process called interesterification. I still consider these to be highly processed non-foods. If you want omega-3 fatty acids, you are far better off with quality eggs or fish.

There's a great quote by the noted nutritionist Joan Gussow: 'As for butter versus margarine, I trust cows more than chemists.' I can only agree.

Thickening agents

KUDZU (KUZU), CORNFLOUR (CORNSTARCH) AND TRUE ARROWROOT are all starch-based thickening agents and have their uses. Of these, I prefer kudzu because of its medicinal properties. The sea vegetable, agar, and gelatine are other useful gelling agents (see pages 62 and 63).

KUDZU

Also called kuzu, this thickening agent is made from the root of the kudzu plant, and is well known in China and Japan for its medicinal qualities—it is traditionally used to treat digestive problems such as an upset stomach or to soothe the nerves. It is also gluten free. When used to thicken sauces, kudzu imparts a beautiful, clear sheen to the finished sauce. It will also set soft puddings. It must be completely dissolved (generally in a little liquid) before being used, and then gently brought to the boil while stirring constantly. Kudzu continues to thicken as it cools.

As a guide, 2 teaspoons of kudzu will set 250 ml (9 fl oz/1 cup) of liquid to a sauce consistency, while 2½ tablespoons will set to a soft pudding consistency. To measure kudzu, which is sold in lumps, grind it with the end of a rolling pin, or use a pestle and mortar. Kudzu is a wonderful choice to settle an upset tummy.

CORNFLOUR

Also called cornstarch, this is a finely ground gluten-free flour made from the endosperm of corn kernels; it is white and has very little nutrient value. It is, however, particularly useful when some 'structure' is required in a finished product and is especially useful in dairy-free desserts. For example, a 'cream' requires more body than a simple sauce. In small quantities, it is also useful to aid binding, especially in gluten-free baking. Check the packet when you buy cornflour as it is often actually made from wheat.

TRUE ARROWROOT

Similar in appearance to cornflour (cornstarch), arrowroot comes from the root of a tropical plant and is gluten free. Make sure you purchase 'true' arrowroot, as much of the arrowroot sold is actually tapioca (cassava) flour, which is not the same thing and behaves very differently. True arrowroot is dried and powdered root, and a rich source of trace minerals and calcium. It has traditionally been used for babies and young children as it's very easy to digest—it's a great choice for baking. When using it to make a custard or sauce, like kudzu (kuzu), arrowroot must be completely dissolved (generally in a little liquid) before using. Unlike kudzu, however, arrowroot thickens at a slightly lower temperature—it's especially important not to over-boil it as this can break it down. It must be gently brought to the boil while stirring constantly, but remove it from the stovetop as soon as you see bubbles forming.

AGAR

Also known as kanten, agar is a nutrient-rich, high-fibre, kilojoule-free gelling agent made from seaweed. It comes in flakes, powder and bars but I prefer flakes or powder—they are easy to measure out and give reliable results. Agar will set at room temperature and can be boiled and reheated without losing its gelling ability. I have specified powder in most recipes as it gives more reliable results. Some batches of flakes are stronger than others, and the consistency of their setting can vary enormously.

To achieve a good but not too solid jelly, the basic equation is 3 teaspoons of agar flakes or ½ teaspoon of agar powder for 250 ml (9 fl oz/1 cup) of liquid.

For a very firm jelly, increase the amount of agar used. However, it does depend on the brand. Sometimes I have found I only need to use 2 teaspoons of agar flakes per cup of liquid. If you're worried about the consistency, test it: when you have cooked and dissolved the flakes or powder, simply place a little in a small bowl, then pop it in the fridge (or freezer) until cold. If it is too soft, add it back to the mix along with a little more agar and cook until dissolved. If it's too firm, add more liquid and cook for a couple more minutes.

Agar dissolves best in high-pectin juices like apple, but works in most fruit juices. Both flakes and powder need to be dissolved slowly over a gentle boil and stirred frequently to stop the agar sticking to the bottom of the pan as it dissolves. Powder is best whisked into the mixture to avoid its tendency to clump; it takes about 8 to 10 minutes from the boil. Flakes take up to 25 minutes.

Agar will not set in distilled and wine vinegars, nor in food containing large amounts of oxalic acid such as chocolate, rhubarb or spinach. When using high-acid juices such as lemon, lime or pineapple juice, double the quantity of agar.

The quality of agar powder will affect your result. Look for agar powder in natural food stores, rather than the more common fine, very white powder seen at supermarkets and Asian grocers.

GELATINE

Traditionally made from the skin and bones of cows, gelatine is one of the most traditional aids to digestion, and one of the reasons stocks made from animal bones are so nourishing. It's very important to use a gelatine that you trust—one that is made from the healthiest of cows. I prefer to use the Bernard Jensen brand, which is made from healthy, A-grade cows and it is readily available on the Internet.

Sea vegetables

SEA VEGETABLES ARE A WONDERFULLY RICH SOURCE of protein, vitamins A, B, C and E, trace elements and minerals such as calcium, zinc and iron (among many others) and, of course, iodine. A little bit goes a very long way.

It is important to choose sea vegetables that are sourced from clean waters, although these will invariably be more expensive than others. Good health food, organic and wholefoods shops are the best places to source quality sea vegetables. Dried, they are easily stored in an airtight container in the pantry and will keep indefinitely.

USING SEA VEGETABLES

As all sea vegetables are rich sources of iodine, you will need to tone down the use of salt in the dish, only adding tamari, miso or salt at the end of the cooking after tasting.

Most dried sea vegetables need rehydrating before use. Cover them completely with water and allow them to sit for approximately 15 to 30 minutes. Strain the soaked sea vegetables, squeeze out the excess water (you could use this nutrient-rich liquid on your garden), then rinse, making them ready to use.

If you are adding sea vegetables to a soup or stock, place the dried portion in the liquid—this will rehydrate it, with all the goodness returning to the broth. Remember, though, that the sea vegetable will not have been strained or rinsed of the strongly flavoured soaking liquid, so you may not want to use too much at first, as you adjust to the flavour the sea vegetables impart. Agar (see page 62), kombu and wakame have the least intrusive flavours and are good ones to start with.

KOMBU

Rich in iodine, calcium, potassium and magnesium, and containing glutamic acid—a 'natural' and safe form of monosodium glutamate (MSG)—kombu is a wonder helper in the kitchen. It enriches and boosts the flavour of stocks, soups, stews and grains, and tenderises beans. A deep green colour, kombu will just about dissolve when cooked for a long time—you'll never know it was there. Use a 10 cm (4 inch) strip for 3–4 litres (105–140 fl oz/12–16 cups) of liquid.

ARAME

Rich in calcium, iodine, iron, potassium and phytohormones, arame is a thin, strongly flavoured, partly cooked and dried almost noodle-like sea vegetable. Soaked and rehydrated, it can be used as an addition to salads and stir-fries and is excellent in small amounts in soups.

DULSE

This is an exceptional sea vegetable which is extremely high in iron as well as calcium, iodine, phosphorus, potassium, magnesium, manganese and vitamins A, B, C and D. Dulse is a beautiful dark purple colour, and easily used. It's handy to buy dulse flakes, which can be sprinkled over anything.

KELP

Rich in calcium, potassium, magnesium and iron, kelp is great added dry to soups and stews, or soaked and added to stir-fries. It expands up to five times its dry size.

NORI

This has the highest protein of any sea vegetable, along with the usual array of minerals. In its original state, nori is a deep reddish purple sea vegetable. When soaked it is great in a salad as it looks so pretty. Once toasted, nori will turn bright green—this is how it looks in its most common use—the toasted nori sheet. As well as being the traditional wrapping for sushi, toasted nori sheets are great to crumble or cut into strips and add to soups (particularly miso), salads or even a bowl of steamed vegies and brown rice. They are very fragile and must be sealed once the packet has been opened—air and moisture make them difficult to roll.

WAKAME

This is a delightful sea vegetable—when rehydrated it is a beautiful green leaf. Wakame is a good choice for salads and stir-fries—dishes that ask for a mild flavour and lovely colour. It is very, very rich in calcium, among the many other minerals it contains, with high levels of B and C vitamins as well.

Salt

GOOD-QUALITY SALT IS AN IMPORTANT PART of a wholesome diet and, like many real foods, has critical roles to play. It stimulates gastric juices, is essential for the production of hydrochloric acid in the stomach and is required for nerve transmissions, to name a few. It is also a rich source of minerals, including iodine. There is a huge difference between a real, mineral-rich, unrefined sea salt and the refined, bleached and concentrated sodium chloride that is sold as salt. I prefer salt from the sea and love Celtic sea salt, which contains 80 minerals. I never use or recommend iodised salt, but prefer to get iodine from its source (sea salt, seafood and sea vegetables). I also like to access salt in other ways—from naturally brewed soy sauces such as miso, umeboshi plums and sea vegetables. *Tamari* and *fish sauce* are both wonderful seasoning agents. Rather than just use salt, I often prefer to add a touch of one of these to provide a salty focus to the dish and reap the benefit of added flavour.

Sweeteners

I BELIEVE WE ARE HARD-WIRED FOR SWEETNESS in our lives, and it's not a bad thing for young children to have small amounts of foods that include whole sweeteners in moderation. It's a deeply delicious and joyous experience to eat foods made with wholesome and real sweeteners, and I suspect a profound imbalance arises from being totally deprived of them. I see lots of parents excluding sweeteners from a child's diet—and while this is not necessarily a bad thing, invariably that same child is likely to be eating large amounts of flavoured yoghurts (mistakenly believed to be healthy) which have been sweetened artificially or with refined white sugar. When children start to socialise with other children and families, refined sugar in its many guises (such as lollies and soft drink) comes into the picture. As I said, I think we are hard-wired for sweetness (we don't call each other sweetheart for nothing) and I'd much rather see you help your child develop a taste for subtle, whole and natural sweetness than for the highly refined and sickly sweet alternatives. By providing your young child (and the entire family) with small amounts of whole and natural sweetness, we help train the taste buds. I've also found that when a little natural sweetness is provided, refined sweet goods are less tempting as the need for sweetness has been met. You might be surprised to know that whole sweeteners are also good sources of vitamins and minerals.

SAP SWEETENERS

Sap is the nourishing fluid that flows through a plant or tree and, in many cases, is sweet. Many plant saps—including birch and pine, sorghum and maize—have been used throughout history. The ones most commonly available today include cane sugar, maple syrup, palm sugars and agave nectar.

CANE SUGAR The best-known sweetener is probably cane sugar—and it is a great example of what makes a food good or bad. Sugar (as most foods) is not necessarily a *bad* thing—it's really more what we *do* to it that makes it so. When you take the natural juice from cane sugar, strip and refine it of everything but the sucrose—which is then bleached—you are going to end up with a highly body-incompatible product that will simply behave like high-octane fuel in the body. It's interesting to note that a very popular health supplement is molasses. This is simply all the goodness (vitamins and minerals) that is stripped from the sugar during processing, and it is often prescribed for children because it is rich in iron.

Fortunately, things are changing in the world of sweeteners, and you can now buy whole sugars.

RAPADURA SUGAR (EVAPORATED CANE SUGAR) Rapadura sugar is made from organic cane sugar, where the juice is filtered, the fibre removed and what remains is crystallised. It retains its valuable vitamins and minerals. Brands vary—some are quite moist, others quite dry. Foods that include rapadura in the ingredients take on some of its rich colouring (it retains the natural molasses) and are less sweet than foods cooked with white sugar. Rapadura contains approximately 75 per cent sucrose, compared with 99 per cent sucrose in refined white sugar.

When a little more sweetness and less colour is required, I prefer to use the washed rapadura sugars—the washing process is sometimes referred to as sifting.

It's important to understand this—1 cup of white sugar will sweeten more than 1 cup of a lighter, unrefined washed or centrifuged sugar (commonly known as unrefined raw sugar, or 'golden' sugars), which in turn will sweeten more than 1 cup of rapadura sugar.

Unrefined sugars are washed to remove the colour and flavour that molasses gives. Another technique for producing a more whole but less-coloured and less-flavoured sugar involves using a centrifuge to spin off varying degrees of molasses. Both techniques will concentrate the sucrose; the resulting sugar is about 85 per cent sucrose.

Brands vary, but a wide range of these unrefined, less-coloured sugars is available. They vary in crystal size—from very fine icing (confectioner's) and caster (superfine) sugars, to the fine and larger all-purpose varieties, such as raw (demerara) sugar.

MAPLE SYRUP I love maple syrup—it's such a beautifully flavoured sweetener to use, and rich in trace minerals, including calcium. It's far cheaper to buy in bulk than in small quantities, but be very particular about the brand you use—I prefer organic, as maple syrup can contain formaldehyde traces from the pellets used in the trees to extend sap flow. (This is not permitted under organic certification, nor by the Canadian Government.) You can also buy maple sugar, which is simply crystallised maple syrup.

PALM SUGAR (JAGGERY) AND COCONUT SUGAR The concentrated saps of the sugar palm or coconut palm are delicious, mineral-rich sweeteners. Grades and colours vary—sugar palm sugars are generally darker in colour than coconut palm sugars. They are sold in a variety of styles: as small logs, wrapped in paper or packed in small plastic containers; and in granulated form. The paper-wrapped logs are generally soft and easy to shave into thin slivers; I prefer not to use the logs packed in plastic containers as the sugar can be very hard. Granulated palm and coconut sugars look similar to a rapadura sugar, varying from a light golden colour for a coconut palm sugar, to a dark brown for a palm sugar.

Apart from being so delicious and mineral rich, one of the huge benefits of these sugars is that they have a low glycaemic index (GI), yet they are not fructose based. Primarily they are sucrose, followed by glucose, then a little fructose.

AGAVE NECTAR To make this sweetener, the juices of the agave cactus are filtered and heated at a low temperature to break down the carbohydrate to sugars. Agave is becoming very popular as a sweetener because it has a low glycaemic index (GI).

Agave nectar is much sweeter than sugar, so I suggest using 125–185 ml (4–6 fl oz/½–¾ cup) agave nectar as a substitute for 220 g (7¾ oz/1 cup) raw (demerara) sugar. It also browns more easily in the oven, so you will need to reduce the oven temperature a little.

However, it does have a high fructose content, so I'm not entirely convinced this is the wonder sweetener it's being sold as (see *Fructose*, page 70), but it does have its uses. Its texture is viscous, like a very runny honey, and it doesn't crystallise or set when cold. It comes in a variety of grades—light (with the most neutral flavour) to the darker version (with a corresponding increase in caramel flavours).

MALTOSE-BASED SWEETENERS

These are some of the most whole and body-compatible sweeteners. They are made by steeping grains with enzymes which break down the starches into simpler sugars. These sugars are still complex, and take much longer to digest than the sugar in sap sweeteners (see page 67).

RICE SYRUP (BROWN RICE MALT) This is one of the least sweet and most whole sweeteners. Although sticky and difficult to use, it also has its place. It retains a syrupy consistency even when cooked, and tends to crisp when directly exposed to heat. As a result, a cake crust will be crisp and the insides a bit chewy, but it is great in biscuits and excellent in creams. It's wonderful to drizzle over yoghurts, porridge and pancakes, and it also works well when cut with maple syrup.

BARLEY MALT This is strongly flavoured (think beer). Use as you would rice syrup but go easy—the flavour really is very strong.

SPELT SYRUP Fairly new to the market, spelt syrup is similar to rice syrup and barley malt. It has a lovely mild flavour—use as described for rice syrup.

AMASAKE (AMAZAKE) This is a fascinating, brilliant, though relatively unknown, sweetener that looks like a puréed rice pudding. It's made using a similar process to the syrups and malts above, only extracted at a far earlier stage. Because this is a fermented food, not only is amasake easy to digest but it also aids digestion. Originally, rice milk was watered-down amasake. It's great for young children as a drink, mixed with coconut cream and served with fruit, or in baking.

OTHER WHOLE SWEETENERS

There are a handful of natural, whole sweeteners that are neither sap sweeteners nor maltose-based.

Always choose raw honey— unfiltered, unprocessed, unrefined and unheated—as it will still have all its goodness and enzymes intact.

RAW HONEY Honey is generally the most easily available local sweetener, and almost certainly, the first used by humans. It's a wonderful food, with many healthful, nourishing and healing properties. Use in any drink or foods which do not require heating. Indeed, ancient Ayurveda teachings consider honey to be indigestible and toxic when heated. Also, honey shouldn't be fed to children less than 12 months, as it is said to contain bacterial spores that produce *Clostridium botulinum* bacteria and can result in infant botulism. Because a baby's digestive and immune systems are still so underdeveloped, this can be deadly. There are people who disagree with this, but I think it's best to err on the side of caution. Honey is a nourishing and healing sweetener. Remember that it's twice as sweet as sugar—so use it sparingly.

STEVIA The leaves of the stevia plant have been used for centuries to sweeten foods and as a remedy for diabetes. Stevia is available as a liquid, as a white powder or in a more whole form, where the leaves are ground into a fine, soft greenish-grey powder. Although it's not a bad thing in the whole form, I'm not mad about stevia. For all its intense sweetness, it also has a bitter taste to it, and a little goes a very long way—too much, and you will end up with a bitter result.

VANILLA Not technically a sweetener, but a flavouring used in sweet foods, vanilla is often described as an essence or an extract, and there are rules that define both. My bottom line is to look for ones that contain only vanilla and alcohol. No sweeteners (generally fructose or glucose) and certainly no preservatives.

Vanilla paste is also very handy, this is the vanilla seed suspended in a thick syrup—generally inulin or tragacanth, which are both tree saps and quite safe.

FRUCTOSE

Fructose is the sugar found in fruits. As with sucrose, nature goes to a lot of trouble to protect fructose and pad it out with a lot of other nutrients—including fibre. Fructose is not such a great sweetener. First, unlike glucose, which is digested in the gut, fructose is metabolised in the liver and can place a strain on that organ. Second, because fructose doesn't stimulate the release of insulin (that's why it's recommended for diabetics), which in turn stimulates the hormone leptin, the brain can't 'hear' the 'I've had enough, thank you' message. It's easy to keep on eating or drinking substances sweetened with fructose. Finally, fructose converts more easily to fat than glucose does. Like any food, it's always going to be better when left whole—in the original apple or grape, for example. I'm not a fan of high-fructose sweeteners for all the above reasons.

FRUIT JUICE CONCENTRATES I am not a fan of fruit juice concentrates as a sweetening tool, but I do use a little for balancing out savoury dishes. I find fruit juice concentrates to be a poor sweetener for baking, preferring the flavour and nutrient richness of other sweeteners, such as rapadura sugar or maple syrup.

HIGH-FRUCTOSE CORN SYRUP (HFCS) Cheap and plentiful, HFCS is the main sweetener used in commercial food products and drinks. It is refined from corn through a convoluted process that transforms glucose into fructose, resulting in a highly processed product. It is even less desirable than fructose as a sweetener.

ARTIFICIAL AND NUTRITIVE SWEETENERS

There is a large range of artificial sweeteners on the market, which includes aspartame, NutraSweet, saccharin, cyclamate and many more. I would not recommend any of these products for children or adults.

There is also a range of products known as 'nutritive sweeteners' on the market—these *sound* natural, and so are very popular, especially because they are not sugar. One of the best-selling are the sugar alcohols—they're pure, white and highly refined. I'm not a fan of sugar alcohols—primarily because they are *highly, highly, highly* refined and fractionalised sweeteners, and do not break down in the stomach. Once in the bowels, they attract water, which can lead to fermentation of bad bacteria—common reactions to sugar alcohol can be stomach cramping and anal leakage. A young digestive system would have even more trouble coping with this sweetener. Many sugar-free foods and drinks are sweetened with these highly questionable artificial or sugar alcohol sweeteners, including all chewing gums. All the unrefined sweetening agents discussed above would be far better options.

Especially for children, I recommend you avoid any food or drink made with HFCS, and definitely reduce the use of fruit juice concentrates and fructose-based sweeteners. Fruit juice itself should always be watered down when given to children.

SPECIAL DIETS

For many reasons, your child
may need a special diet.
We are all individuals and what might
suit one, will not suit another—children
are no exception. There may be health
issues to consider or philosophical
or religious reasons to take into
account. It is important that you
approach such a diet with as much
information as possible, so that you
replace the food being removed,
with a healthy substitute.

Raising a vegetarian child

WHILE VEGETARIANISM IS NOT MY PREFERRED OPTION, I do believe you can raise a whole and healthy child without meat—but not without animal products. This is a dietary decision that should never be made lightly, but with a great deal of consideration regarding how the child will be provided with adequate key nutrients, particularly protein, iron and vitamin B12.

PROTEIN

Vegetarian sources of protein are generally not complete—that is, they don't contain all eight essential amino acids. A broad variety of whole grains and legumes is an important part of any vegetarian diet, because in combination they can provide a complete range of the essential amino acids. The whole grains amaranth and quinoa should especially be included, as they are as complete a protein as a grain can be. You should also take care to include sea vegetables (especially kelp and nori, see pages 64 and 65), as well as nuts and seeds (see page 48). Soy is considered to be the highest protein of the legume family, but you do need to think carefully about how and in what forms you will include it (see page 50). Too much soy is not always a good thing for a young and growing child. Take into account also that a young child's digestion can be delicate, and too much fibre from a large amount of whole grains and legumes is not good when they are very young. Make sure to liberally include eggs and, if possible, fish to provide complete protein.

IRON

Red meat is an exceptionally rich source of bioavailable haem iron. When relying on vegetable sources for this critical growth nutrient, you will need to make sure you include a broad range of foods rich in iron, and supply a quality vitamin C to help its absorption. Good non-flesh sources of iron include sea vegetables (especially arame, dulse and kelp), molasses, dark leafy green vegetables, nuts, apricots, peaches, figs, seeds and avocados.

VITAMIN B12

This critical B vitamin is primarily found in animals. The grass they eat is fermented in the gut—B12 comes from fermented sources. B12 can also be made by good bacteria in the gut—which is another reason lacto-fermented foods (see page 98) are so important. Other animal sources include oily fish, eggs and milk products. Non-animal sources include fermented soy (tempeh and miso), spirulina and sprouts, although all these claims are debated.

I strongly encourage you to include fish and fish stock, good-quality eggs, full-cream (whole) milk (cow's or goat's), butter, cream and cheese (sheep's, cow's or goat's) in your child's diet. Include sea salt and sea vegetables for iodine. Also plenty of lacto-fermented foods to encourage beneficial bacteria in the gut.

It is also important to remember that fat and protein sate. When meat is removed, it's very easy to pad out the diet with too much carbohydrate, and typically, this is what can happen in a vegetarian diet.

For all the above reasons, I strongly believe that a vegan diet (no animal products) is *not* suitable for young and growing children.

Raising a dairy-free child

THE MOST COMMON DAIRY-FREE MILK, cheese, yoghurt and ice cream substitution used is soy—and for all the reasons described on page 50, this can be a poor choice, especially for growing boys. These products are especially damaging because they are almost always made from highly refined soy protein isolate with numerous additives, including refined sugars and oils, to give it mouthfeel and flavour. Indeed, there is little nourishment in many of these products.

MILKS

Not all children thrive on cow's milk and its products. But before moving on to the alternatives, read the information on page 34. If you've given cow's milk a good try, using it in the most body-compatible ways (whole, raw and/or cultured), and also tried goat's milk with no luck, then it is worth looking at the following alternatives.

SOY MILK Any soy milk you buy should be derived from the whole soya bean, and preferably have the sea vegetable kombu in it. Using sea vegetables with soy products is a wise thing to do—traditional cultures depending on soy included plenty of sea vegetables, which are very rich in minerals and help to make up for some of the mineral deficiencies that can be caused by soy. Brands do vary in flavour—generally you get what you pay for.

OAT MILK This is a lovely alternative to dairy, but it is important to look for oat milks that contain as few additives as possible.

RICE MILK Traditionally this was made from watered-down amasake (amazake, see page 69). However, this is not the case for the rice milks you will find on the shelves today—it would be prohibitively expensive. I do love rice milk and, because it's slightly sweeter than most other milks, it's a great choice for baking or dessert work. It is best enriched with coconut milk to add fat and give body.

NUT MILKS I consider these (especially almond milk) to be the most nutritious of the milk alternatives. I always prefer to make my own nut milks (see page 105) rather than buy them—the commercially available nut milks are stabilised and can contain added flavours, refined sweeteners and oils. For baking, they are best enriched with coconut milk to add fat and give body.

FORTIFIED MILK ALTERNATIVES Many milk alternatives are fortified with vitamin D and/or calcium and there are sure to be other additives in the future. As you might guess, I'm not a fan. As with iodine deficiencies, calcium and vitamin D deficiencies result from eating refined and processed foods. As far back as the 1920s, Dr Weston A Price called such foods 'the displacing foods of modern commerce'. Also, many drinks are fortified with vitamin D2, which behaves very differently in the body than vitamin D, and has been linked to hyperactivity, heart disease and allergies. I am entirely unconvinced that adding these fractionalised vitamins and minerals makes any positive difference, or that they are even absorbed and able to be used—especially by children whose systems are not all that adept at conversions. Whole and real food sources of these nutrients do exist and include the following:

- Non-dairy sources of vitamins A and D:
  - cod liver oil
  - good-quality eggs
  - pork fat
  - grass-fed animal fat.
- Non-dairy sources of calcium:
  - bone stocks are the best source, followed by sea vegetable stocks
  - sea vegetables—especially wakame
  - dark leafy green vegetables
  - dried fruits
  - nuts and seeds.

Remember that calcium also needs vitamin D and good-quality fats from both animal and non-animal sources for absorption and utilisation.

CHEESES

If your child cannot tolerate cheese made from cow's milk, consider goat's milk and sheep's milk cheeses. Soy cheeses are highly refined damaged non-foods and I do not recommend them at all. Cheese made from milk (in a traditional manner) provides a comforting sweetness and mouthfeel that you will need to replace if you remove all cheeses from your child's diet. Hulled tahini, avocado, coconut (cream, milk, butter and oil) and nut creams are great alternatives. None of them can replicate grilled cheese, but they do create deliciousness in other ways.

YOGHURT

Consider goat's milk and sheep's milk yoghurt as alternatives to cow's milk yoghurt. Soy yoghurts are highly refined non-foods, masquerading as probiotics. We turn to yoghurt for the beneficial bacteria within them—but there are much richer sources: unpasteurised miso, cultured or pickled vegetables, water-based lacto-fermented drinks, such as water-based kefir or kombucha (a colony of friendly bacteria and yeasts) and cultured dried fruits are all rich in beneficial bacteria and are all dairy free. Amasake (amazake) mixed with coconut cream is another great replacement for yoghurt, while coconut-based yoghurts are also beginning to come onto the market and can be a great option.

It is important to note that sesame seeds are indeed a rich source of calcium, but this is bound in the hull with oxalic acid and is not bioavailable. Soaking sesame seeds then lightly roasting them (see page 104), will help to make the calcium more available. When using tahini, I prefer to use hulled as it has a milder flavour. Using an unhulled tahini will not deliver any more calcium, unless the seeds were pre-soaked.

ICE CREAM

There are great dairy-free alternatives for ice cream—my favourites are based on coconut (see page 209) and rice, rather than soy. There are also lots of other iced treats, including homemade creamy frozen fruit and fruit sorbets.

BUTTER AND SPREADS

Ghee is pure butterfat, with all the milk protein removed. Many children who can't tolerate milk are fine with ghee. It's a huge bonus if your child can tolerate ghee, which is great as a spread and for cooking (see page 107). If not, look to hulled tahini, avocado, coconut (cream, milk, butter and oil) and nut butters and creams. Don't be tempted by the quaint-sounding margarines (see page 61) and oil-based spreads, which are highly refined, damaged and will offer little goodness.

NIGHTSHADES

In a dairy-free diet, you will also need to consider nightshades. This vegetable family includes the potato, capsicum (pepper), tomato and eggplant (aubergine) all of which are high in alkaloids, which interfere with the absorption of calcium. When you look at most traditional dishes made with these vegetables, they generally include a rich calcium source—most often dairy. If you cannot include milk or cheese, make sure you provide plentiful calcium in other ways.

Raising a wheat-free or gluten-free child

THE TWO MOST DIFFICULT PROTEINS FOR HUMANS to digest are the protein in cow's milk (casein) and the protein in wheat (gluten). This difficulty is compounded by a child's immature digestive system and many children find wheat very difficult to digest, with problems ranging from bloating to allergic reactions. Shifting to other grains that are not wheat can help this. They may be able to tolerate the other gluten grains, such as barley, oats, rye or spelt—which is the most water-soluble.

They will also be able to tolerate the gluten-free grains, amaranth, buckwheat, maize, millet, quinoa and rice.

There are other things you can do to aid the digestion of grains:

- ⊛ soak all grain used (see page 88)
- ⊛ cook the grain in a bone stock (see page 89)
- ⊛ provide a rich source of lacto-fermented foods to enrich the gut bacteria and thus aid digestion (see page 98)
- ⊛ give preference to whole grains rather than refined
- ⊛ reduce the amount of grain in the diet.

For some children, these measures will be enough. Others, though, will not be able to tolerate any gluten at all. There are varying degrees of intolerance to gluten—some people simply find it incredibly difficult to digest (generally because they have a poor digestive system); others have coeliac disease, where gluten triggers an autoimmune response, damaging the stomach. In both cases all grains containing gluten should be avoided. The gluten-free grains are amaranth, buckwheat, maize, millet, quinoa and rice. Some gluten-sensitive people can also tolerate oats that have been certified free from gluten contamination.

There is a lot of confusion about wheat-free diets and gluten-free diets—they are not necessarily the same thing. As you can see, some people just need to avoid the particular gluten found in wheat, and they will be fine. Spelt, oats and barley are easy to use and wonderful for people in this category. Those on a gluten-free diet, however, will need to avoid all gluten grains.

The other aspect I'd like to discuss here is this: if your child is gluten intolerant, be careful what you replace the gluten grains with. Baking with gluten-free grain flours is tricky—they don't really stick together; thus, most gluten-free pasta, noodles, pastry, cakes or biscuits are in fact made from highly refined starches and gums. Potato, rice, tapioca (cassava) and cornflour (cornstarch) are all very popular for gluten-free baking. They give a lovely light result, but are not ideal as food. Cast your mind back to when you were a child and mixed a white starch with water—you made glue. These highly refined starches will do the same thing in your child's stomach and compound their digestive problems by breaking down into sugars too quickly, thus feeding bad bacteria. They have their place, but it is wise to avoid them as much as possible and become comfortable with using the gluten-free whole grains and their flours.

RECIPE FOUNDATIONS

The recipes you will find in this chapter are some of the most important in the book, as they represent fundamental and invaluable wisdoms handed down from generations past. If you're wondering where to start, this is a good place.

Cooking essentials

THROUGHOUT THE FOLLOWING RECIPES, there are some things that remain consistent. For every recipe, you can assume the following:

- All ingredients, including spices, where at all possible, are organic. Food that is organic will, almost always, have a better and deeper flavour, and this will impact on the finished dish.
- Nuts and seeds are more digestible when soaked, especially for young ones. Once soaked, lightly roasting them ensures they keep well (see page 103).
- To peel or not to peel? For many root vegetables, especially potatoes, much of the goodness is just under the skin. If your carrots, potatoes and orange sweet potatoes are fresh and have lovely skin, simply scrub them well and don't worry about peeling. If there are any dodgy bits, just cut those off.
- Olive oil is always extra virgin.
- Coconut oil is always extra virgin (unrefined, full flavour).
- Coconut milk is always full-cream, not light, and never stabilised.
- Milk is always non-homogenised and full-cream (whole), and preferably raw when the recipe does not involve heat.
- Tamari is always wheat free.
- Honey is always raw and unfiltered.
- Apple juice is always unfiltered.
- Salt is always Celtic sea salt and black pepper is always freshly ground.
- All dried fruit is sulphur free.
- Natural vanilla extracts vary in strength so adjust according to your taste.

Beans

BEANS CONTAIN LONG-CHAIN SUGARS CALLED OLIGOSACCHARIDES, which the human stomach is not able to break down, so these ferment in the stomach and cause gas.

The method for preparing beans, and also the cooking of them, aims to break these long-chain sugars down. A slow cooker is perfect for most beans (apart from red kidney—these need to be cooked at higher temperatures to ensure their naturally occurring toxin is destroyed). When cooking beans, make more than you need, and freeze the rest in portions for another time. If you are adding frozen beans to a soup or stew, you won't need to thaw them first as they will simply thaw in the hot pot.

In this section, you'll find all the information you need for cooking a large variety of beans. Before you know it, you'll be finding it very simple to cook them yourself rather than relying on tinned beans. It's true that beans take a long time to cook, but once they are ready, you have either a great meal or the beginnings of one. Beans take planning, that's all. If you are cooking them from scratch, you'll need to organise soaking and cooking time. There are many ways to use beans; as a rule, deeply flavoured stews and soups benefit from the addition of uncooked beans, while pre cooked beans are great for spreads, dips, stir-fries and lighter, quicker-cooking stews.

TINNED BEANS

These are a great standby and handy to have in the cupboard, but they shouldn't be the only beans you use. Tinned beans are often harder to digest than home-cooked beans, due to the reliance on pressure to create a soft bean rather than long soaking and cooking times. When using tinned beans, it's best to rinse them well and to take away some of the 'tinned' taste. Brands vary enormously; a very few do actually soak the beans and cook them with kombu—even though they are more expensive, these are the brands I prefer. Another thing to consider is the tin itself—most are lined with plastic and can transfer xenoestrogens—in particular bisphenol A—into the food when heated, so I choose a brand that uses bisphenol A-free tins.

SOAKING

Pre-soaking dried beans for 6 to 8 hours helps to leach out the oligosaccharides, making them more digestible. A useful routine is to soak them overnight in a large bowl, well covered with water that has 1 tablespoon of whey (see page 99), buttermilk or yoghurt stirred gently through. Soaking at room temperature is recommended, allowing a little fermentation to occur.

When preparing beans, if you need to hurry the soaking process, bring the soaking water (with the beans in it) to the boil, then remove from the heat and leave them to soak for a few hours.

Dried beans must be well cooked to ensure optimum digestion; they can take between 1 and 4 hours to cook on the stove. Make sure they are well covered with liquid as they swell considerably. Here are a few tips that make cooking beans easier, and help to ensure a good result every time.

 Kombu Adding a small portion of this sea vegetable at the beginning of cooking will soften the beans and improve their digestibility. A 3–5 cm (1¼–2 inch) piece will be adequate for the quantities of beans cooked in the following recipes.

 Do not add salt Salt only serves to toughen beans. If you must add salt, do it when they have finished cooking. Usually, though, the addition of kombu will add sufficient saltiness.

 Think small Beans are concentrated and powerful foods—a little goes a long way. Serve very small portions to young children, building up to a serving of ¼–½ cup of cooked beans for a seven-year-old child.

How to cook beans

GLUTEN FREE / DAIRY FREE
Serves 4–6

After the beans have soaked, discard the water, drain the beans well and put them in a large heavy-based saucepan. Add enough water to cover the beans by 10 cm (4 inches) and bring to the boil over medium heat.

As soon as the water reaches boiling point, turn the heat down very low (a heat diffuser is useful). Begin timing from this point based on the cooking times opposite. Check the pan regularly to ensure that the beans are always well covered with liquid. Some beans, particularly chickpeas, produce a large amount of froth, foam and scum, which needs to be removed as they cook.

You can tell when the beans are cooked—they begin to yield their soft, starchy centres to light pressure, and there should be no hard, pebbly bits. The following quantities indicated for cooked beans are approximate as they depend on various factors, including the age of the beans and the length of soaking time.

Beans cook very well in a pressure cooker. Cover them with about 3 cm (1¼ inch) of water, bring them to the boil, then skim off any foam before beginning to cook under pressure. Your cooking times will be radically shorter than in a normal cooking pot; about 20 minutes for lighter beans, such as adzuki, pinto, borlotti (cranberry), great northern and cannellini (white); and about 50 minutes for hardier beans such as red kidney, soya and chickpeas.

dried adzuki beans (1–1½ hours)
    220 g (7¾ oz/1 cup) makes 520 g (1 lb 2½ oz/3 cups)

dried black (turtle) beans (1–1½ hours)
    200 g (7 oz/1 cup) makes 450 g (1 lb/2¼ cups)

dried borlotti (cranberry) beans (1–1½ hours)
    200 g (7 oz/1 cup) makes 450 g (1 lb/2¼ cups)

dried cannellini (white) beans (1–1½ hours)
    200 g (7 oz/1 cup) makes 500 g (1 lb 2 oz/2½ cups)

dried chickpeas (2½–4 hours)
    200 g (7 oz/1 cup) makes 450 g (1 lb/3 cups)

dried broad (fava) beans (1½–2 hours)
    175 g (6 oz/1 cup) makes 480 g (1 lb 1 oz/3 cups)

dried great northern beans (1½ hours)
    200 g (7 oz/1 cup) makes 450 g (1 lb/2¾ cups)

dried red kidney beans (2–3 hours)
    200 g (7 oz/1 cup) makes 450 g (1 lb/2½ cups)

dried butter (lima) beans (1–1½ hours)
    190 g (6¾ oz/1 cup) makes 400 g (14 oz/2 cups)

dried navy beans (1–1½ hours)
    200 g (7 oz/1 cup) makes 480 g (1 lb 1 oz/2½ cups)

dried pinto beans (1–1½ hours)
    190 g (6¾ oz/1 cup) makes 420 g (15 oz/2⅓ cups)

dried soya beans (3–4 hours)
    60 g (2¼ oz/1 cup) makes 550 g (1 lb 4 oz/3 cups)

 KITCHEN NOTE

Why don't my organic beans cook in the suggested time?
Your beans may be exceptionally old or they may have been heat-treated which is standard practice for organic beans imported into Australia. Try soaking them for a long time—at least 24 hours. And you will need to cook organic beans for longer than indicated —about twice as long. Finally, don't add any salt or acid, such as tomato, until the beans are cooked. If, after all this, you find your beans are still uncooked, it is unlikely they will ever cook.

Lentils and peas

LENTILS OR PEAS THAT HAVE BEEN HUSKED AND SPLIT are also known as dhal, and there are many varieties. These legumes are handy to have in your pantry—quick to cook and, even without pre-soaking, much easier to digest than beans.

RINSING AND SOAKING

Rinse lentils and peas well, making sure you pick out any stones that may be mixed in with them. While pre-soaking is not essential, it is desirable, as it makes them more digestible—especially any lentils with their skins on: whole red, brown, green and black, split peas, chana dhal and black-eyed peas. A useful routine is to soak them overnight in a bowl, covered with water mixed with 1 tablespoon of whey (see page 99), buttermilk or yoghurt stirred gently through. Soaking at room temperature is recommended, as this allows a little fermentation to occur.

COOKING

Many things will affect cooking time: pre-soaking, age, being whole as opposed to split, or having the skins left on. Most are cooked when tender to the bite. Split lentils, split peas, mung (moong) and chana dhal are very soft when cooked (in some cases completely collapsed), and split lentils and split dhal without skins will become quite mushy when cooked.

How to cook lentils and peas

GLUTEN FREE / DAIRY FREE
Serves 4–6

If the lentils or peas have been soaked, discard the water and drain well. If unsoaked, rinse and drain well. Place in a large heavy-based saucepan. Cover with about 4 cm (1½ inches) of water and bring to the boil over a medium heat.

As soon as the water reaches boiling point, turn the heat down as low as possible (a heat diffuser is useful). Begin timing from this point, based on the cooking times below, and adding more water, if necessary, to keep the dhal covered. I suggest you check them as they cook, and rely on mouthfeel rather than a strict time.

Yields are approximate as they will depend on the age of the lentils or peas.

dried brown lentils (soaked 12–15 minutes; unsoaked 30–45 minutes)
185 g (6½ oz/1 cup) makes 500 g (1 lb 2 oz/2½ cups)

dried green lentils (soaked 12–15 minutes; unsoaked 30–45 minutes)
185 g (6½ oz/1 cup) makes 500 g (1 lb 2 oz/2½ cups)

dried black lentils (soaked 12–15 minutes; unsoaked 30–45 minutes)
200 g (7 oz/1 cup) makes 500 g (1 lb 2 oz/2½ cups)

dried split red lentils (do not soak, unsoaked 25–30 minutes)
200 g (7 oz/1 cup) makes 500 g (1 lb 2 oz/2½ cups)

dried whole red lentils (soaked 12–15 minutes; unsoaked 1½–2 hours)
200 g (7 oz/1 cup) makes 480 g (1 lb 1 oz/2¾ cups)

dried split peas
(soaked 15 minutes – 1½ hours; unsoaked 45 minutes – 2 hours)
220 g (7¾ oz/1 cup) makes 420 g (15 oz/2½ cups)

dried black-eyed peas
(soaked 35–50 minutes; unsoaked 45 minutes–1 hour)
180 g (6½ oz/1 cup) makes 450 g (1 lb/2¾ cups)

dried mung (moong) dhal
(do not soak, unsoaked 30 minutes–1 hour, longer if whole)
200 g (7 oz/1 cup) makes 500 g (1 lb 2 oz/2½ cups)

dried chana dhal (must be soaked: split 2–2½ hours; whole 2½–3 hours)
200 g (7 oz/1 cup) makes 480 g (1 lb 1 oz/2½ cups)

dried toor (toovar) dhal (do not soak, unsoaked 40 minutes–1½ hours)
200 g (7 oz/1 cup) makes 450 g (1 lb/2½ cups)

dried urad dhal (do not soak, unsoaked 40 minutes–1½ hours)
200 g (7 oz/1 cup) makes 480 g (1 lb 1 oz/2¾ cups)

Grains

GOOD ORGANIC WHOLE GRAINS HAVE AS MUCH as possible of their natural, edible parts intact and provide slow-release fuel and fibre that enables the body to function properly. They also deliver nutrients as nature designed them—in the correct proportions for optimum usage.

SOAKING

Most whole grains benefit from soaking. This is because grains contain phytic acid and enzyme inhibitors in the outer layer, or bran, which interferes with the absorption of many minerals, notably calcium, magnesium and zinc. During soaking and fermentation, lactobacilli bacteria begin to break down the phytic acids and enzyme inhibitors, creating lactic acid as a by-product. The bacteria also break down gluten—a protein that is very difficult to digest. Because of this, soaking often increases tolerance to wheat, and increases the vitamin content in the grain, especially B vitamins. It can also dramatically reduce cooking times.

Cook extra grain to use in porridge the next morning, in a salad for lunch, or to include in a stuffing or dessert.

Whole grains, except for buckwheat and hulled millet, are best soaked for 6 to 12 hours. I recommend soaking all whole grains, especially the harder grains, such as barley, rye, spelt and wheat. A useful routine is to soak them overnight in a large bowl. For 1 cup of grain, cover with water mixed with 2 teaspoons of whey (see page 99), buttermilk or yoghurt (see page 98) stirred gently through. Soaking should be done at room temperature, allowing a little fermentation to occur.

COOKING

The following basic techniques for cooking grains will give you a fluffy and generally intact grain, though some grains such as millet and buckwheat do tend to lose their form. The cooked grain can then be served with a meal, included in stuffing or patty mix, or used for a wealth of other applications limited only by your imagination. The yields given for cooked grains are approximate, and will vary depending on the age of the grain, growing conditions and other factors.

How to cook grains

DAIRY FREE
Serves 4–6

If using soaked grains, drain well, pour the grains into a sieve and rinse under running water, shaking gently. Pat dry with a tea towel to remove excess moisture. If using unsoaked grains, rinse well and pat dry with a tea towel. Put in a heavy-based saucepan, add the required amount of water or stock (see below), cover with a lid and bring to the boil. As soon as it reaches boiling point, turn the heat down as low as possible, leaving the lid on the pan (a heat diffuser is useful). Begin timing from this point, based on the cooking times below.

At the end of the cooking time (or about 5 minutes before for longer-cooking grains), remove the lid and check if there is any water left by tipping the pan at an angle. If there is, replace the lid and continue to cook until no liquid remains. When the grain is ready, small steam holes should appear in the surface. Generally, the steam holes are more noticeable for the smaller grains, than for the larger grains.

Remove from the heat and place a tea towel or paper towel over the grains to absorb excess moisture, resulting in a fluffier grain. Cover with the lid and stand for 5 minutes, allowing the internal steam to finish the cooking process. If using the grain cold, let it sit in the pan covered with the paper towel and lid until cool.

Soaking beans, lentils, peas and grains with a little buttermilk, whey, yoghurt, or an acid such as lemon juice or vinegar breaks down the phytic acid and enzyme inhibitors. In the case of many grains, it also helps to break down gluten. Cooking any grain in a bone stock rather than water will make it easier to digest.

pearled barley
220 g (7¾ oz/1 cup) makes 680 g (1 lb 8 oz/3–4 cups)
soaked, add 560 ml (19¼ fl oz/2¼ cups) liquid (50–70 minutes)
unsoaked, add 625 ml (21½ fl oz/2½ cups) liquid (60–80 minutes)

kasha (toasted buckwheat)
200 g (7 oz/1 cup) makes 680 g (1 lb 8 oz/2½–3½ cups)
soaked, add 435 ml (15¼ fl oz/1¾ cups) liquid (15–20 minutes)
unsoaked, add 500 ml (17 fl oz/2 cups) liquid (15–20 minutes)

hulled millet
200 g (7 oz/1 cup) makes 550–650 g (1 lb 4 oz–1 lb 7 oz/2½–3 cups)
soaked, 435 ml (15¼ fl oz/1¾ cups) liquid (15–20 minutes)
unsoaked, 500 ml (17 fl oz/2 cups) liquid (15–20 minutes)

wheat or spelt berries
   200 g (7 oz/1 cup) makes 600 g (1 lb 5 oz/2–3 cups)
   soaked, add 1 litre (35 fl oz/4 cups) liquid (2 hours)

long-grain brown rice
   200 g (7 oz/1 cup) makes 450 g (1 lb/2½ cups)
   soaked, add 375 ml (13 fl oz/1½ cups) liquid (30–40 minutes)
   unsoaked, add 435 ml (15¼ fl oz/1¾ cups) liquid (40–50 minutes)

short- or medium-grain brown rice
   200 g (7 oz/1 cup) makes 450 g (1 lb/2½ cups)
   soaked, add 435 ml (15¼ fl oz/1¾ cups) liquid (30–40 minutes)
   unsoaked, add 500 ml (17 fl oz/2 cups) liquid (40–50 minutes)

Wild brown rice

GLUTEN FREE / DAIRY FREE

Makes about 425 g (15 oz/2½ cups)

Richer in protein, minerals and B vitamins than many other grains, wild rice adds a delicious nuttiness to cooked brown rice.

   100 g (3½ oz/½ cup) long-grain brown rice
   100 g (3½ oz/½ cup) wild rice
   1 tablespoon yoghurt (see page 98) or buttermilk or 2 teaspoons whey
      (see page 99) or lemon juice
   375 – 435 ml (13–15¼ fl oz/1½ – 1¾ cups) stock (see pages 93–97)

If possible, soak the rice overnight covered with water with the yoghurt gently stirred in. Put the rice in a sieve and rinse well. Pat dry with a tea towel and place in a small saucepan. Add 375 ml (13 fl oz/1½ cups) of stock, if soaked, or 435 ml (15¼ fl oz/1¾ cups), if unsoaked. Cover and bring to the boil. As soon as it reaches boiling point, turn the heat down as low as possible, so no steam escapes through the lid (you may need to use a heat diffuser).

Cook for 35 minutes, if soaked, or 45 minutes, if unsoaked, or until the grains are tender—cooking time often varies for wild rice. If it isn't cooked, or if the stock has all evaporated, add a little boiling water and cook until the rice is tender.

If you can't find wild rice, or it's too expensive, just use 200 g (7oz/1 cup) long-grain brown rice instead.

Quinoa

GLUTEN FREE / DAIRY FREE
Makes about 480 g (1 lb 1 oz/3 cups)

Quinoa is the best friend of the time poor, cooking in only 25 minutes. It is exceptionally high in protein, B vitamins, iron, potassium, zinc, calcium and vitamin E. Rather than turning to couscous (which is generally only the starchy endosperm of semolina wheat—white pasta in another form) for a quick dinner grain, do give quinoa an opportunity to prove itself to you. If you soak it beforehand, you will ensure optimum absorption of minerals—and given it has so many, this is a worthwhile option.

200 g (7 oz/1¼ cups) quinoa
1 tablespoon yoghurt (see page 98) or buttermilk, or 2 teaspoons whey
   (see page 99) or lemon juice
560–625 ml (19¼–21½ fl oz/2¼–2½ cups) stock (see pages 93–97)

If desired, soak the quinoa overnight covered with water with the yoghurt, buttermilk, whey or lemon juice gently stirred in. Rinse the quinoa and drain well. Pat dry with a tea towel (dish towel), then place in a saucepan with 560 ml (19¼ fl oz/2¼ cups) stock or water, if soaked, and 625 ml (21½ fl oz/2½ cups), if unsoaked. Add some sea salt, if needed (remember, there may already be salt in your stock), then cover and bring to the boil. As soon as it reaches boiling point, turn the heat down as low as possible (a heat diffuser is useful), leaving the lid on the pan.

Simmer for 15–25 minutes, or until the quinoa is soft. About 5 minutes before the end of the cooking time, lift the lid and check if there is any water left by tipping the pan at an angle. If there is, replace the lid and continue cooking until there is no water left. When the quinoa is ready, small steam holes should appear on the surface.

Remove from the heat, place a clean tea towel or sheet of paper towel on top of the grain, then replace the lid. Allow to sit for 5 minutes before serving.

Quinoa takes well to spices such as, cumin, coriander, cinnamon, turmeric, cardamom and ginger, added to the cooking liquid, and also to toasted seeds and nuts tossed through the cooked grain.

Polenta

Serves 4

The key to good polenta is to cook it for at least 20 minutes; this ensures full softening of the grain. It also helps to use a good-quality, deep saucepan with a heavy base, and to stir the polenta with a large wooden spoon. The end result should be beautifully creamy.

> 1 litre (35 fl oz/4 cups) stock (see pages 93–97) or water
>   for a firm polenta, or 250 ml (9 fl oz/1 cup) extra for a soft polenta
> 150 g (5½ oz/1 cup) polenta

In a large, deep, heavy-based saucepan, bring the stock or water and salt to the boil. Add the polenta slowly, stirring as you go. Lower the heat to a gentle simmer and cook, stirring frequently (especially as the polenta starts to thicken), for 20–30 minutes or until the polenta starts to pull away from the sides of the pan.

 VARIATIONS

Polenta benefits enormously from the addition of extra flavourings. At the end of the cooking time, add any or all of the flavourings below and stir well to combine:

- 2 teaspoons finely chopped rosemary leaves
- 2 teaspoons finely chopped basil leaves
- 2 tablespoons butter
- 25–50 g (1–1¾ oz/¼–½ cup) grated parmesan.

Stocks

HOMEMADE STOCKS ARE AMONG THE MOST nourishing foods you can offer a young child. Stock is an easily digestible, nutrient-dense food. It is an incredibly rich source of minerals—especially calcium and trace elements pulled from bone, cartilage, sea vegetables and vegetables as they cook—all in a bioavailable form. Bone stocks are especially valuable, as they contain gelatine, which enables food to be digested more easily. Bone stocks have been used by just about all traditional cultures for nourishment and healing—Dr Alfred Vogel, one of the early organic, wholefood and natural food advocates, describes their use in Europe for healing; in New York, chicken soup is known as Jewish penicillin (chicken fat contains palmitoleic acid—a powerful immune-boosting monounsaturated fat); and throughout Asia, fish stock is believed to be the restorer of chi (life force), and is also a rich source of iodine.

I recommend you avoid using commercial stocks. They are overbearing in flavour, and those made from bones (such as fish, chicken and beef) carry none of the rich, nutrient-dense bounty of gelatine contained in homemade stocks. If you get caught out and need to use a commercial stock, salt-reduced is my preferred option.

Stocks are so easy to make, simply requiring a large, deep saucepan and, if you are using bones, some acid (such as wine or vinegar) to help draw all the gelatine and minerals from inside the bone. You can't muck them up and they freeze brilliantly.

It's very handy to freeze a portion of your homemade stock in easy-to-use 125 ml (4 fl oz/ ½ cup) and 250 ml (9 fl oz/1 cup) quantities, so all you have to do is defrost and add to recipes without measuring. As baby gets older, freeze in larger quantities because you'll be making bigger portions.

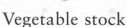

Vegetable stock

GLUTEN FREE / DAIRY FREE
Makes about 1½ litres (52 fl oz/6 cups)

This is the vegetarian stock I invariably make—I like it, it works and it's easy. It has a great flavour and the sea vegetables enrich the broth with minerals. If leek is in season, or if I have some left-over greens, I add those, too. I like to use kombu, but wakame and kelp sea vegetables are also good.

  1 tablespoon olive oil
  1 large onion, roughly chopped
  5 small–medium carrots, roughly chopped
  1 medium–large orange sweet potato, roughly chopped
  2–3 celery stalks, roughly chopped
  5 small–medium dried shiitake mushrooms
  5 cm (2 inch) piece kombu or 2 teaspoons agar flakes
  3–4 parsley sprigs, with or without leaves
  1 bay leaf
  2 thyme sprigs

Heat the olive oil in a large, heavy-based saucepan over medium heat, add the onion, carrot, sweet potato and celery and cook for 6–8 minutes or until the vegetables are lightly coloured. Add the remaining ingredients and 3 litres (105 fl oz/12 cups) of water and bring to the boil.

Reduce the heat to low and simmer gently for 1–1½ hours. Make sure the stock remains at a gentle simmer and does not boil rapidly. After 1 hour, the stock will have reduced to about 1½ litres (52 fl oz/6 cups).

Strain the stock and discard the solids. At this point you can use the stock as is, or return it to a clean pan and simmer rapidly for another 30 minutes for a richer, more concentrated flavour.

Cool the stock to room temperature, then place in airtight containers and refrigerate for up to 1 week or freeze for up to 3 months.

Chicken stock

GLUTEN FREE / DAIRY FREE
Makes about 2½ litres (87 fl oz/10 cups)

Chicken (or duck) stock is one of the most valuable to have around—its sweet flavour enhances any foods you cook, and I prefer its lighter taste to lamb or beef. It's best made with head, feet or wings—these parts deliver the most goodness to the broth—but any or all other bony parts of an organic chicken can be used.

2–3 chicken carcasses
6–8 chicken wings
6–8 chicken feet
3 carrots, roughly chopped
3 celery stalks, roughly chopped
1 onion, quartered
4 thyme sprigs
4 bay leaves
4 parsley sprigs
2 sage leaves
4 black peppercorns
60 ml (2 fl oz/¼ cup) white wine or 2 teaspoons apple cider vinegar

If you are able to access the head, gizzards or heart of an organic chicken, add those to the stock as well.

Place the ingredients in a large, heavy-based saucepan and add 3 litres (105 fl oz/ 12 cups) of water or enough to cover. Bring to just below boiling point, then reduce the heat to very low, cover with a lid, slightly ajar, and simmer for 3–12 hours (the longer the better), skimming the scum—but not the valuable fat—from the surface regularly. You may need to top up with more water several times during cooking.

Strain the stock and discard the solids. Cool the stock to room temperature, then place in airtight containers (retaining the valuable fat) and refrigerate for up to 1 week, or freeze for up to 3 months.

 KITCHEN NOTES

* *While organic chickens are expensive, it's useful to buy a whole chicken, remove the legs, thigh and breasts and freeze them,*

then use the remaining carcass, neck and wings for the stock. (If you buy a frozen chicken, once the meat has been thawed and cooked, it cannot be refrozen. However, it's fine to freeze stock made from the thawed carcass and wings.)

 Alternatively, make the stock in two stages. First, cook a whole chicken along with the other ingredients. Remove after 30–40 minutes or when cooked. Remove the breast and leg meat (to use for lunches or other meals), return the remaining skin and bones to the broth and continue cooking your stock as above.

Fish stock

Makes about 2 litres (70 fl oz/8 cups)

Fish makes a surprisingly delicious and sweet stock. It is particularly rich in minerals, especially iodine and thyroid-strengthening substances.

1 tablespoon butter or ghee (see page 107)
1 large brown onion, roughly chopped
1 carrot, roughly chopped
2–3 tablespoons white wine or 2 teaspoons apple cider vinegar
2–3 thyme sprigs
2–3 parsley sprigs
1 bay leaf
1 fish carcass, head detached and halved

Melt the butter in a large heavy-based saucepan over low heat. Add the onion and carrot and cook for 15 minutes or until lightly coloured. Add the wine and allow to boil for 1 minute, then add the remaining ingredients and about 2½ litres (87 fl oz/10 cups) of water, or enough to cover. Bring to a gentle boil, then reduce the heat to low and simmer for 30 minutes to 1 hour, skimming the scum from the surface regularly.

Strain the stock and discard the solids. Cool the stock, then place in airtight containers and refrigerate for up to 1 week or freeze for up to 3 months.

Avoid oily fish, as their flavour will overpower the stock. If I can get whole red mullet, I'll ask the fishmonger to fillet it and give me the head and bones—they make a lovely stock. Other good options include snapper, flathead, whiting and bream bones.

Beef or lamb stock

GLUTEN FREE / DAIRY FREE
Makes about 3 litres (105 fl oz/12 cups)

The inclusion in a stock of just a couple of beef or lamb marrow bones adds a large amount of nutrients—especially vitamin A, phosphorus and iron. You may need to ask your butcher to cut the bones down the middle to expose the marrow. If desired, to deepen the flavour of the stock, you can slowly brown the bones in the saucepan over low heat or roast in the oven before adding the other ingredients. The addition of an acid, such as wine or vinegar, helps the nourishing minerals, protein and cartilage leach from the bones into the stock.

- 2½ kg (5 lb 8 oz) beef or lamb bones, including 1–2 marrow bones
- 1 onion, unpeeled and quartered
- 5 small–medium carrots, roughly chopped
- 2–3 celery stalks, roughly chopped
- 3 bay leaves
- 60 ml (2 fl oz/¼ cup) white wine or 1 tablespoon apple cider vinegar or white wine vinegar

Place all the ingredients in a large, heavy-based saucepan, add about 3 litres (105 fl oz/12 cups) or enough water to cover everything well and bring to the boil. As soon as the stock comes to the boil, reduce the heat to very low and simmer, covered or uncovered, for 8–12 hours (the longer the better), skimming the scum from the surface regularly and topping up with extra water, as necessary. The longer you cook this stock, the better the result.

Strain the stock and discard the solids. You can use the stock as is, or return to a clean pan and simmer rapidly for 30–40 minutes or until you have a richer, more concentrated flavour. Cool the stock. Much of the fat will have solidified—scoop it off and keep this rendered fat for cooking—then place the stock in airtight containers and refrigerate for up to 1 week or freeze for up to 3 months.

Lacto-fermentation

LACTO-FERMENTATION IS NOT AS SCARY AS IT SOUNDS, and is easy to do at home. Fundamentally, it is the process of encouraging the growth of lactic acid-producing bacilli. As they proliferate, they produce lactic acid. This is one of the oldest ways of preserving food. During the growth or culturing process, many good things happen—B vitamins and enzymes are created, proteins are pre-digested, phytic acid is broken down and in milk products the sugars are consumed—all making lacto-fermented foods a rich source of beneficial bacteria and a superb digestive aid.

Yoghurt

GLUTEN FREE

Makes about 625 g (1 lb 6 oz/2½ cups)

The only equipment you need for making your own yoghurt is a large, clean, glass preserving jar or jam jar with a lid. The jar must be made of tempered glass that can withstand heat. A sugar (candy) thermometer is handy, but not essential.

Many people are lactose intolerant or allergic to the protein in milk and other dairy products. Good-quality yoghurt contains live bacteria that break down many of the reaction-causing properties of milk and make it easier to digest.

1 litre (35 fl oz/4 cups) milk
1 tablespoon yoghurt—it must say 'live cultures' on the label

Wash a heatproof glass jar and lid, rinse with very hot water and drain to dry.

Put the milk in a saucepan and bring just to the boil—82°C (180°F) on a sugar (candy) thermometer—stirring occasionally. Remove from the heat and cool the milk to 43°C (110°F), or until it's cool enough for you to put your finger in it and keep it there. Stir the milk a couple of times to prevent a skin forming.

Spoon the yoghurt into a clean jar and pour in a little of the warmer milk. (Don't be tempted to add a little extra yoghurt, thinking more is better; the bacteria need lots of room to grow and play.) Stir to combine well, then add the remaining milk and replace the lid. Leave the jar to sit overnight, or for at least 8 hours, in a warm, but not too hot place, approximately 20–25°C (68–77°F). (I wrap mine in a blanket and place it next to the warm part of the fridge where the motor is. You can also put it in the oven, if it has a very low temperature setting.) The next morning you will have lovely, thick, yoghurt. Allow it to cool a little, then refrigerate. It will keep for about 6 days.

Labne

GLUTEN FREE
Makes about 400 ml (14 fl oz)

Drained for 12 hours or more, plain yoghurt or kefir milk can be transformed into a light and tangy cheese called labne. Many little ones will find labne more digestible than other cheeses as much of the proteins and sugars have been digested by the bacteria. Yoghurts that do not contain milk solids are preferable and will take longer to firm up.

600 ml (21 fl oz) yoghurt (see opposite) or kefir milk (see page 100)

Line a sieve with four layers of muslin (cheesecloth)—don't worry if the corners hang over the edge of the sieve. Set the sieve over a bowl to catch the whey.

Spoon the yoghurt or kefir milk into the muslin-lined sieve and refrigerate for 12–24 hours. The labne will be soft, but still quite dense. If you want a firmer cheese, fold the muslin corners over the yoghurt and weight it down with something heavy before refrigerating it—I use a tin of tomatoes placed on a small plate. It will keep for up to 3 days in an airtight container in the fridge, or cover with a layer of olive oil and it will keep for up to 2 weeks in the fridge.

 VARIATIONS

- *Savoury labne* Sprinkle with chopped herbs, salt and olive oil, or shape firm labne into small balls and roll in chopped herbs. Place in a clean glass jar, cover with olive oil and store in the fridge for up to 1 month.
- *Sweet labne* Add ground cinnamon, natural vanilla extract, honey or a drizzle of maple syrup to taste and mix until smooth.

The whey that drips off can be stored in a clean glass jar and will keep for approximately 4 months in the fridge—it's excellent to use when soaking grains and beans.

Kefir milk

GLUTEN FREE
Makes about 435 ml (15¼ fl oz/1¾ cup)

Kefir grains look like little cauliflowers, and you can buy them on the Internet, or get them from someone who has some extras to spare. Each 'grain' is actually a little colony of friendly bacteria and yeasts. You use the grains to culture milk—as the bacteria grow, they consume much of the milk sugar (lactose) and protein, the longer it's left, the more it consumes making it more easily digestible. When ready, you strain the grains (putting them aside for another batch), and use the kefir milk. Many people consider kefir milk to have a broader spectrum of good bacteria than yoghurt, and to be superior. Culturing is aerobic, that is, it needs oxygen, so does not require a lid, but does need to be covered with muslin (cheesecloth).

1 tablespoon kefir grains
500 ml (17 fl oz/2 cups) milk

This recipe is for milk, but you can also use kefir grains to culture the juice from fresh young coconuts, or grape juice (see variations, page 102).

Place the grains in a clean jar, pour the milk over them, and cover the top of the jar with a small piece of muslin.

Leave to culture in a warm place. The rule here is: the warmer it is, the quicker it will culture. The longer it cultures, the more sour the taste becomes. Thus, in summer it may only take 5 or so hours and in winter 24 hours or more. As the culture develops, it will begin to separate into curds and whey. I prefer my kefir milk when the curds and whey are not too pronounced, but rather just beginning to separate and the texture is more like yoghurt. I find the taste a little too sour when it has fully separated.

Place a sieve over a jug and tip the entire contents of the jar into it. Use a stainless steel spoon to gently push the grains to the sides, allowing the liquid to seep through the sieve, until you only have grains left in the sieve. What is in the jug is yours to drink or use (if your kefir milk is stinky, see kitchen notes). Wash out the jar, then add the kefir grains with some new milk—you are ready to go again (if you want to store your kefir grains, see kitchen notes).

Place the cultured milk in a clean bottle and store in the fridge. At this stage the bacteria continue to proliferate and consume lactose and protein—this is known as ripening. As the milk ripens, it will become increasingly sour, but it will still be delicious. It will keep for 3–4 days in the fridge. You will easily be able to tell when it is off, as it will smell nasty.

KITCHEN NOTES

- Why is my kefir milk sometimes stinky and awful?

  Invariably, your first kefir milk batch is made with a small amount of grain—about 1 tablespoon. If you give it too much milk, it can't make enough lactic acid to preserve the milk, and putrefying bacteria will proliferate more quickly. If you only have a small amount of grain, start with just a little milk and you will be fine. The grains grow very, very quickly and before you know it, you'll have plenty. This problem is also much more common when pasteurised milk is used, and rarely happens with raw. Approximately 250 ml (9 fl oz/ 1 cup) to 1 tablespoon kefir grains is a good place to start.

- How do I store my kefir grains if I don't want to make kefir milk regularly?

  As your grains grow, you can end up with rather a lot of them—all demanding to be fed and loved, just like your children. One can only use so much cultured milk and this is what I do when I want to slow down the production of my kefir milk: when you have strained the milk and are left with the kefir grains, place them in a smaller jar with just enough milk to cover them. Cover the jar with muslin and place in the fridge. When ready to use them, place them in a sieve and rinse with filtered water until clean. Place the clean grains in a jar and you're ready to go.

- How do I keep my kefir grains 'alive', if I'm going away?

  Follow the above procedure. The kefir grains might be a bit cheesy when you get back, but they're hard to kill. Many people also give them to a friend to look after and enjoy.

VARIATIONS

- *Kefir coconut milk* Replace the milk with coconut milk and follow the same method as described. The consistency of the end product will vary: light and fluffy (similar to kefir cream, see below) with effervescence; luscious like yoghurt; or it may fully separate into curds and whey.
- *Kefir grape juice* Replace the milk with grape juice. You might like to water it down (but by no more than 50 per cent water, 50 per cent juice). Follow the method as described, but it may take a couple of days, if the weather is a little cool. The end product will be effervescent. You will see little bubbles on the walls of the jar and if you give the jar a shake, they will bubble up.

Kefir cream

GLUTEN FREE
Makes about 185 ml (6 fl oz/¾ cup)

Holly Davis is one of Australia's pioneering whole and natural food chefs. She introduced me to the idea of using kefir grains to culture cream. Oh my goodness it is so delicious. All the same rules apply here as with kefir milk (see kitchen notes, page 101)—basically you are using cream as the medium, rather than milk.

½–1 tablespoon kefir grains
250 ml (9 fl oz/1 cup) cream

Place the kefir grains in a clean jar, pour the cream over them and cover the top of the jar with a small piece of muslin (cheesecloth).

Leave to culture in a warm place. The rule here is: the warmer it is, the quicker it will culture. The longer it cultures, the more sour the taste becomes. Thus, in summer it may only take 5 or so hours and in winter 24 hours or more. As the culture develops, it will begin to lighten, looking and feeling like whipped cream—it does not separate into curds and whey. I like it when it's only lightly cultured.

Place a sieve over a jug and tip the entire contents of the jar into it. Use a stainless steel spoon to gently push the grains to the sides, allowing the cream to seep through the sieve, until you only have grains left in the sieve. What is in the jug is yours to use.

Place the cream in a clean jar and store in the fridge. At this stage the bacteria continue to proliferate and ripen. It will last for 2–3 days if stored in the fridge.

Soaked and lightly roasted nuts and seeds

NUTS AND SEEDS ARE A GOOD SNACK FOR YOUNG CHILDREN—rich in good fats and proteins. Nuts do contain enzyme inhibitors though, so many traditional cultures soak their nuts and seeds before eating them. Ayurveda, for example, believes almonds should always be soaked to make them digestible and also recommends removing almond skins, as they are considered to be irritating to the stomach.

It won't be the end of the world if you can't manage to soak and dry out your nuts and seeds, but if you can, your child will get more goodness from them. You can prepare large quantities and store them in a clean glass jar, somewhere cool.

 KITCHEN NOTES

- *When preparing a variety of nuts and seeds, soak and toast each kind separately. For example, almonds in one bowl and then on one tray, sesame seeds in their own bowl and on their own tray.*
- *When drying the soaked nuts or seeds, the temperature of the oven needs to be low enough—about 140°C (275°F/Gas 1) —to fully dry but not cook them and this takes time—about 6 hours. A dehydrator is also a great tool for this.*

Soaked and lightly roasted nuts

GLUTEN FREE / DAIRY FREE
Makes 2 cups

2 cups raw nuts, such as almonds, pecans, walnuts or hazelnuts

Place the nuts and 1 teaspoon sea salt in a bowl, cover with cold water and soak overnight at room temperature. Strain and rinse well.

Preheat oven to 140°C (275°F/Gas 1). Spread nuts on a baking tray, ensuring they're not clumped together. Bake until dry and slightly crisp but not golden. Check frequently that the oven is not too hot, and use your hands to move the nuts around, so they're exposed to the warm air. Cool completely, then store in a glass jar.

Soaked and lightly roasted sesame seeds

GLUTEN FREE / DAIRY FREE
Makes 310 g (11 oz/2 cups)

Sesame seeds are a rich source of calcium, but this is bound in the hull with oxalic acid. Soaking and lightly roasting the seeds breaks down the acid and makes the calcium bioavailable.

310 g (11 oz/2 cups) unhulled sesame seeds

Place the seeds and 1 teaspoon sea salt in a bowl, cover with cold water and soak overnight at room temperature. Strain and rinse well.

Preheat the oven to 140°C (275°F/Gas 1). Spread out the seeds on a baking tray, ensuring they are not clumped together. Bake in the oven until they are dry and slightly crisp but not golden. Check frequently that the oven is not too hot, and use your hands to move the sesame seeds around, so they are exposed to the warm air. Cool completely, then store in a clean glass jar.

If using almonds, after soaking, remove the skins—they should slip off easily. If they don't, cover them with boiling water and let them sit for a minute—the skins should then be easy to remove.

If you don't have time to lightly roast the almonds, you can serve them as they are to children.

NUT MILKS

Nut milks are nutritious and delicious. While they can be made in advance and stored in the fridge, they are best made as close as possible to using. They will separate as they sit, but will easily reconstitute when stirred. As a general rule, almonds need to have the skins removed, and nuts that have been soaked will be more nutritious than unsoaked nuts.

Do play with these recipes—you can add more nuts for a richer milk, or a little rice syrup, maple syrup or fresh pitted dates to sweeten.

Almond or cashew nut milk

GLUTEN FREE / DAIRY FREE

Makes about 375 ml (13 fl oz/1½ cups)

75 g (2¾ oz/½ cup) raw almonds, with skins on, or raw cashew nuts

Place the almonds or cashews and a pinch of salt in a small bowl, add enough water to cover the nuts well and soak overnight at room temperature. Strain and rinse well. If you are using almonds, remove the skins—they should slip off easily. (If they don't, cover them with boiling water and let them sit for a minute—the skins should now be easy to remove.)

Place the almonds or cashews in a blender with 435 ml (15¼ fl oz/1¾ cups) of water and process until smooth.

Peg four layers of muslin (cheesecloth) onto a jug or bowl and pour the almond milk through. Pick up the muslin and twist to squeeze out the remaining milk.

Use immediately or store in a clean jar in the fridge for up to 2 days. After a time the almond or cashew milk will separate, so just give it a stir before using.

Sesame-enriched almond milk

DAIRY FREE / GLUTEN FREE
Makes about 375 ml (13 fl oz/1½ cups)

40 g (1½ oz/¼ cup) raw almonds, with skins on
40 g (1½ oz/¼ cup) unhulled sesame seeds

Place the almonds, sesame seeds and a pinch of sea salt in a small bowl, then add enough water to cover the nuts and seeds well and soak at room temperature overnight. Strain and rinse well. Remove the skins from the almonds—they should slip off easily. (If they don't, cover them with boiling water and let them sit for a minute—the skins should now be easy to remove.)

Place the almonds and seeds in a blender with 375 ml (13 fl oz/1½ cups) of water and process until smooth.

Peg four layers of muslin (cheesecloth) onto a jug or bowl and pour the almond milk through. Pick up the muslin and twist to squeeze out the remaining milk.

Use immediately or store in a clean jar in the fridge for up to 2 days. After a time the nut milk will separate, so give it a stir before using.

 **KITCHEN NOTE**

To gain the full benefit of the calcium in the unhulled sesame seeds, soak and lightly roast them (see page 104) before adding to the blender.

Ghee

GHEE IS VERY SIMPLE TO MAKE AND, AS IT IS A SATURATED FAT, is also very stable. Do give it a try as it adds such lovely flavour to your cooking and is an extremely health-supportive fat.

Ghee

GLUTEN FREE

Makes about 225 g (8 oz/1 cup)

250 g (9 oz) butter, preferably unsalted

Melt the butter gently in a small saucepan over low heat. Once it has melted, increase the heat so there is a gentle simmer—as the water evaporates, there will be a gentle gurgling sound and the butter will be covered with white foam. Continue to simmer, uncovered, for 20–25 minutes, or until the milk solids start to brown on the bottom of the pan—tilt it to check—and there is little foam left on top of the butterfat. The time will vary for different butters as they contain differing water and fat ratios; be careful not to leave it unattended towards the end as it can burn.

Remove from the heat and leave to cool until any milk solids left on top have sunk to the bottom. When cool, spoon off any remaining milk solids left floating on top. Gently pour the butterfat into a bowl, stopping when you get to the milk solids at the bottom of the pan. Discard the solids. To make sure all the milk solids are removed—this is especially important for people who are intolerant to the milk protein, casein—strain the ghee through two or three layers of muslin (cheesecloth). Refrigerate in a container until needed—ghee will keep indefinitely in the fridge.

FIRST TASTES,
PURE *and* SIMPLE

6–8 MONTHS

*First foods should be simple
and undemanding of baby, letting
them taste the pure and simple
essence of food. When the vegetable
or fruit is fresh, ripe and organic,
it will be delicious and nourishing,
and baby will develop the taste
for good food.*

Delicious food foundations

BREAST MILK IS NATURE'S MOST PERFECT AND COMPLETE FOOD, and has everything required for your baby's healthy growth and development. But from about six months, baby will begin to require more than your breast milk can offer, especially iron. It's time to introduce baby to the world of food and all the nourishment and deliciousness it offers. If you are wondering where to start, have a look at the composition of breast milk—which is complex nutrient-dense food. Up to 60 per cent of its kilojoules come from fat: lauric acid for immune protection, long-chain polyunsaturated docosahexaenoic acid (DHA) and eicosapentaenoic acid (EPA) and cholesterol. Complete protein, easy-to-digest carbohydrates, antibodies and beneficial bacteria for the gut make up the other 40 per cent. First foods for baby should follow along these lines.

Introducing your baby at this early stage to delicious, real, wholefood is one of the best ways to lay down the foundation for the later years.

Because a very young baby lacks the enzymes required to digest carbohydrate, grain flours are not a good first food—better to leave these a few weeks and let baby's digestive system have some time to get used to food. When my mother was asked what were the first baby foods she used, she said mashed vegetable and brains; my aunt said, egg yolk and liver! Many traditional cultures consider egg yolk and raw liver the best first foods, followed by cooked brains—all are exceptionally rich in the fats that are so critical for baby's brain and nervous system. Following lightly cooked egg yolks, vegetables and fruits are other great first foods. First vegetables should not include the nightshade family: potato, tomato, eggplant (aubergine), capsicum (pepper); it's better to start with simple root vegetables, puréed and enriched with ghee or coconut oil.

Please don't use a microwave to cook baby's (or your) food, as this will destroy a large amount of life force and goodness within the food. Steaming is just as easy, and retains a large amount of nutrients.

If you must microwave, do not use plastic wrap or plastic containers, as this transfers large amounts of xenoestrogens into the food.

When storing food in the fridge, preferably store it in glass.

Simple, singular food is also exceptionally grounding. And don't think this is just for baby—you and the rest of your family will love the taste of healthy vegetable or fruit purées.

In this busy world, I know it makes great sense to make up batches of food (puréed carrots, for example) and freeze them in iceblock sizes, but try to make and serve food as fresh as possible for baby. This offers them the best opportunity for digestion and gaining life force from their foods, and is one of the foundations of Ayurveda. On the other hand, don't beat yourself up if you can't do this—food you have cooked at home and frozen absolutely has its place (frozen fruit purées, for example) and is still far superior to commercial (even organic) foods that have all been pasteurised and taste pretty much the same.

🫖 KITCHEN NOTES

When preparing and cooking the recipes in this chapter, take into account:

- *Vegetables and fruit will be fresh and ripe when they are in season. Apples, for example, should be eaten in autumn and winter, not spring and summer. Dried and frozen fruit can be a great help in this regard.*
- *It's best to use a small saucepan, 14–16 cm (5½–6¼ inch) is perfect, so that the specified quantity of stock or liquid will completely cover the ingredients in the pan—using too much liquid can dilute the pure flavour.*
- *Because we are working with such small quantities, puréeing is best done using a mini food processor, a mouli, or by pushing it through a sieve. As baby develops, you can simply use a fork to roughly mash it.*

Nutrient-dense first foods

EGG YOLK, BRAIN AND LIVER ARE ALL EXCEPTIONALLY RICH sources of the fat-soluble vitamins A and D, cholesterol and a wide range of other nutrients baby will require for development of the brain and nervous system. They are easily digested, and are well known as first foods in most traditional cultures and even up until 50 years or so ago were commonly used in ours.

Egg yolk

GLUTEN FREE / DAIRY FREE
Makes 1 baby serve

1 egg, at room temperature

Place egg in a saucepan of boiling water and cook for 3 minutes, a little longer if it is a large one. Place in an egg cup and cut the top off. The yolk should be warm and slightly runny. Spoon out the yolk and discard the white. Add the cooked yolk to vegetable purées (see page 114).

Liver

GLUTEN FREE / DAIRY FREE
Makes 2–3 baby serves

Any offal given to young children must be organic or biodynamic; free range is not good enough and open to parasites and bacteria, especially in the case of chicken liver. If you are happy to give your child finely chopped or grated raw liver, it must be frozen for 14 days before using.

> 1 organic liver (any type is fine)
> squeeze of lemon juice

Remove any connective tissue and veins from the liver. Place in a bowl, cover with water and add the lemon juice. Allow to soak for 1 hour to remove impurities and soften the flavour. Use it fresh, or slice and freeze it. Add a small amount of very finely chopped, or grated if frozen, liver onto warm egg yolk (see opposite) or onto warm vegetable purée (see page 114). The warmth of the egg or the vegies will lightly cook the liver.

Brains

GLUTEN FREE / DAIRY FREE
Makes 2–3 baby serves

> 1 set very fresh, organic lamb's brains

Soak the brains in salted water for 1–1½ hours, changing the water once. Drain, then place in a small saucepan and cover with water (or stock, see pages 93–97). Simmer for 10–15 minutes or until firm to the touch but still slightly springy. Drain and allow to cool slightly. Using a small, sharp knife, remove any traces of skin or connective tissue. Mix a small amount of cooked brain with warm vegetable purée (see page 114) and serve. The remaining brain will keep, refrigerated, for 24 hours.

After 8 months, liver can be added to minced meat dishes, such as Bolognese and meatballs. Keep in mind, though, the mince needs to be cooked and blended, otherwise it's too dangerous for baby. After 12 months, there's no need for blending. You can also serve liver like we used to have it, as lamb's fry (even though it was cow's liver) with bacon. Lamb's fry is a good first food. In both minced meat and lamb fry dishes, the liver is lightly cooked.

Vegetable purées—nature's rainbow

BEETROOT, CARROT, PARSNIP, PUMPKIN, sweet potato and zucchini (courgette) are all good vegetables to begin baby on, moving on to broccoli, cauliflower and peas. Vegetables purées can and should be enriched by adding butter, ghee (see page 107) or coconut oil. This will ensure the vitamins and minerals in the vegetables are easily assimilated by baby. Do keep an eye on your baby's reactions to first foods— any discomfort at this stage may come from the milk solids in butter rather than the vegetables themselves. If so, use ghee instead of butter.

At this early stage, baby's vegetables should be puréed. I've kept the quantities of all the purées to 1 cup, as baby will only eat a little at a time. You will need to increase the amount if you plan on feeding the rest of the family.

Remember also:

- It's important at this stage that the vegetables are well cooked and offer no resistance when a fork or skewer is inserted.
- It's a good idea to reserve some of the cooking liquid, so you can add it to the purée to thin it out, if necessary.
- Purée the vegies while they are still hot, so the fat can melt through.

After trying the purées by themselves, egg yolk, liver or brain can be added to enrich them (see pages 112–113).

After a couple of weeks or so, when baby has experienced the taste of a good range of pure vegetables, try adding some avocado (although, technically a fruit)— combined with cooked beetroot, it makes a great coloured purée.

Then, after a few more weeks, try adding just a little labne (see page 99) or yoghurt (see page 98) to the vegetables, keeping an eye out for any adverse reactions to the dairy products, albeit cultured.

 VARIATIONS

Other uses for vegetable purées include:

- binding for vegetable or grain patties
- toppings for pies
- bubble and squeak.

Roasted sweet potato purée

GLUTEN FREE / CAN BE DAIRY FREE

Makes 1 scant cup

1 orange sweet potato, about 450 g (1 lb)
1 teaspoon ghee (see page 107) or coconut oil
1 teaspoon coconut oil, extra

Preheat the oven to 180°C (350°F/Gas 4). Place the sweet potato on a baking tray, rub all over with the ghee or coconut oil and bake for 20–30 minutes or until a knife inserted into the thickest part meets no resistance. Cool a little, then halve lengthways, scoop out the flesh, place in a bowl and add the extra coconut oil. Purée in a small food processor or mouli until smooth.

This is a great purée to make when you are cooking stuffed sweet potatoes for the rest of the family. Set a roasted sweet potato aside to purée for baby.

Autumn harvest purée

GLUTEN FREE / CAN BE DAIRY FREE

Makes 1 scant cup

100 g (3½ oz) carrot, finely diced
60 g (2¼ oz) parsnip, peeled, core removed and finely diced
120 g (4¼ oz) pumpkin, peeled, seeded and finely diced
½ green or red apple, peeled, core removed and finely diced
1 teaspoon ghee (see page 107) or coconut oil

Steam the vegies and apple together for 20 minutes or until soft. Transfer to a bowl and, while they are still hot, add 2 tablespoons of the cooking liquid and fat of your choice. Purée in a small food processer or mouli until smooth, adding extra cooking liquid, if necessary.

※

Carrot purée

GLUTEN FREE / CAN BE DAIRY FREE

Makes 1 scant cup

300 g (10½ oz) carrots, finely diced
1 teaspoon butter, ghee (see page 107) or coconut oil

Steam the carrot for about 20 minutes or until soft. Transfer to a bowl and, while they are still hot, add fat of your choice. Purée in a small food processor or mouli until smooth.

※

Carrot and parsnip purée

GLUTEN FREE / CAN BE DAIRY FREE

Makes 1 scant cup

200 g (7 oz) carrots, finely diced
100 g (3½ oz) parsnip, peeled, core removed and finely diced
1 teaspoon butter, ghee (see page 107) or coconut oil

Steam the vegies for about 20 minutes or until soft. Transfer to a bowl and, while they are still hot, add 2 tablespoons of the cooking liquid and fat of your choice. Purée in a small food processor or mouli until smooth, adding extra cooking liquid, if necessary.

Carrot, beetroot and ginger purée

GLUTEN FREE / CAN BE DAIRY FREE
Makes 1 scant cup

This recipe calls for cooked beetroot, and I prefer roasting, rather than boiling, as I feel it keeps a more intense flavour that is otherwise lost to the cooking water. It's also easier to cook a whole beetroot rather than a part of one, so if you can't find baby beetroots, just cook larger ones for longer and reserve the remainder to use in a salad for the family.

1 small beetroot, about 100 g (3½ oz)
1 teaspoon olive oil
200 g (7 oz) carrot, finely diced
½ thin, small slice ginger, peeled
1 teaspoon butter, ghee (see page 107) or coconut oil

Preheat the oven to 180°C (350°F/Gas 4). Place the beetroot in a small ovenproof dish with a little water, drizzle with oil and cover with foil. Bake for 20 minutes or until tender when pierced with a knife tip. Remove from the oven and while still warm, remove the skin, then place the beetroot in a bowl.

Your ginger slice should be just enough to give a hint of flavour (it should equal no more than ¼ teaspoon if finely grated). Steam the carrot and ginger for about 20 minutes or until the carrot is tender. Add to the beetroot and, while the carrot is still hot, add 2 tablespoons of the cooking liquid and fat of your choice. Purée in a small food processor or mouli until smooth, adding extra cooking liquid, if necessary.

To prepare the beetroot, cut off the leaves (you can keep any very young leaves to use in a salad for the rest of the family) and wash the bulb to remove any sand or grit. Removing the skin from the roasted beetroot is best done when they are warm; it will just slip off with a bit of help from your fingers. A word of warning, you might like to wear gloves!

Fruit purées—pure essence

Good first fruits include banana, avocado, mango and melon, all of which can be served raw. For babies, high-pectin fruits such as apples, apricots, cherries, peaches, plums, nectarines and berries should be cooked. Citrus fruit should not be introduced until after 12 months.

THESE FRUIT PURÉES ARE GORGEOUS—THE CONCENTRATED PURE essence of fruit. It is especially important the fruit is ripe, as this will provide flavour and natural sweetness. Unripe fruit will be tart, indigestible and taste awful, and may turn your child off these foods. Dried fruits also offer an especially rich source of iron—a critical mineral at this stage. Any dried fruit should be sulphur free—they are darker, but taste delicious. At this stage, fruits should be puréed, and again, I've kept the quantities of all the purées to 1 cup, as baby will only eat a little at a time. When cooking fruit, add as little water as possible—use a lidded saucepan and a very gentle heat to sweat the juices out before increasing the heat a little. While this takes longer than simmering the fruit in liquid, it will result in an intensely flavoured fruit purée that everyone in the family will love—you will definitely want to make larger quantities! Also, avoid substituting fruit juice for water—good, ripe fruit is sweet enough, and keeps the flavours pure.

After a couple of weeks when baby has experienced the taste of the individual pure fruits, try adding a little avocado, amasake (amazake) or coconut milk to add creaminess and fat. A bit later you can begin to add small quantities of plain or kefir cream (see page 102), kefir milk (see page 100) or yoghurt (see page 98) to the fruit, keeping an eye out for any sensitivity to the dairy products, albeit cultured.

Fruit purées are delicious on their own, but other uses include:
- adding to breakfast porridges (see page 158)
- toppings for pancakes and pikelets (see page 154)
- adding to baked goods for moistness
- serving with custard (see page 132) or pudding.

RAW FRUITS

There are a few fruits which offer an ideal first taste experience to babies who have until this point been nourished by breast milk only. While these fruits can safely be served raw to your little one, it's best to purée them first. Purée just enough for baby to eat at one sitting, as puréed raw fruits, in general, do not freeze or keep well.

Banana purée

GLUTEN FREE / DAIRY FREE

Makes 1 cup

1 small ripe banana

Banana is an excellent first fruit. Purée in a small food processor or mouli until smooth. Once your baby has grown accustomed to the taste, you can mix in other puréed fruits to vary the flavour—mango, papaya and melon are all good. Next, try including a little coconut milk to add creaminess and fat, or avocado.

COOKED FRUITS

As well as serving your baby a variety of puréed raw fruits, you can introduce the broad range of high-pectin fruits that are best cooked before puréeing. They just take a little longer to prepare.

Apple purée

GLUTEN FREE / DAIRY FREE

Makes 1 cup

4 small ripe apples (red or golden delicious are perfect), peeled, core removed and finely diced

Place the apple in a small saucepan with 80 ml (2½ fl oz/⅓ cup) of water. Cover with a lid and cook over very low heat, stirring regularly, for 10 minutes or until the juices have been released, then cook for another 5–8 minutes or until soft. Check occasionally that there is enough liquid to stop the apples burning, as different varieties of apples tend to have more or less juice. If necessary, add a tiny amount of water. Purée in a small food processor or mouli until smooth.

As your baby gets a little bit older, spices such as cinnamon and nutmeg (introduce at 8 months), and finely grated lemon rind (introduce at 12 months), are delicious additions.

Apple and dried apricot or peach purée

GLUTEN FREE / DAIRY FREE
Makes 1 cup

80 g (2¾ oz) dried apricots or peaches, roughly chopped
4 ripe apples, peeled, core removed and finely diced

Place the apricot or peach and apple in a small saucepan with 125 ml (4 fl oz/ ½ cup) of water. Cover with a lid and cook over very low heat for 10–15 minutes or until the dried fruit has soaked up the cooking juices and is plump and soft and the apple is soft. Stir once or twice, checking you have enough liquid—some dried fruits absorb more than others. Purée the mixture in a small food processor or mouli until smooth.

Peach purée

GLUTEN FREE / DAIRY FREE
Makes 1 cup

3 ripe peaches

Drop the peaches into a saucepan of boiling water for 10 seconds, then remove with a slotted spoon. When they are cool enough to handle, remove the skins and cut the flesh into small dice.

Put the peach in a small saucepan with 1 tablespoon of water. Cover and cook over very low heat, stirring frequently, for 10–15 minutes or until the peach is soft. Check a couple of times that you have enough water, as different varieties of peaches tend to have different amounts of juice. Purée the mixture in a small food processor or mouli until smooth.

Pear purée

GLUTEN FREE / DAIRY FREE

Makes 1 cup

4 small ripe pears, peeled, core removed and finely diced
2 drops natural vanilla extract

Place the pear in a small saucepan with the vanilla extract and 1 tablespoon of water. Cover with a lid and cook over very low heat, stirring frequently for 10 minutes or until the pear is soft. Check a couple of times that you have enough water, as different varieties of pears tend to have different amounts of juice. Purée the mixture in a small food processor or mouli until smooth.

Strawberry purée

GLUTEN FREE / DAIRY FREE

Makes 1 cup

500 g (1 lb 2 oz) very ripe strawberries, washed, hulled
and roughly chopped

Place the strawberries in a small saucepan, cover with a lid and cook over very low heat, stirring frequently for 10 minutes or until soft. You should end up with a large amount of liquid. Pour the juice off into a small bowl—you should have about 125 ml (4 fl oz/½ cup). Set aside this juice to make jelly (see page 204). Purée the strawberries in a small food processor or mouli. Because they have tiny seeds, push the purée through a fine sieve to obtain a lovely smooth texture.

Pretty in pink purée

GLUTEN FREE / DAIRY FREE
Makes 1 cup

3 ripe plums—choose those with a dark red flesh, such as
     mariposa or ruby blood
2 figs, peeled and roughly chopped
small pinch ground cinnamon

Drop the plums into a saucepan of boiling water for 10 seconds, then remove with a slotted spoon. When they are cool enough to handle, remove the skins and cut the flesh into small dice.

Put the plum and fig in a small saucepan with the cinnamon and 2 tablespoons of water. Cover with a lid and cook over very low heat, stirring frequently, for 10 minutes or until the fruit is cooked and soft. Purée the fruit in a small food processor or mouli. Because figs have tiny seeds, push the purée through a fine sieve to obtain a lovely smooth texture.

Cultured dried apricot and fig purée

GLUTEN FREE
Makes 1 cup

This is a delicious way to enjoy good bacteria and include the iron-rich dried fruits, especially apricot. It's based on recipes from wholefood writers Holly Davis and Sally Fallon. I find the smaller amount enables me to use it all before it becomes a little ripe, and almost alcoholic—it shouldn't, but mine often does. If this happens, use it in cooking (cakes, puddings) for yourself, but don't give it to baby.

As baby grows, you can increase the sweetener to taste; once baby is 12 months old, I suggest using raw, unfiltered honey instead of the maple syrup.

135 g (4¾ oz/¾ cup) dried apricots
¼ cup dried figs, sultanas or seedless raisins
2 teaspoons maple syrup
1 tablespoon whey (see page 99)

Place the dried fruits and 250 ml (9 fl oz/1 cup) of water in a small saucepan and cook over low heat for 15 minutes or until the fruit is soft and plump, and the liquid has been absorbed.

Remove from the heat, allow the fruit to cool, then place it in a blender or food processor with the maple syrup, whey and ¼ teaspoon of sea salt. Process until smooth, then spoon into a glass jar which has a good lid that seals properly, making sure there's about 4 cm (1½ inches) between the top of the purée and the lid.

Stand at room temperature for 2–4 days or until the mixture becomes soft and fluffy. If the weather is very cold, you may need to leave it a little longer. If the weather is very hot, it will take less time and you may even need to do this entirely in the fridge. Remember, in such a sugar medium, too much fermentation will end up alcoholic and too much heat will result in over-fermentation, so the fridge is best. It should taste lightly soured and delicious when ready. It will taste alcoholic and fizzy when over-fermented. Store in the fridge for up to 4 weeks, tasting before using to double check.

First grains, for grounding and wholeness

AMARANTH, QUINOA, BROWN RICE AND HULLED MILLET are all excellent first grains and can be served to your baby in small quantities once she is 6 or 7 months old and has been eating puréed fruit and vegetables, and some nutrient-dense foods, for a few weeks. Amaranth and quinoa are particularly high in protein and are considered to be complete—they are perfect grains to start with, although I especially recommend quinoa as it's far easier to cook. For optimum digestion, all grains should be pre-soaked, although this is not necessary for hulled millet.

Once cooked, the grain needs to be puréed. Adding a little butter or ghee will ensure the vitamins and minerals in the grain are easily assimilated. Do keep an eye on your baby—any discomfort at this stage may come from the milk solids in the butter rather than the grains themselves. If so, use ghee instead of butter.

After a couple of weeks, you can cook grain in bone stock—this will make it even easier to digest and enrich the flavour. While vegetable stock does not aid digestion, it will provide flavour and added nutrients.

Here are some serving suggestions:

- mix a little cooked grain with breast or formula milk
- add amasake (amazake) to gently sweeten and aid digestion
- serve grains with vegetables or fruit purées
- after a few weeks, you could also add cream, kefir cream (see page 102), labnc (see page 99), kefir milk (see page 100) or yoghurt (see page 98) to the grains, but do keep an eye on how your baby responds to the dairy products, albeit cultured.

KITCHEN NOTE

Don't be tempted to cook grains over a high heat to speed up the process, or you will end up with grain that looks creamy but is still al dente.

Baby grain

GLUTEN FREE / CAN BE DAIRY FREE
Makes 1 cup

¼ cup amaranth, quinoa, brown rice or hulled millet
1 teaspoon whey (see page 99) or lemon juice
1 teaspoon butter, ghee (see page 107) or coconut oil

If using amaranth or quinoa Place the grain, whey or lemon juice and 125 ml (4 fl oz/½ cup) of water in a small bowl and stir to combine. Cover with a tea towel and stand for 6 hours or overnight, preferably at room temperature. Strain the grain, then put it in a small saucepan with 250 ml (9 fl oz/1 cup) of water. Simmer over very low heat, stirring frequently, for 25 minutes or until the grain is soft and creamy. Note that amaranth will look quite sticky, and not at all like lovely individual grains. This is not a problem, as it will blend up just fine.

If using brown rice Blend the brown rice in a small food processor or a mortar and pestle until a fine flour forms. Place the brown rice flour, whey or lemon juice and 125 ml (4 fl oz/½ cup) of water in a small bowl and stir to combine. Cover with a tea towel and stand for 6 hours or overnight, preferably at room temperature. Pour mixture into a small saucepan, add 250 ml (9 fl oz/1 cup) of water and cook it over low heat, stirring frequently to prevent it sticking to the bottom of the pan, for 30–35 minutes or until the mixture is soft and creamy and not at all al dente.

If using hulled millet Place the grain in a small saucepan and toast over a low heat for 1–2 minutes, shaking the pan from time to time to ensure the grain is evenly toasted. Add 375 ml (13 fl oz/1½ cups) of water and simmer over very low heat, stirring frequently, for 25 minutes or until the grain is soft and creamy and not at all al dente.

For all grains Process the grain in a small food processor or mouli, thinning to a runny consistency with breast milk or formula milk as desired, then stir in the fat of your choice.

Banana and dried apricot quinoa

GLUTEN FREE / CAN BE DAIRY FREE

Makes 1 cup

50 g (1¾ oz/¼ cup) quinoa
1 teaspoon whey (see page 99) or lemon juice
5 dried apricots, finely chopped
½ banana, roughly chopped
1 teaspoon butter, ghee (see page 107) or coconut oil

Place the quinoa, whey or lemon juice and 125 ml (4 fl oz/½ cup) of water in a small bowl and stir to combine. Cover with a tea towel and stand for 6 hours or overnight, preferably at room temperature.

Strain the quinoa, then put it in a small saucepan with the apricots and 250 ml (9 fl oz/1 cup) of water. Simmer over very low heat, stirring frequently, for 20 minutes or until the grain is soft. Add the banana and cook for a further 5–10 minutes or until the porridge is soft and creamy.

Process in a small food processor or mouli, thinning it to a runny consistency with breast milk or formula milk as desired, then stir in the fat of your choice.

Apple and blueberry rice

GLUTEN FREE / CAN BE DAIRY FREE

Makes 1 cup

50 g (1¾ oz/¼ cup) brown rice
1 teaspoon whey (see page 99) or lemon juice
50 g (1¾ oz) apple, peeled, core removed and grated
40 g (1½ oz/¼ cup) fresh or frozen blueberries
1 teaspoon butter, ghee (see page 107) or coconut oil

Place the rice, whey or lemon juice and 125 ml (4 fl oz/½ cup) of water in a small bowl and stir to combine. Cover with a tea towel and allow to stand for 6 hours or overnight, preferably at room temperature.

Strain the rice, then put it in a small saucepan with 375 ml (13 fl oz/1½ cups) of water and cook it over very low heat for 35 minutes or until soft and creamy and not at all al dente. Add the apple and blueberries and cook for another 10 minutes. Don't worry if the mixture seems thin at this stage—it will thicken when you blend it.

Process in a food processor or mouli, thinning to a runny consistency with breast milk or formula milk as desired, then stir in the fat of your choice.

First stews—combining flavours

AFTER A FEW WEEKS ON SIMPLE AND COMBINED VEGETABLES, fruits and grains (with or without egg yolk, liver or brain) we can begin to develop a little complexity. Baby can now be introduced to a range of complete proteins—the following recipes include chicken, fish and a vegetarian stew that combines grains and legumes. All these stews include quality fats to aid assimilation of vitamins and minerals. Where chicken or bone stock has been used, this will also aid the digestion of any grain and protein. As baby progresses, a broader variety of vegetables can be added to the stews.

Other than these dedicated baby stews, you can create your own for baby by setting aside a small amount of meat and vegetables from your meal and pulsing them up with a little stock, or even breast milk or formula milk, to thin them out. If you are having a roast for dinner, adding a little of the gravy to baby's puréed mix provides flavour as well as gelatine from the meat juices to aid digestion.

Baby kichari

GLUTEN FREE
Makes 1 cup

1 tablespoon quinoa
½ teaspoon whey (see page 99) or lemon juice
1 tablespoon split red lentils or mung (moong) dhal
1 teaspoon ghee (see page 107)
1 teaspoon coconut oil
50 g (1¾ oz) jap or butternut pumpkin, peeled, seeded and finely diced
30 g (1 oz) carrot, finely diced
small pinch each ground ginger, cumin, coriander and turmeric
125 ml (4 fl oz/½ cup) vegetable stock (see page 94)

Place the quinoa, whey or lemon juice and 60 ml (2 fl oz/¼ cup) of water in a small bowl and stir to combine. Cover with a tea towel and stand for 6 hours or overnight, preferably at room temperature. Drain.

Pick over the lentils and check for any stones, then rinse well.

Heat the ghee and coconut oil in a small saucepan over low heat. Add the pumpkin and carrot and cook for 5 minutes, then add the spices, lentils, drained quinoa and stock. Stir to combine, then cover and cook for 25 minutes or until the vegetables are soft and the quinoa is cooked.

Process in a small food processor or mouli until smooth.

Baby chicken stew

GLUTEN FREE
Makes 1 cup

1 tablespoon brown rice
½ teaspoon whey (see page 99) or lemon juice
1 teaspoon ghee (see page 107)
50 g (1¾ oz) chicken thigh fillet, skin on
35 g (1¼ oz) jap or butternut pumpkin, peeled, seeded and finely diced
15 g (½ oz) carrot, finely diced
1 thyme sprig—about 15 small thyme leaves
185 ml (6 fl oz/¾ cup) chicken stock (see page 95)
1 large broccoli floret, cut into small pieces
1 tablespoon green peas

Place the rice, whey or lemon juice and 60 ml (2 fl oz/¼ cup) of water in a small bowl and stir to combine. Cover with a tea towel and stand for 6 hours or overnight, preferably at room temperature. Drain.

Heat the ghee in a small saucepan over medium heat. Add the chicken thigh, skin-side down, and brown for 2 minutes—this will render out some of the valuable chicken fat. Remove the chicken, reduce the heat to low, then add the pumpkin, carrot and thyme. Remove and discard the chicken skin. Cut the meat into small pieces and add to the pan with the drained rice and stock. Cover and cook for 40 minutes or until the rice is soft. Add the broccoli and peas and cook for another 8 minutes or long enough to cook them through, but not dull their colour.

Process the mixture in a food processor or mouli until smooth.

Baby fish stew

GLUTEN FREE / CAN BE DAIRY FREE
Makes 1 cup

Use a fish that is sustainable where you live—an oily, high-omega fish, such as sea mullet, is great for this recipe. Ask your fishmonger to skin the fillet. Carefully check for any bones and remove them.

1 teaspoon ghee (see page 107) or coconut oil
½ small carrot, finely diced
125 ml (4 fl oz/½ cup) coconut milk, plus a little extra, if required
60 ml (2 fl oz/¼ cup) vegetable cooking broth or stock (see pages 93–97)
75 g (2¾ oz) skinless fish fillet, cut into small pieces
1 large broccoli floret, cut into small pieces
1 tablespoon green peas
2 drops fish sauce

Heat the ghee in a small saucepan over low heat, add the carrot and cook for 1 minute. Add the coconut milk and broth, cover and cook for 10 minutes, or until the carrot is tender. Add the fish, broccoli and peas—adding a little extra coconut milk, if there is not enough liquid to cover the vegetables. Cover and cook for 8 minutes or long enough to cook the vegetables through, but not dull their colour. Add the fish sauce and remove from the heat.

Process the mixture in a food processor or mouli until smooth.

Custard and fools

USING FRUIT AND A SMALL AMOUNT OF WHOLE SWEETENER, custards and fools are a wonderful and nourishing way to introduce baby to the concept of sweetness.

Stone fruit fool

GLUTEN FREE / DAIRY FREE

Makes 1½ cups / about 6 baby serves

A fool is simply stewed or puréed fruit whipped into a cream base. Here, I've used a non-dairy custard base enriched with coconut milk.

2 peaches or nectarines, or 360 g (12¾ oz) apricots
1½ tablespoons kudzu (kuzu) or true arrowroot
60 ml (2 fl oz/¼ cup) rice or almond milk
185 ml (6 fl oz/¾ cup) coconut milk
2 teaspoons maple syrup, or to taste
½ teaspoon natural vanilla extract

Drop the fruit into a saucepan of boiling water for 10 seconds, then remove with a slotted spoon. When cool enough to handle, peel and chop the flesh into small dice. Place the fruit in a small saucepan with 60 ml (2 fl oz/¼ cup) of water, cover and cook over low heat until soft. Check a couple of times that you have enough water, as different varieties of fruit tend to have different amounts of juice. Set aside.

Place kudzu and rice milk in a small saucepan and mix to a smooth paste. Add remaining ingredients and whisk until combined. Place over medium heat and, stirring continuously, bring just to the boil. As soon as bubbles form, give it a couple more stirs, then remove from heat and cool for 5 minutes. It should be thick and smooth.

Transfer to a blender along with the cooked fruit and process until light and airy. Divide among 6 small bowls or 1 large bowl and refrigerate for 1–2 hours or until set. The fool will keep for up to 2 days in the fridge.

Using fruit purée that you have made a little ahead of time cuts down your preparation time significantly. If you are making fruit purée (see page 118) for baby, consider making a double batch so that you can use the leftovers to make this fool later in the day. Simply substitute the stone fruit with ¾ cup of fruit purée and add to the hot custard in the blender.

For an even quicker fool, simply whip the fruit purée into cream or yoghurt.

Baked coconut cream and banana custard

GLUTEN FREE / CAN BE DAIRY FREE
Makes 1 cup / 4−6 baby serves

The most delicious custard will be that made with cream—but if you prefer to use full-cream (whole) milk instead, try adding another egg yolk—this will give you a smoother custard.

The dairy-free version won't be quite as smooth, and may split a little, but is still delicious. Make sure to use coconut cream (and not more coconut milk) to substitute for the cream, as this provides the fat required for good texture.

- 125 ml (4 fl oz/½ cup) coconut milk
- 125 ml (4 fl oz/½ cup) cream or coconut cream
- 3 egg yolks
- 1 tablespoon maple syrup
- ½ teaspoon natural vanilla extract
- 1 small banana

Preheat the oven to 170°C (325°F/Gas 3).

Place all the ingredients except the banana in a bowl and whisk gently until smooth and combined. Thinly slice the banana and divide the slices between four 80 ml (2½ fl oz/⅓ cup) capacity ramekins and place these in a deep roasting pan. Pour the custard mixture over the banana. Pour enough hot water into the roasting pan to come two-thirds of the way up the side of the ramekins.

Bake for 30–35 minutes or until the custard is just set but still a little wobbly in the centre. (Check the custards after 15 minutes, and if you see any bubbling whatsoever, reduce the heat.) When cooked, the banana rises to the top, and the custard will shrink away from the side. Remove the ramekins from the pan and allow to stand until the custards have cooled to blood temperature—they will firm as they cool.

These custards are best served warm. If they are cold from the refrigerator, steam for 5 minutes or until lightly warmed before serving.

- *I've used ramekins measuring 8 x 4 cm (3¼ x 1½ inch), but you can also use smaller ones, if desired.*
- *For a quicker cooking time, steam the custards on top of the stove for 15–20 minutes.*

VARIATION

Simple coconut cream custard Instead of a baked custard, you can use the same ingredients (omitting the banana) to make a simple custard on top of the stove. Place the ingredients in a bowl and whisk gently until smooth. Place the bowl over a saucepan of simmering water and cook, stirring continuously, until the mixture is thick enough to coat the back of a wooden spoon. Serve with fresh or stewed fruit.

EXPLORING *and* LEARNING

8–12 MONTHS

*With more control over their bodies,
babies will now begin to physically
interact with the world and everyone in
it. Smelling, looking, touching, tasting
and hearing—these are the tools they will
use to explore and learn.*

A wider range of foods

ONCE BABY IS EIGHT MONTHS OLD, YOU CAN BEGIN to introduce a wider range of foods into their diet. Milk (preferably raw), cultured milk and milk products (see *Lacto-fermentation*, page 98) can be used more freely, and you can introduce soft cheeses and a little hard cheese. Most vegetables and fruits can now be used, including garlic and onion and the nightshades, in moderation. Vegetables should still be cooked; as baby begins to become more independent and wants to grab and hold foods, you can lightly cook vegetables like carrot sticks. Other great finger foods are thick slices of avocado and banana.

High-pectin fruits, such as apples, peaches, plums, nectarines and cherries are still best cooked, although as your baby gets older you can begin to include the softer peaches, plums, nectarines and cherries raw. Berries can also begin to be used raw. Continue to avoid citrus fruits.

Egg whites should also still be avoided, as should gluten grains, but flavours can begin to develop more complexity. A little quality sea salt can now make an appearance, along with more herbs and spices—just go easy on chilli and pepper. Foods can be mashed rather than puréed.

Recipes in this section are for larger quantities, as baby begins to eat more food which the family will enjoy, too.

This is the stage where it can be very tempting to give bread to your baby—try to hold out until after 12 months, relying on whole grains in porridges or stews instead. This will give baby time for her digestive system to mature a little more, and will go a long way to helping avoid allergies.

Kefir or yoghurt smoothie

GLUTEN FREE
Makes about 1½ cups

This smoothie is a powerhouse of nutrients, all of them easy to digest. It has no added sweeteners (I find the banana does the job) but as baby gets closer to 12 months, you could add a touch of maple syrup and, after 12 months, raw honey. Any fruits can be used, though the softer stone fruits, berries, banana and mango are the best.

185 ml (6 fl oz/¾ cup) kefir milk (see page 100) or yoghurt (see page 98)
60 ml (2 fl oz/¼ cup) coconut milk
40 g (1½ oz/¼ cup) blueberries
1 small banana
½ teaspoon spirulina (optional)

Place all the ingredients in a food processor or blender and process until smooth. Smoothie will keep in the fridge for 1 day.

Sardine pâté

GLUTEN FREE
Makes ¾ cup

Strong-flavoured, oily fish is exceptionally high in omega-3 essential fatty acids and it's a good idea to introduce this taste to baby when she is young. The labne and ghee both help to soften the assertive fishy flavour.

100 g (3½ oz) tinned sardines packed in olive oil, drained
3 teaspoons lemon juice
2 drops fish sauce
2 tablespoons yoghurt (see page 98) or labne (see page 99)
2 teaspoons ghee (see page 107), melted and cooled

Place all the ingredients in a bowl and mash together well. Taste and adjust flavour as desired. Pâté will keep in an airtight container in the fridge for 2–3 days.

 KITCHEN NOTE

When baby is more than 12 months old (and for the rest of the family), add finely chopped chives, parsley or dill to the pâté. Mayonnaise is another lovely addition when baby is older—it can be substituted for the yoghurt or labne.

Liver pâté

Makes about 3½ cups

500 g (1 lb 2 oz) organic chicken liver
1 teaspoon lemon juice
125 g (4½ oz/½ cup) ghee (see page 107),
    plus 2 tablespoons extra, melted
1 large onion, finely diced
3 lemon thyme sprigs, leaves picked
180 g (6¼ oz) mushrooms, preferably Swiss browns, thinly sliced
1 garlic clove, finely chopped
125 ml (4 fl oz/½ cup) mirin (Japanese rice wine)
125 g (4½ oz/½ cup) sour cream

Remove any connective tissue and veins from the livers. Place in a bowl, cover with water and add the lemon juice. Allow to soak for 1 hour to remove any impurities.

Heat the ghee in a large frying pan over low heat. Add the onion and cook for 10 minutes or until soft and lightly coloured. Add the thyme leaves, mushroom, garlic, a good pinch of sea salt and a pinch of freshly ground black pepper. Stir through and cook for another 5 minutes or until the mushroom is just starting to soften. Add the mirin and cook for another 10 minutes or until the liquid is reduced by half.

Drain the livers and pat dry. Add to the pan, stir through and simmer gently for 10 minutes or until they are just cooked through and the liquid has almost reduced, but the mixture is still very moist. Remove from the heat and cool slightly.

Place the mixture in a blender with the sour cream and process until smooth. Check the seasoning, adding more salt or pepper, as desired.

Transfer to a 1 litre (35 fl oz/4 cup) capacity ceramic or glass dish and smooth the top. (If you prefer, you can use several smaller bowls.) Pour the extra ghee over to cover and seal the surface completely, then refrigerate for 2–3 hours or until set. Pâté will keep in the fridge for up to 2 weeks.

Creamy coconut vegetable broth

GLUTEN FREE / DAIRY FREE

Makes 3 adult serves and 1 baby serve

This is an exceptionally nourishing quick and easy breakfast, lunch or dinner. You can use any seasonal vegetables, cooking the root vegetables first, and adding the lighter ones towards the end. It's a great way to use dark leafy greens, such as Tuscan black kale—the broth softens their sturdy texture, and the fat ensures their powerful store of minerals (especially calcium) has optimum opportunity to be assimilated. Coriander (cilantro) leaves and spring onions (scallions) are wonderful added at the last minute.

50 g (1¾ oz/¼ cup) quinoa or amaranth
1 teaspoon whey (see page 99) or lemon juice
1 tablespoon coconut oil
1 small carrot, finely diced
1 litre (35 fl oz/4 cups) chicken or fish stock (see pages 95 and 96)
1 zucchini (courgette), finely diced
50 g (1¾ oz) Tuscan black kale (cavolo nero), thinly sliced
185 ml (6 fl oz/¾ cup) coconut milk
1 tablespoon fish sauce

Place the grain, whey or lemon juice and 250 ml (9 fl oz/1 cup) of water in a small bowl and stir through. Cover with a tea towel and allow to stand for 6 hours or overnight, preferably at room temperature. Drain.

Heat the coconut oil in a heavy-based saucepan over medium heat. Add the carrot and cook for 1 minute, then add the drained grain and the stock. Reduce the heat to low, cover and cook for 20 minutes or until the carrot is just tender. Add the zucchini, kale and coconut milk, and simmer, uncovered for 10 minutes. Stir in the fish sauce and remove from the heat.

Process in a food processor or mouli or mash baby's portion before serving.

For a quick version of this, use rolled quinoa or amaranth instead of whole grains. Although grains are always best soaked, you can skip that step, if you're in a rush, and simply add the rolled grains directly to the broth—they will only take 10 minutes or so to cook.

Lismore corn chowder

GLUTEN FREE (IF WHEAT-FREE TAMARI USED)
Makes 3 adult serves and 1 baby serve

A delicious, quick and easy dinner in summer when the corn is abundant. The recipe is so-called because, when I visit my dearest friend Jeanie and her daughter Violet in Lismore, it also happens to be corn season. We go to the organic farmers' market where the vegetables and greens are glorious and cheap.

2 tablespoons ghee (see page 107), butter or olive oil
1 large onion, finely diced
2 garlic cloves, roughly chopped
4 celery stalks, finely diced
4 carrots, finely diced
2 potatoes, finely diced
generous handful basil leaves, roughly chopped
4 cobs of corn, kernels cut off
1 litre (35 fl oz/4 cups) chicken or vegetable stock (see pages 94 and 95)
45 g (1¾ oz) Tuscan black kale (cavolo nero), thinly sliced
½–1 teaspoon mirin (Japanese rice wine) or tamari, or to taste

Heat the ghee in a heavy-based saucepan over low heat. Add the onion, garlic, celery, carrot, potato, basil, corn kernels and a pinch of sea salt and cook, stirring occasionally, for 8–10 minutes or until just beginning to soften. Add the stock, cover with a lid, slightly ajar, and simmer gently for 30 minutes or until the vegetables are soft.

Process one-third to one-half of the mixture in a food processor until smooth, then return to the pan with the remaining chowder. Stir in the kale and simmer gently for another 10 minutes, then remove from the heat. Check for taste, adjusting the flavours if need be—chicken stock will generally be sweeter than vegetable stock. Add a little mirin or tamari, if needed.

Process baby's portion in a blender to a chunky or fine purée, then pass it through a sieve to remove the tough outer skin of the corn kernels.

Fish pie

GLUTEN FREE

Makes 2 adult serves and 1 baby serve

This is one of the quickest meals to make. I use crème fraîche or kefir cream, not only because it's a great source of lactic acid (which aids digestion), but also because the saturated fat ensures optimum usage of omega-3 fatty acids.

2 potatoes, cut into 2–3 cm (¾–1¼ inch) dice
100 g (3½ oz) broccoli, coarsely chopped
2 tablespoons butter or ghee (see page 107)
2 spring onions (scallions), roughly chopped or 1 small onion, finely diced
2 tablespoons chopped herbs, such as lemon thyme,
    flat-leaf (Italian) parsley or basil
zest of 1 small lemon
handful of seasonal green vegetables, such as peas and asparagus,
    trimmed and cut into small pieces, as necessary
80–115 g (2¾–4 oz/⅓–½ cup) crème fraîche
    or kefir cream (see page 102)
¼ teaspoon wholegrain mustard
300 g (10½ oz) fish fillet, skin and bones removed,
    and cut into 3 cm (1¼ inch) pieces (see side bar)

Preheat the oven to 190°C (375°F/Gas 5).

Steam the potatoes for 5 minutes or until nearly tender, then add the broccoli and steam for 3–4 minutes or until the broccoli is just tender. Take care not to overcook, as that will dull the colour of the broccoli. Place in a bowl, add 1 tablespoon of butter or ghee and roughly mash. Set aside.

Melt the remaining butter or ghee in a small saucepan over low heat and cook the spring onion for 1 minute or onion for 5 minutes or until soft. Add the remaining ingredients, season to taste with salt and black pepper and stir gently—the cream will 'melt' and relax. Spoon into a shallow, ovenproof dish and top with the mashed potato. Bake for 20 minutes or until golden. Mash or purée baby's portion.

Use a fish that is sustainable where you live—this is a great recipe for an oily, high-omega fish, such as sea mullet or red mullet, although black bream is also great. Ask your fishmonger to skin your fillet. Carefully check for any bones.

Garden vegetable tomato sauce

Makes 4 – 5 cups

This is a brilliant base for many meals—it's great to have in the freezer.

    2 teaspoons butter, ghee (see page 107) or olive oil
    ½ onion, finely chopped
    1 – 2 garlic cloves, finely chopped
    1 celery stalk, finely diced
    1 carrot, finley diced
    1 small–medium zucchini (courgette), finely diced
    1 small piece jap or butternut pumpkin (about 150 g/5½ oz),
        peeled, seeded and finely diced
    handful fresh herbs, including basil, oregano, marjoram—all or any,
        roughly chopped
    1 teaspoon dulse flakes
    800 g (1 lb 12 oz) tinned chopped tomatoes or fresh tomatoes
    ¼ – ½ teaspoon apple juice concentrate (optional)

Melt the butter in a heavy-based saucepan over medium heat. Add the onion, garlic, celery, carrot and a pinch of sea salt, and cook for 10 minutes or until soft and lightly coloured (you are not frying, just developing a little flavour).

If using tinned tomatoes Add the zucchini, pumpkin, herbs, dulse flakes and the tinned tomatoes. Add 60 ml (2 fl oz/¼ cup) of water (or you can use stock) to the empty tomato tins, swish around and pour into the pan. Reduce heat to low, cover and simmer for 20–30 minutes or until the vegetables are soft.

If using fresh tomatoes Bring a large saucepan of water to the boil. Cut a small cross into the base of each tomato and drop them into the boiling water for 10 seconds. Remove with a slotted spoon, drop into cold water until cooled a little, then drain and peel. Squeeze out all the liquid from the peel into the onion mixture. Finely chop the tomato flesh and add it to the onion mixture along with all the tomato juices.

The sauce at this stage will look a lot drier than if you have used tinned tomatoes—the fresh tomatoes are uncooked and their juices have not yet sweated out. Cover and cook on very low heat for 20 minutes—the juices will now be sweated out. Add the zucchini, pumpkin, herbs and dulse flakes, cover and simmer for 20–30 minutes or until the vegetables are soft. If you feel the sauce is still slightly dry, add a little water or stock.

For both tinned and fresh tomatoes Check the flavour and adjust—you might like to add a little freshly ground black pepper or the apple juice concentrate, but the pumpkin should have balanced out the acidity of the tomatoes.

Serve as is, or blend in a food processor, thinning out with stock, if required. Either way, baby's portion should always be puréed or mashed. The sauce will keep in an airtight container for up to 2 days in the fridge or up to 6 weeks in the freezer.

SERVING SUGGESTIONS

- Leave chunky and serve as a soup, with the addition of a little pasta. Add chopped bacon to the pan along with the onion at the beginning. Sprinkle over a little parmesan or pecorino.
- Serve as a sauce with pasta (see page 144)—with or without other vegetables.
- Delicious as a sauce for gnocchi.
- Add cooked lentils, and borlotti (cranberry) or cannellini (white) beans once baby is more than 12 months old.
- Serve with fish balls (see page 189) or meatballs (see page 197) when baby is older.

Baby pasta marinara

Makes 1 cup

This is a great place to use a strong-flavoured, oily fish such as sea mullet or red mullet.

  1 teaspoon spelt stelline or other soup pasta
  250 ml (9 fl oz/1 cup) garden vegetable tomato sauce (see page 142),
      unblended
  60 ml (2 fl oz/¼ cup) fish stock (see page 96)
  1 small fillet oily fish, skin and bones removed, and roughly chopped
  1–2 teaspoons finely grated cheese, such as cheddar or parmesan,
      or crumbled soft goat's cheese

Cook the pasta in a small saucepan of boiling salted water according to the packet instructions or until al dente. Drain and keep warm.

Heat the sauce and the stock in a small saucepan over low heat. Add the fish and cook for 5 minutes or until the fish is just cooked. Mash the sauce, if you wish, and break up the fish, as necessary. Add the desired amount to a bowl, and serve with the pasta and the cheese.

Mama's palak spinach

GLUTEN FREE

Makes 2 cups

This is my take on the Indian classic palak paneer, but I've toned down the spices, and used an uncooked cheese (labne) to make it a bit easier on baby.

200 g (7 oz) picked English spinach (about 2 bunches)
2 teaspoons coconut oil
2 teaspoons ghee (see page 107)
2 tablespoons finely chopped onion
pinch each ground cumin, coriander and turmeric
2 tablespoons coconut milk
2 tablespoons yoghurt (see page 98) or kefir labne (see page 99)

Wash the spinach well and make sure there is no grit left. Lift it out of the water and place it in a large frying pan over low heat. Cook for 1–2 minutes or until wilted (you don't need to add anything else to the pan; the water on the leaves is enough to help wilt them). Place the wilted spinach into a colander and leave it to drain well. When it is cool enough to handle, squeeze the excess liquid out of the spinach and roughly chop it.

Heat the coconut oil and ghee in a frying pan over low heat, add the onion and cook for 5–6 minutes or until soft but not coloured. Stir in the spices and cook for 30 seconds, then add the chopped spinach and coconut milk and cook for another 1–2 minutes or until heated through. Remove from the heat, fold in the labne, season to taste with sea salt and freshly ground black pepper and serve warm. It will keep in an airtight container for 1 day in the fridge.

🍵 SERVING SUGGESTIONS
- Serve with a simple whole grain and vegetables.
- Serve with baby kichari (see page 128) or, after 12 months, serve with vegetable and red lentil coconut dhal (see page 174).

Gravy

GRAVY IS A PROFOUND THING—MUCH MORE THAN JUST A SAUCE. It not only adds flavour and nutrition to a simple meal, but when made with bone stock, also provides a rich source of gelatine that facilitates digestion. It's a great food for young children.

I've included two gravy recipes here—a vegetarian option and a meat-based one. Wherever possible, use stock rather than water for the liquid when making either; although the water from steamed vegetables will suffice, stock is more nutrient-dense and will add more flavour.

With regard to the amount of steamed vegetable water or stock used—the great thing is that it doesn't matter. If you add lots and the gravy is too thin, just reduce it over high heat—you will end up with a more nutrient-dense and better-tasting stock as you reduce and concentrate the sauce to your desired consistency.

As you get to the end of making the gravy, you will need to taste it and adjust the flavours accordingly. If adding mirin, make sure to boil the mix well for at least 2–3 minutes to cook off the alcohol. There are some handy tricks to balancing the flavour of your gravy.

- If it's too sweet, try adding small amounts of:
  - tamari
  - herbs, such as thyme, oregano and flat-leaf (Italian) parsley; mint works well with lamb or mutton.
- If it's too savoury, try adding small amounts of:
  - mirin
  - mashed roasted pumpkin
  - apple juice concentrate
  - quince paste.

Shiitake mushroom gravy

GLUTEN FREE (IF WHEAT-FREE TAMARI USED) / DAIRY FREE
Makes 1 cup

Rich with immune system-boosting shiitake mushrooms and sea vegetable minerals in the stock, this gravy is a store of goodness. You can use true arrowroot or cornflour (cornstarch) to thicken, but kudzu will support baby's digestive system and give you a better texture.

> 2 small dried shiitake mushrooms
> 250 ml (9 fl oz/1 cup) vegetable stock (see page 94)
> 2 thyme sprigs
> 1 teaspoon dulse flakes
> 2 teaspoons kudzu (kuzu) or true arrowroot
> 1 teaspoon mirin (Japanese rice wine)
> ½–1 teaspoon tamari

Soak the mushrooms in 250 ml (9 fl oz/1 cup) of hot water for 20 minutes, then drain. Reserve the soaking water and discard the mushrooms. (Afer baby is 12 months, the mushroom caps can be thinly sliced and added back to the stock.)

Put the stock, thyme sprigs, dulse flakes and 185 ml (6 fl oz/¾ cup) of the soaking water in a small saucepan and cook over a high heat until reduced by half.

Meanwhile, place the kudzu in a small bowl, add the remaining soaking water and stir until a smooth paste forms. Whisk into the stock mixture, reduce the heat to medium and stir continuously until the mixture boils and thickens. Add the mirin and tamari and cook for another minute. This gravy is delicious with roasted or steamed vegetables, and with roasted, barbecued or grilled meats.

Nonna's roasted rack of lamb with mashed potato and gravy

GLUTEN FREE

Makes 2 adult serves and 1 baby serve

According to my Mum, this is how I was fed when I was an older baby—the family enjoys a great roast, and baby gets to try nutrient-rich gravy over mashed vegetables. Supervised, she can also hold the meaty cutlet bone while sucking on the juices. Because I use grass-fed meat, I prefer my rack of lamb to have the fat left on, rather than trimmed, as it renders out nutrient-rich fat I can use in other ways.

2 carrots, peeled and cut into small pieces
180 g (6¼ oz) jap or butternut pumpkin, peeled, seeded
    and cut into 4 pieces
1 small orange sweet potato, cut into 4 pieces
1 parsnip, peeled, core removed and cut into small pieces
5 garlic cloves, unpeeled
2 tablespoons rosemary leaves
2 teaspoons olive oil
420 g (15 oz) rack of lamb, with the fat left on
2–3 potatoes, cut into chunks
20 g (3¾ oz) butter
seasonal green vegetables, such as peas, green beans, asparagus
    and broccoli, to serve
2 teaspoons true arrowroot
500 ml (17 fl oz/2 cups) lamb, beef or chicken stock (see pages 95–98)

Preheat the oven to 200°C (400°F/Gas 6).

Place the carrot, pumpkin, sweet potato and parsnip in a large heavy-based heatproof roasting pan. Add 3 garlic cloves, half the rosemary leaves, a pinch of sea salt and the olive oil, toss well, then roast for 30 minutes.

Peel and finely chop the remaining 2 garlic cloves and chop the remaining rosemary leaves. Using a small sharp knife, make a few shallow incisions all over the fat on the rack of lamb. Press a little garlic, rosemary and a pinch of salt into each incision. Place the lamb on top of the vegetables and roast for 40–45 minutes or until the fat is crisp and golden and the meat is cooked but still a little pink in the middle.

Meanwhile, steam the potato until tender. Return to the drained saucepan, add the butter and a pinch of sea salt, mash and keep warm.

Just before the meat comes out of the oven, steam the green vegetables, and reserve a little of the steaming water to add to the gravy, if desired. Keep warm.

When the lamb is cooked, remove it from the roasting pan, place it in a shallow dish, cover loosely with foil and rest in a warm place for 15 minutes. Remove and reserve the whole garlic cloves, then transfer the remaining roasted vegetables to an ovenproof dish and place in the oven, with the heat turned off, to keep warm.

Drain off most, but not all, of the fat from the roasting pan. Place the pan over low heat, add the arrowroot and use a wooden spoon to combine it with the juices and scrapings. Add a small amount of the stock or vegetable steaming water and stir until smooth, then squeeze out the garlic flesh from the reserved cloves into the pan, add the remaining stock and mix well. Transfer the gravy to a small saucepan and simmer over medium heat until it is reduced to 250 ml (9 fl oz/1 cup). Taste and adjust the seasoning, if necessary.

Cut the lamb rack into individual cutlets. (The meat will have released some juices while resting—make sure you add them to the gravy.) For the adults, serve with the mashed potato, roasted vegetables and steamed greens and gravy. For baby, mash some of the roasted and steamed vegetables into the mashed potato, and top with gravy. After she has eaten this, give her the cutlet (trimmed along the bone for ease of holding, and trimmed of the back fat) to suck on.

🫖 KITCHEN NOTE

When cutting vegetables for roasting, you will need to take their shape and size into account. For example, small, thin carrots will simply need to be topped and tailed, halved lengthways and, if long, cut again crossways. Baby carrots can be left whole. For a quick cooking roast, such as a rack of lamb, the vegetable pieces will all need to be small.

DEVELOPING COMPLEXITY

1–3 YEARS

*As a baby passes the age of
12 months and becomes a toddler,
much is changing. This is the time of
rapid learning and much
development.*

New foods and experiences

BUILDING A BODY, BEING AND LEARNING REQUIRE a great deal of complexity and your baby will reflect this in many ways. She now understands food, and is able to chew—she will almost certainly want to feed herself. As her digestive system begins to develop, many new foods can be introduced, although it's a good idea to do this gradually at first and observe how she reacts.

At this stage, a toddler's food begins to look very much like the food the whole family will be eating, although it may be cut in smaller pieces or roughly mashed.

Egg whites are better tolerated. Yoghurt, kefir milk and cheeses of all varieties can now be used more freely. Raw vegetables can be offered, but always with quality fats. High-pectin fruits like apple and pear can now be eaten raw, and citrus fruits can be introduced. You can begin to use a wider variety of grains—especially oats and spelt, and quality bread can also be introduced. Muesli, however, is still not included, as this can be a very difficult food to digest. Pasta and noodles can be used, though in moderation.

From the legume family, beans make a welcome addition to lentils and split peas—it's best to begin with the more easily digestible adzuki before moving on to borlotti (cranberry), pinto, black (turtle), chickpea and cannellini (white). You should continue to avoid soya or red kidney beans—both must be very well cooked, and can still offer problems to an immature digestive system. Serving any legume dish with a food rich in lactic acid—such as kefir milk (see page 100), yoghurt (see page 98), labne (see page 99) or sour cream—will enhance the digestibility of the dish. But do remember that beans are heavy-duty foods—a toddler will only need very small amounts. You won't see a recipe for hummus in this age bracket— that should be left until closer to three years.

To round it all off, the principle of sweetness is introduced and small amounts of a whole sweetener, including raw honey, can now be used.

While many new foods are being introduced, the basics discussed in the previous chapters should still be considered—stocks (especially bone) are still one of the most important ways to provide nutrient density and enhance digestion. Quality fats of all description are still critically important. And it's still a good idea to provide the bulk of your toddler's diet without relying on too much grain or grain products. Many recipes from the earlier sections will still hold true as your baby becomes a toddler.

It pays to bear in mind that as dietary complexity develops, simple food can be exceptionally grounding—and the recipes in this chapter intentionally reflect this principle.

Your toddler's eating during these years can also be erratic—there is a lot going on for a child during these years. As well as growing, they are working out how to be in the world—learning how to communicate and interact. It's natural for you as a parent to worry that your child might not be eating enough—they will certainly go through those stages. Children tend to eat when they're hungry—they are not going to starve, though some days they may not eat as much as other days. I've included a couple of very simple recipes and nutrient-dense suggestions for those kind of days, so that you know they are getting some goodness.

This is also the time it becomes easy for a child to slip into the habit of eating snacks, rather than meals. Primarily, the bulk of your child's nutrients should still come from breakfast, lunch and dinner. When this is adhered to daily, you will develop a rhythm and routine for your child, and the foundation for all her eating patterns right into adulthood.

I have recommended serving sizes for these recipes, where appropriate, but use your judgement as to how much to feed your child. A one-year-old baby will not eat as much as a three-year-old toddler. A good guide is ½ cup for a one year old, increasing to 1–1½ cups for a three year old.

Breakfasts

MANY OF THESE 'BREAKFAST' RECIPES DO DOUBLE DUTY as quality, nutrient-dense snacks—especially pikelets, which can easily be held in a little hand. Don't get too hung up, either, on having porridge as a breakfast food only—if your toddler has had egg for breakfast, porridge can make a great morning or afternoon tea snack.

PIKELETS AND TOMBOLAS

Any of the following recipes are a great way to introduce new grains, such as oats and buckwheat, to young children. If at all possible, soak the grains overnight (see page 88)—this will ensure easier digestion and maximum goodness. When making the following recipes with grains that have not been soaked, you can omit the salt because it is added to control the rate of lacto-fermentation during the overnight soaking process.

A tombola is similar to a frittata, but with less egg, and relies more on a flour-based batter. They are delicious cold, topped with butter, avocado, labne (see page 99) or feta or funky bright green broad bean dip (see page 164).

All these pikelets and tombolas can be served warm with or without butter, ghee (see page 107), cream or kefir cream (see page 102), yoghurt (see page 98) or labne or, for a dairy-free topping, coconut milk mixed with a little amasake (amazake).

Also note that as these pikelets and tombolas are more dense than those made from white flour, they need to cook more slowly so that the batter will be cooked the whole way through.

Oat and apple pikelets

WHEAT FREE
Makes about 25

Top with berries or other fruits, or if you'd like to make these pikelets slightly softer so you can roll them up, add a little milk or an egg to thin down the batter.

70 g (2½ oz/½ cup) oatmeal (see kitchen note, page 156)
80 g (2¾ oz/½ cup) buckwheat flour
250 ml (9 fl oz/1 cup) milk or 125 ml (4 fl oz/½ cup) coconut milk
    and 125 ml (4 fl oz/½ cup) rice milk
2 teaspoons whey (see page 99), yoghurt (see page 98)
    or kefir milk (see page 100)
¼ teaspoon ground cinnamon
1 tablespoon rapadura sugar
2 tablespoons melted butter, ghee (see page 107) or coconut oil
170 g (6 oz) apples (1–2 small apples), peeled and finely grated
¾ teaspoon baking powder
butter, ghee (see page 107) or coconut oil, for frying

Place the oatmeal, buckwheat flour, milk, whey and a tiny pinch of sea salt in a small bowl and combine well. Cover with a tea towel and allow to stand overnight at room temperature or in the fridge, if the weather is very warm.

Place the cinnamon, sugar, melted fat of your choice and grated apple in a bowl and sift in the baking powder. Add to the flour mixture and gently stir together.

Place enough butter, ghee or coconut oil in a large frying pan to coat the base and place over medium heat. When the fat is hot enough that a small drop of batter sizzles when it is dropped into the pan, cook 2 tablespoons of mixture for 2½ minutes or until the base is golden and small bubbles appear on the surface. Flip the pikelet and cook for another minute. Repeat for the remaining batter, adding a little more fat to the pan in between every batch.

KITCHEN NOTE

If you can't find oatmeal, it's easy to make your own. Place the same quantity of rolled oats in a food processor and process until coarsely ground. You may have a little more oatmeal than you need, so measure out the required amount.

VARIATION

If you don't have time to soak the flours, simply combine all the dry ingredients in a bowl, omitting the salt, then combine with the remaining ingredients and continue as per the recipe.

Buckwheat and brown rice vegetable pikelets or tombolas

GLUTEN FREE
Makes about 25

This mix is a great way to offer vegetables to children and is very adaptable.

    65 g (2½ oz/½ cup) buckwheat flour
    40 g (1½ oz/¼ cup) brown rice flour
    30 g (1 oz/¼ cup) true arrowroot
    250 ml (9 fl oz/1 cup) milk or 125 ml (4 fl oz/½ cup) coconut milk
        and 125 ml (4 fl oz/½ cup rice milk)
    2 teaspoons whey (see page 99), yoghurt (see page 98)
        or kefir milk (see page 100)
    1 egg
    1 teaspoon dulse flakes
    1 tablespoon melted butter, ghee (see page 107), coconut oil or olive oil,
        plus extra if making tombolas (see kitchen note)
    130 g (4¾ oz) mixed vegetables, finely chopped or grated, such as
        zucchini (courgette), carrot, cauliflower, broccoli, capsicum (pepper)
    1 tablespoon chopped herbs, such as basil, thyme, flat-leaf (Italian) parsley
    ¾ teaspoon baking powder
    ghee (see page 107) , butter or coconut oil, for shallow-frying,
        if making pikelets

Place the buckwheat and rice flours, arrowroot, milk, whey and a pinch of salt in a small bowl and combine well. Cover with a tea towel and stand overnight at room temperature or in the fridge, if the weather is very warm.

The next morning, whisk together the egg, dulse flakes, a pinch of salt and your choice of fat until well combined (see kitchen note). Add to the flour mixture along with the vegetables and herbs. Sift in the baking powder and gently stir together.

To make pikelets Place enough ghee, butter or coconut oil in a large frying pan to coat the base and place over medium heat. Cook 2 tablespoons of the mixture for 1–2 minutes or until the base is golden and small bubbles appear on the surface. Flip the pikelet and cook for another minute or until golden and cooked through. Repeat with the remaining batter, adding a little more fat to the pan in between every batch. Pikelets are best eaten on the day of making but will keep in an airtight container for up to 2 days in the fridge.

To make tombolas Preheat the oven to 180°C (350°F/Gas 4). Add 1–2 tablespoons extra fat of your choice to the batter and mix well. Line two 12-hole mini-muffin tins with cupcake papers or squares of baking paper folded to fit. Divide the mixture among the holes and bake for 20 minutes or until a skewer inserted into the centre comes out clean. Cool a little in the tins, then turn out. Tombolas are best eaten on the day making but will keep in an airtight container for up to 2 days in the fridge.

🫖 KITCHEN NOTE

When making this mixture as pikelets, frying provides the extra fat they require. When baking as tombolas, you will need to add extra fat to the batter.

🫖 VARIATION

If you are not soaking the flours, simply combine all the dry ingredients in a bowl, omitting the salt, then combine with the remaining ingredients and continue as per the recipe.

PORRIDGE

Rather than looking to highly processed puffed and flaked cereals, go closer to the source—whole grain. Porridges are simple, nourishing wholefoods and provide your growing toddler with a wealth of goodness and energy.

 SERVING SUGGESTIONS

- Serve with melted ghee (see page 107), butter, cream, kefir cream (see page 102), yoghurt (see page 98) or labne (see page 99) to ensure all the nutrients are optimally utilised.
- For a dairy-free topping, use coconut milk mixed with amasake (amazake).

Apple and fig buckwheat porridge

GLUTEN FREE

Makes 2 adult serves and 1 toddler serve

A fabulous breakfast for when the weather starts to cool. You can easily make up more than you need and store it in the fridge for the next day, just add a little liquid to it when warming up. Once baby is a bit older, hazelnuts and pistachio nuts are a delicious topping for buckwheat.

90 g (3¼ oz/½ cup) buckwheat groats (see glossary)
250 ml (9 fl oz/1 cup) milk, or 125 ml (4 fl oz/½ cup) coconut milk
   and 125 ml (4 fl oz/½ cup) rice milk
3 dried figs, finely chopped
1 large apple, peeled and grated

Place the buckwheat groats in a heavy-based saucepan over medium heat and toast, shaking the pan often, for 1 minute or until they smell fragrant and are lightly coloured. Add the milk, fruit and 250 ml (9 fl oz/1 cup) of water, reduce the heat to low and cook, stirring frequently, for 30 minutes. If you find the porridge is too thick, simply add a little more milk.

Everyday creamy rolled oat porridge

WHEAT FREE
Makes 2 adult serves and 1 toddler serve

A basic porridge made from rolled oats is a quick, easy and nutritious breakfast. Simply soak the oats and cook them in their soaking liquid, serving the porridge with stewed fruits or berries. You can also add dried fruits (sultanas are especially delicious and provide natural sweetness) and chopped or grated apple or pear to the oats as they cook. Sweeten with a little honey or maple syrup, if desired.

    100 g (3½ oz/1 cup) rolled oats (see side bar)
    2 teaspoons whey (see page 99), yoghurt (see page 98)
        or kefir milk (see page 100)

Place the oats in a bowl with 500 ml (17 fl oz/2 cups) of water, the whey and a pinch of salt. Cover and allow to stand overnight at room temperature or in the fridge, if the weather is very warm.

Place the mixture in a small saucepan and cook over low to medium heat, stirring frequently, until the mixture comes to a gentle boil. Reduce the heat to low and cook for 10 minutes, stirring frequently, or until the grain is soft and creamy. If your rolled oats are not stablised, you may need to cook the porridge for another 10 minutes. Any dried fruits will be swollen and soft. If the porridge is too thick, thin to your desired consistency by adding milk. If too thin, cook at a higher heat for a little longer.

Most rolled oats sold are stabilised—this means they have been steamed before rolling, to stop them going rancid. If at all possible, use rolled oats that have not been stabilised for making porridge, but make sure they are fresh. They will have more goodness in them.

Left-over rolled oat pudding

Makes 2 cups

Quick and delicious, this is great to serve as a dessert after a vegetable- or protein-based meal that has little carbohydrate.

    100 g (3½ oz/1 cup) cold everyday creamy rolled oat porridge
        (see page 159)
    110 g (3¾ oz/½ cup) stewed pears or apples
    125 ml (4 fl oz/½ cup) milk—any type is fine, but coconut
        is especially creamy
    1 tablespoon maple syrup
    ½ teaspoon natural vanilla extract
    pinch ground cinnamon

Place all the ingredients in a blender and process until smooth. If the pudding is too thick, add more milk and adjust to the desired consistency. Pudding is best eaten on the day of making, but it will keep in an airtight container for up to 2 days in the fridge.

EGGS

The protein and fat in eggs help provide one of the most sustaining breakfasts. How you present that egg will often depend on how busy you are in the morning, the age of your toddler and how much mess you can cope with. Where possible, leave the egg yolk soft—it will be more digestible this way—and don't forget to serve the egg with a small amount of good-quality sea salt or a sprinkle of dulse flakes. Here are some good egg ideas:

- When your toddler is very little, simply adding a soft-boiled egg to some mashed vegetables makes a nourishing and delicious meal.

- Though messy, a soft-boiled egg presented to your toddler in an egg cup with 'soldiers' (thin pieces of buttered toast for dipping) is great for encouraging independence.

- Left-over vegetable and red lentil coconut dhal (see page 174) is a brilliant base for an egg breakfast. Add a little coconut oil or ghee (see page 107) to a small frying pan and cook the left-over dhal for 5 minutes or so, then make a clearing in the middle and fry an egg in it.

- To add extra vegetable goodness to an egg, in a small frying pan, gently cook a small amount of grated or finely chopped vegetables in a little coconut oil or ghee. Add 1 lightly beaten egg to the mix and gently stir until the egg is just set or scramble, as desired. This is a great way to include greens in your toddler's diet as the fat in the egg and ghee or coconut oil ensures the many minerals are utilised by the body.

Dips and spreads

DIPS AND SPREADS ARE INVALUABLE TO HAVE ON HAND, providing a nutrient-dense addition to raw vegetables and small amounts of good bread. Quality butter or ghee (see page 107) is always the first thought for topping bread, but when this is not tolerated, any of the following dips and spreads would make a great alternative.

Delicious avocado

GLUTEN FREE

Makes about 1 cup

Avocados are handy to have around. They are a highly concentrated food, often described as a nut rather than a fruit. They are rich in potassium, iron, vitamins A, the B family, C and E, and high-quality fat. A simple dip will provide a large amount of energy and goodness.

I hesitate to give a recipe for avocado dip—really you just need to mash it up and flavour it with a little lime juice. A good avocado should need nothing else, and I prefer the taste not to be diluted. This is delicious with a little wakame gomasio (see page 168) sprinkled over it, the salt lifting the flavour of the avocado. Flavour it with finely chopped coriander (cilantro) leaves or 1 finely chopped or puréed tomato, if desired, but it's a good idea to keep raw garlic and onion out of it.

 VARIATIONS

The following suggestions are good ways to add beneficial bacteria to mashed avocado:

- *Dairy* Choose from yoghurt (see page 98), labne (see page 99) or sour cream. Add 125 g (4½ oz/½ cup) to 1 mashed avocado.
- *Non-dairy* Add 2 teaspoons to 1 tablespoon unpasteurised genmai (brown rice) miso (see glossary) or similar mellow miso to 1 mashed avocado.

Vegetable and nut pâté

GLUTEN FREE
Makes 1½ cups

This is a lovely vegetarian pâté for a young child, with nuts and seeds to provide protein and quality fats. If you can, use soaked and lightly roasted nuts and seeds (see page 103). For very young toddlers, try mixing a little of this pâté with delicious avocado (see opposite), as a wonderful introduction to nuts and seeds. For the older toddler, serve with a small piece of wholegrain bread, and some avocado.

1 tablespoon ghee (see page 107) or butter
1 tablespoon olive oil or coconut oil
½ onion, finely chopped
1 celery stalk, finely chopped
½ small leek, white part only, thinly sliced and washed well
1 carrot, finely diced
generous pinch each dried thyme and sage
80 g (2¾ oz) broccoli, including some stem, roughly chopped
125 ml (4 fl oz/½ cup) vegetable stock (see page 94)
40 g (1½ oz/⅓ cup) walnuts or pecans
50 g (1¾ oz/⅓ cup) sunflower seeds
1 teaspoon genmai (brown rice) miso (see glossary)
     or similar mellow miso, preferably unpasteurised

Heat the ghee and oil in a large frying pan over low heat. Add the onion, celery, leek, carrot, dried herbs and a pinch of sea salt. Cook, stirring regularly, for 6–8 minutes or until soft and very lightly coloured.

Add the broccoli and stock, cover with a lid and simmer over very low heat for 10 minutes or until the vegetables are just cooked. Remove the lid and simmer until all the liquid has evaporated.

Place the cooked vegetables, nuts, seeds and miso in a food processor and process until smooth. Will keep in an airtight container in the fridge for up to 3 days.

Funky bright green broad bean dip

GLUTEN FREE
Makes 1 cup

With the funkiest of colours, this dip is fabulous just about anywhere—with raw vegetables, heaped onto fritters, tossed into cooked pasta, even scooped onto cooked fish (see baked cherry tomato, basil and olive fish parcels, page 184). It's also a great way to use older beans, frozen will work just fine, too.

185 g (6½ oz/1 cup) shelled broad (fava) beans (see kitchen note)
1 garlic clove, crushed
1–2 tablespoons finely grated parmesan or pecorino cheese
60 ml (2 fl oz/¼ cup) olive oil
3 teaspoons lemon juice

Bring a saucepan of salted water to the boil. Place the shelled broad beans in the boiling water and cook for 1 minute, for small, young beans, or 3 minutes, for larger, older beans. Drain, then refresh in cold water and, when cool enough to handle, peel off their white skins.

Place the peeled broad beans and the remaining ingredients in a food processor, add a pinch of salt and process until a thick paste forms. Taste, and add a little more salt, cheese or lemon juice as required. Store in a sealed, clean glass jar in the fridge for up to 3 days.

 KITCHEN NOTE

If using fresh broad beans, you'll need to shell the beans from their fleecy, snug pods. Shelling broad beans is a wonderful thing to do with your child. You will need about 450 g (1 lb) fresh broad beans in their long pods for this recipe.

Egg and olive spread

Makes ½ cup

A quick and easy, nutrient-dense dip for raw vegetables, or great to spread on a piece of good bread as a snack.

    10 pitted black or green olives
    2 hard-boiled eggs
    ½–1 anchovy fillet
    1–2 teaspoons finely snipped chives
    1 tablespoon labne (see page 99) or yoghurt (see page 98)

Finely chop the olives, eggs and anchovy together, then place in a bowl. Add the chives and labne or yoghurt and combine well. Store in a sealed, clean glass jar in the fridge for up to 1 week.

Mayonnaise

Makes ⅓ cup

Homemade mayonnaise is one of the most flexible foods to have on hand. Used to enrich a salad or snack or to add flavour to meals, mayonnaise is a profoundly rich source of quality fats and antioxidants. I prefer to make my mayonnaise in the traditional way—using organic extra virgin olive oil. Unfortunately, because of the cost and strong flavour, most mayonnaise available today is made with refined, lighter-tasting oils which are nutritionally inferior.

It's best to make mayonnaise by hand, rather than using a food processor or blender because it gives you more control—you can stop adding oil when you feel the mayonnaise is looking good. This is particularly important when using organic oil, and it's good to keep in mind that you may need to use less. This is because organic extra virgin olive oils typically have more density than their conventional counterparts.

The other important thing to remember when making mayonnaise is to start with all your ingredients at room temperature. If your mayonnaise happens to split while you are making it, simply place another egg yolk in a clean bowl and slowly whisk in the split mayonnaise.

Mayonnaise is made with raw egg yolk, so it's critical for you to know the source of your eggs —they should be from organic, free-ranging chickens eating their natural foods.

1 egg yolk, at room temperature
1 garlic clove, crushed
½ teaspoon white wine vinegar
½ teaspoon wholegrain mustard
80 ml (2½ fl oz/⅓ cup) conventional extra virgin olive oil
    or 65 ml (2¼ fl oz) organic extra virgin olive oil

Place a damp cloth on a work surface and put a small heavy mixing bowl on top (the cloth stops the bowl from slipping). Place the egg yolk, garlic, vinegar and mustard in the bowl and whisk to combine well. While whisking continuously, gradually add the oil, drop by drop at first, then in a slow steady stream. Stop adding oil every now and then and give the mixture a thorough whisk before adding more. Continue until the mixture is thick and emulsified. Season to taste with sea salt and adjust with more vinegar, if desired. Store in a sealed, clean glass jar in the fridge for up to 2 weeks.

Mayonnaise made with bacon fat

GLUTEN FREE / DAIRY FREE
Makes ⅓ cup

When you have organic, nitrate-free bacon it's a pity to waste the nutrient-dense fat that renders out during cooking, especially as this fat is a great source of vitamin D. Mayonnaise made with bacon fat is so delicious, and a great addition to any sandwich. This mayonnaise has a slightly different texture—it is not quite as thick as the one opposite.

60 ml (2 fl oz/¼ cup) rendered bacon fat, melted, but not too hot
25 ml (1 fl oz) extra virgin olive oil
1 egg yolk, at room temperature
1 garlic clove, crushed
½ teaspoon white wine vinegar
½ teaspoon wholegrain mustard

Place a damp cloth on a work surface and put a small heavy mixing bowl on top (the cloth stops the bowl from slipping). In a separate bowl, whisk the slightly warm bacon fat and olive oil together.

Place the egg yolk, garlic, vinegar and mustard in the heavy bowl and whisk to combine well. While whisking continuously, gradually add the combined fat and oil, drop by drop at first, then in a slow steady stream. Stop adding fat every now and then to give the mixture a thorough whisk before adding more. Continue until the mixture is thick and emulsified. Season to taste with sea salt and a little more vinegar, if desired. Store in a sealed, clean glass jar in the fridge for up to 2 weeks.

Wakame gomasio

GLUTEN FREE
Makes ½ cup

A powerhouse of minerals—especially calcium—this is great to sprinkle over anything you can imagine. If you have time, soak and lightly roast your sesame seeds (see page 104) to increase the amount of bioavailable calcium.

80 g (2¾ oz/½ cup) sesame seeds
1 strip wakame sea vegetable

If the sesame seeds are not already soaked and lightly roasted, lightly toast them in a dry frying pan over low heat, then remove them from the heat and cool.

Preheat the oven to 165°C (320°F/Gas 3). Place the wakame on a baking tray and bake for 10 minutes or until crisp and completely dried out. Grind the wakame in a mortar with a pestle, discarding any stem.

Add the sesame seeds to the wakame and pound to break the seeds and release the oils but do not grind into a paste. The mixture should begin to smell fragrant and glisten. Add ½–1 teaspoon sea salt and combine well. Store in a sealed, clean glass jar in a cool spot for up to 1 month.

Salads

SALADS MAKE GREAT FINGER FOODS, and can provide a nourishing snack or meal. Any raw vegetables should always be served with a dressing that includes fat—this will enable utilisation of the many vitamins and minerals in the vegetables. A dressing also 'softens' the salad and provides moisture in the mouth, which is important for little ones. Winter salads are often best made with cooked root vegetables, and a more unctuous (thick and creamy) dressing. You'll find I generally use apple cider vinegar in the dressing—it's a great choice for young children, helping to maintain the body's acid–alkaline balance, and has long been valued for its healing powers.

Crunchy apple salad

GLUTEN FREE
Serves 4 as a side salad

Children will very often take to greens when fruit is included. In this salad they are deliciously coated with a nutrient-dense and creamy dressing and slightly sweetened with fresh apple. Make sure the apple is fresh, sweet and ripe. You can easily make a smaller version of this salad, as desired—the dressing will keep in the fridge for 2 3 days.

25 g (1 oz/¼ cup) pecans
1 small lettuce or about 65 g (2½ oz) mixed salad leaves
30 g (1 oz/¼ cup) sultanas
2 celery stalks, thinly sliced
1 small apple, quartered, cored and thinly sliced

Creamy dressing
60 ml (2 fl oz/¼ cup) mayonnaise (see page 166)
60 g (2¼ oz/¼ cup) yoghurt (see page 98)
¼ teaspoon sweet curry powder
1 teaspoon lime juice
1 teaspoon honey

Preheat the oven to 180°C (350°F/Gas 4).

Place the pecans on a baking tray and roast for 6 minutes or until lightly golden and fragrant. Remove and cool.

To make the creamy dressing Place all the ingredients in a small bowl, combine well, then adjust as desired to taste.

Wash and dry the lettuce well and cut into chunky slices or smaller so it is manageable for a young toddler. Place in a bowl with the sultanas, celery, apple and pecans, pour the dressing over and toss together to coat well.

Iron and energy!

GLUTEN FREE / DAIRY FREE
Makes 2 toddler serves

This avocado, arame, beetroot, carrot and lentil salad is what I like to call iron and energy! Arame sea vegetables and lentils are both rich sources of iron, but not in a form that makes them easily bioavailable. The citrus dressing provides a large dose of vitamin C, which helps maximise usage of the vegetable-based iron, and a sprinkle of currants adds delicious sweetness. I generally leave carrots unpeeled, as they will have more goodness, but for salads I prefer to peel and grate them. Don't go overboard on the arame, as it swells considerably when soaked—you only need a little to provide a lot of goodness.

1 tablespoon green lentils
1 teaspoon whey (see page 99) or lemon juice
pinch arame sea vegetable
1 small carrot, peeled and grated
1 small beetroot, peeled and grated
1 small avocado, roughly chopped
1 tablespoon currants

Tangy citrus dressing
2 tablespoons orange juice
1 tablespoon olive oil
1 teaspoon flax (linseed) oil
¼ teaspoon apple cider vinegar
¼ teaspoon wholegrain mustard
2 drops toasted sesame oil (optional)
pinch finely grated ginger (optional)

Place the lentils, whey or lemon juice and 125 ml (4 fl oz/½ cup) of water in a small bowl and allow to stand for 6 hours or overnight at room temperature.

Drain the lentils and place in a small saucepan with 250 ml (9 fl oz/1 cup) of water. Simmer over low heat for 12 minutes, or until the lentils are soft, then drain. Set aside to cool.

Meanwhile, soak the arame in 125 ml (4 fl oz/½ cup) of water for 10–15 minutes, then drain.

To make the tangy citrus dressing Place all the ingredients in a small bowl, season with a little sea salt and whisk until well combined.

Place the cooled lentils, arame, carrot, beetroot, avocado and currants in a bowl. Pour the dressing over, gently toss together and serve.

KITCHEN NOTES

- *Soaking the lentils makes them easier to digest, but best of all, cuts their cooking time by one-third. If you're not soaking the lentils, they will take approximately 35–45 minutes to cook.*
- *For extra deliciousness, try marinating the currants and cooked lentils in the dressing for a couple of hours before serving. They are a great standby to have in the fridge to add nutrient density and iron to a handful of grated vegetables at the drop of a hat.*

Warm potato, green bean, roasted beetroot and egg salad

GLUTEN FREE / DAIRY FREE
Makes 2 toddler serves

Some children will prefer their salads cooked and slightly warm, and from an Ayurvedic perspective, this is entirely healthful for some body types. This salad is a perfect way to showcase whatever vegetables may be in season, and if you can get them as young and as small as possible, they will be all the sweeter. Feel free to add any other vegetables, as desired—lightly steamed baby carrots, or fresh peas or very young broad (fava) beans (shelled and peeled) which will need no cooking.

2–4 very small (or 1 medium) waxy potatoes
3–6 green beans, preferably stringless
1 small cooked beetroot (see kitchen note)
4–6 cherry tomatoes, halved if large
3–5 pitted Kalamata olives, roughly chopped
1 hard-boiled egg, peeled and quartered
1 tablespoon roughly chopped flat-leaf (Italian) parsley leaves

Mediterranean basil dressing
3 teaspoons olive oil
1 teaspoon flax (linseed) oil
1 teaspoon apple cider vinegar
1 small garlic clove, crushed
3 small basil leaves, thinly sliced
¼ teaspoon wholegrain mustard
¼ teaspoon honey

To make the Mediterranean basil dressing Place all the ingredients in a small bowl, add a pinch of sea salt and whisk together well. Adjust for taste.

Bring a saucepan of salted water to the boil. Add the potatoes and cook until just tender. If they have been freshly dug, this will only be a few minutes. Using a slotted spoon, remove the potatoes and allow the water to return to the boil.

Cut the potato into smaller chunks, as desired, then place in a bowl with the dressing and toss through gently.

Top and tail the beans and if necessary remove any side strings. If the beans are long, cut into 5 cm (2 inch) lengths. Drop the beans into the boiling water, allow the water to return to the boil, then cook for 1 minute or until tender. Drain the beans and add to the potato.

Cut the beetroot into small pieces and add to the bowl along with the tomato and olives. Gently toss together well and divide the mixture onto two plates (or reserve half for later). Place 2 egg quarters on each salad, sprinkle with a little parsley and serve.

 KITCHEN NOTE

This recipe calls for cooked beetroot, and I prefer to roast, rather than boil it, as the flavour is more intense. Cut off any leaves—you could keep any very young, small leaves to use in the salad, if desired. Wash the beetroot to remove any sand and grit. Place in an ovenproof dish with about 60 ml (2 fl oz/¼ cup) of water, drizzle over a little olive oil and cover with foil. Bake in a preheated 180°C (350°F/Gas 4) oven until the beetroot is tender when pierced with a knife tip. It is best to remove the skin when the beetroot is warm; it should just slip off using your fingers. A word of warning—you might like to wear gloves!

Substantial meals

IN THIS SECTION YOU WILL FIND A BROAD RANGE OF NUTRIENT-DENSE, nourishing whole meals for toddlers and, indeed, the whole family. They typically have little grain and provide complete protein in a range of ways. Legumes are paired with whole grains, nuts, seeds and sea vegetables. Fish, chicken and red meats provide protein in their own right, and the red meats (especially beef) provide a rich and bioavailable source of iron.

Vegetable and red lentil coconut dhal

GLUTEN FREE

Makes 2 adult serves and 1 toddler serve

Based on vegetables rather than lentils, this makes a delicious meal for the whole family, offering complete protein when served with a small amount of whole grain. Leftovers are brilliant for breakfast—add a little coconut oil or ghee to a small frying pan and cook it all up for 5 minutes or so, then make a clearing in the middle and fry an egg.

90 g (3¼ oz/⅓ cup) split red lentils
2 teaspoons ghee (see page 107) or coconut oil
½ onion, finely diced
1 teaspoon finely grated ginger
large pinch each ground cumin, ground coriander, turmeric
    and garam masala
½ small carrot, finely diced
100 g (3½ oz) jap or butternut pumpkin, peeled, seeded and finely diced
100 g (3½ oz) orange sweet potato, peeled and finely diced
½ apple, peeled, core removed and finely diced
1 teaspoon dulse flakes
2 cm (¾ inch) strip kombu, cut into rough pieces
250 ml (9 fl oz/1 cup) vegetable stock (see page 94)

250 ml (9 fl oz/1 cup) coconut milk
1 tablespoon finely chopped coriander (cilantro) leaves and stems
100 g (3½ oz) cauliflower, cut into small pieces
60 g (2¼ oz) green beans, cut into small pieces
40 g (1½ oz/¼ cup) fresh or frozen peas
1 teaspoon fish sauce
squeeze of lime juice

Check through the lentils for any stones, and rinse well.

Heat the ghee in a heavy-based saucepan over low heat. Add the onion and ginger and cook for 2–3 minutes. Stir in the spices, carrot, pumpkin, sweet potato, apple, lentils, dulse flakes, kombu, stock, coconut milk and 3 teaspoons of the chopped coriander. Make sure the kombu is submerged in liquid, cover with a lid and simmer gently for 15–18 minutes. Add the cauliflower, green beans and peas, then simmer, uncovered, stirring from time to time, for another 20 minutes or until the vegetables are very tender. Remove from the heat and mash any bits of kombu into the stew. Stir in the fish sauce, remaining coriander and the lime juice.

Creamy adzuki bean and vegetable stew

GLUTEN FREE (IF WHEAT-FREE TAMARI USED)
Makes 3 adult serves and 1 toddler serve

Adzuki beans are easily digested, and a perfect first bean for a young toddler. The beans are best soaked overnight at room temperature, although when the weather is very hot, they can be soaked in the fridge. Serve with a small amount of whole grain to complete the protein and a dollop of yoghurt to aid digestion.

   55 g (2 oz/¼ cup) dried adzuki beans
   1 teaspoon whey (see page 99) or lemon juice
   1 tablespoon coconut oil
   ½ onion, finely chopped
   1 garlic clove, finely chopped
   1 teaspoon finely grated ginger
   3 cm (1¼ inch) strip kombu
   280 g (10 oz) jap or butternut pumpkin, peeled, seeded
      and cut into 3 cm (1¼ inch) dice
   500 ml (17 fl oz/2 cups) vegetable stock (see page 94) or water
   1 small cob of corn, kernels removed
   30 g (1 oz) Tuscan black kale (cavolo nero), thinly sliced
   1–2 teaspoons tamari, or to taste
   1 tablespoon finely chopped coriander (cilantro)
      or flat-leaf (Italian) parsley leaves
   yoghurt (see page 98), to serve

Place the beans, whey or lemon juice and 500 ml (17 fl oz/2 cups) of water in a bowl and allow to stand at room temperature overnight. Drain and rinse the beans. Set aside.

   Heat the oil in a heavy-based saucepan over low heat. Add the onion, garlic and ginger and cook, stirring occasionally, for 5–6 minutes or until soft but not coloured. Add the beans, kombu, pumpkin and stock or water, cover with a tight-fitting lid and simmer gently for 1 hour or until the beans are soft. There should be ample liquid, so resist the temptation to add more, as this will dilute the flavour of the stew. Just make sure there is not too much steam escaping around the lid. If your beans are taking longer than 1 hour, you may need to add a little more liquid (see page 85).

Add the corn and kale, and cook, uncovered, for another 10 minutes. Add the tamari to taste and the coriander. Using a potato masher or fork, mash the kombu and some of the beans to thicken the sauce. If desired, simmer, uncovered, over high heat to thicken a little more—the stew should be nice and thick.

 **KITCHEN NOTE**

This stew is best made with dried rather than tinned beans, as the bean cooking liquor provides depth of flavour to the broth's end result.

Cowboy beans and quinoa stew

GLUTEN FREE
Makes 3 adult serves and 1 toddler serve

Tinned beans work fine in this dish, but make sure you drain and rinse them before using. Follow the same cooking method as for cooked beans.

Made with both legumes and whole grains, this quick and easy-to-put-together stew is complete in protein. It's delicious too! Feel free to add other vegetables as desired—zucchini (courgette) and corn would both be lovely. I've kept chilli out of the recipe, but if you'd like to add a bit in, please do so. In some cultures, it's common for very young children to eat small amounts of chilli. Go for a soft and mellow chilli, such as the New Mexico or ancho, which gives beautiful flavour as well as warmth. Serve with yoghurt or kefir cream to aid digestion.

50 g (1¾ oz/¼ cup) quinoa
1 teaspoon whey (see page 99) or lemon juice,
    plus 1 teaspoon extra if using dried beans
100 g (3½ oz/½ cup) dried pinto or borlotti (cranberry) beans
    or 300 g (10½ oz/1½ cups) cooked pinto or borlotti beans
5 cm (2 inch) strip kombu or 1 teaspoon dulse flakes
375–500 ml (13–17 fl oz/1½–2 cups) vegetable stock (see page 94)
1 tablespoon olive oil
1 onion, finely diced
½ green capsicum (pepper), seeded and finely diced
¼ teaspoon each dried oregano, dried thyme and ground cumin
small pinch ground cinnamon
1 carrot, finely diced
1 orange sweet potato, peeled and finely diced
400 g (14 oz) tinned chopped tomatoes
1–2 teaspoons apple juice concentrate or rapadura sugar, or to taste
yoghurt (see page 98) or kefir cream (see page 102), to serve

Place the quinoa in a small bowl. Add the whey or lemon juice plus 125 ml (4 fl oz/½ cup) of water and stir to combine. Leave to stand for 6 hours or overnight at room temperature. Drain and set aside.

If using dried beans Place the beans in a bowl. Add the extra teaspoon of whey or lemon juice plus 750 ml (26 fl oz/3 cups) of water and stir to combine. Leave to stand for 6 hours or overnight. This is best done at room temperature. Drain and rinse the beans. Place the drained beans in a saucepan with the kombu or dulse flakes and 500 ml (17 fl oz/2 cups) stock. Bring to the boil, then cover—with the lid slightly ajar—and cook over low heat for 1 hour. Heat the oil in a frying pan over medium heat. Add the onion, capsicum, dried herbs and spices and cook for 5–6 minutes or until a little colour has developed. Add to the beans, along with the carrot, sweet potato, tomato and drained quinoa.

If using cooked beans Heat the oil in a saucepan over medium heat. Add the onion, capsicum, dried herbs and spices and cook for 5–6 minutes or until a little colour has developed. Add the cooked beans, carrot, sweet potato, tomato, kombu or dulse flakes, 375 ml (13 fl oz/1½ cups) stock and drained quinoa.

For both dried and cooked beans Cover the pan with the lid slightly ajar and simmer for 35–50 minutes or until the vegetables and the beans are soft and the quinoa is cooked. Stir from time to time to check there is enough liquid. It may need a little more depending on how much the beans absorb as they cook, but go easy—too much liquid can dilute the flavour.

Taste and add a little apple juice concentrate or sugar, as required. If the stew is too thin, remove the lid and bring to a robust boil, stirring often, until you have the desired consistency. Serve with yoghurt or kefir cream.

Sweet potato patties with peach salsa and raita

GLUTEN FREE
Makes 20

A humble and delicious little patty that offers so much. Lentils are a good source of iron for vegetarians, but it is in a format that makes it less bioavailable. Serving lentils with vitamin C-rich fruit, tomato and capsicum in the salsa increases iron's bioavailability. Patties are best fresh, as is the salsa, but you can store the patties for up to 2 days in the fridge. The raita will keep for up to 3 days in the fridge.

220 g (7¾ oz/1 cup) split red lentils
2 orange sweet potatoes, about 1 kg (2 lb 4 oz), peeled
1 tablespoon coconut oil
½ onion, finely chopped
¼ teaspoon each ground coriander and ground cumin
1 teaspoon finely grated ginger
40 g (1½ oz/⅓ cup) maize flour (golden cornflour) (see glossary)
50 g (1¾ oz/⅓ cup) sesame seeds
extra coconut oil, for shallow frying

Quick peach salsa
1 peach
1 tablespoon finely diced capsicum (pepper)
1 small tomato, finely diced
1 tablespoon roughly chopped coriander (cilantro) leaves
1 teaspoon lime juice
finely chopped long red chilli (optional, for adults)

Raita
250 g (9 oz/1 cup) Greek-style yoghurt
1–2 tablespoons roughly chopped coriander (cilantro) leaves
1 tablespoon finely chopped mint leaves
1–2 teaspoons lime juice
90 g (3¼ oz/½ cup) peeled, seeded and finely diced cucumber

You can substitue ½ mango for the peach in the salsa. Remove the skin and cut the flesh into small dice and combine with the remaining ingredients.

Preheat the oven to 180°C (350°F/Gas 4).

Check through the lentils for any small stones, and rinse well. Place in a small saucepan with 435 ml (15¼ fl oz/1¾ cup) of water, bring to the boil over medium heat, then reduce the heat to low and simmer gently, stirring occasionally, for 30 minutes or until just cooked and dry. Take care to cook the lentils over a gentle heat—too high and the water will evaporate off before they are cooked. Remove from the heat and set aside to cool.

While the lentils are cooking, cut the sweet potatoes into 2 cm (¾ inch) thick wedges. Place in a heavy-based roasting pan, drizzle with half of the coconut oil and toss to coat. Bake for 45 minutes or until just lightly coloured and soft to the touch. Be careful not to overcook the sweet potato or it will become too dry.

Heat the remaining coconut oil in a small frying pan over low heat. Add the onion, dried spices and ginger and cook for 6–8 minutes or until the onion is soft but not coloured. Season to taste with a little sea salt and freshly ground black pepper, then remove from the heat.

Transfer the onion mixute to a bowl and add the cooled lentils. Roughly break the sweet potato into the bowl. Using a spoon, mix together, roughly mashing the sweet potato into the lentils and onion mixture and season to taste. Shape 2 tablespoons of the mixture into a patty and place on a tray. Repeat with the rest of the mixture.

Combine the maize flour and sesame seeds in a shallow bowl. Coat the patties in the mixture, then place on a tray and refrigerate for 30 minutes.

To make the quick peach salsa Drop the peach into boiling water for 10 seconds, then into iced water to cool. Peel off the skin, cut the flesh into small dice and combine with the remaining ingredients. Leave at room temperature until needed.

To make the raita Combine all the ingredients and refrigerate until needed.

To cook the patties Pour enough coconut oil into a large frying pan to cover the base to about 1 cm (½ inch) deep and place over medium heat. When the oil is hot, but not at all rippling or smoking, cook the patties, in batches, taking care not to overcrowd the pan, for 5–6 minutes or until golden. (You may need to strain the oil in between batches to remove any cooked pieces.) Remove and drain on paper towel. Serve with the salsa and raita.

For extra goodness, sprinkle the patties with a tiny bit of wakame gomasio (see page 168). For adults, these patties make a delicious panini filling, with a touch of chutney and raita.

Simple winter vegetable ragoût

GLUTEN FREE (IF WHEAT-FREE TAMARI USED)
Makes about 1½ cups / 2–3 toddler serves

While this is a delicious vegetable stew for a young toddler, it's just as grounding and delicious for an adult. Enriched with dulse and thickened with kudzu to soothe the digestive system, it can be served with a little cooked whole grain, such as quinoa or brown rice, to complete the protein.

2 teaspoons ghee (see page 107), butter or olive oil
½ small leek, white part only, thinly sliced and washed well
100 g (3½ oz) jap or butternut pumpkin, peeled, seeded and finely diced
½ carrot, finely diced
1 small potato, finely diced
1 sage leaf, thinly sliced
1 teaspoon thyme leaves
1 teaspoon dulse flakes
1 small dried shiitake mushroom, stem discarded, cap halved
1 teaspoon tamari
250 ml (4 fl oz/1 cup) vegetable stock (see page 94)
1 small cauliflower floret, cut into small pieces
40 g (1½ oz/¼ cup) fresh or frozen peas
2 teaspoons kudzu (kuzu)

Heat the fat of your choice in a small saucepan over medium heat. Add the leek, pumpkin, carrot, potato, sage and thyme and cook for 5 minutes or until just lightly coloured. Add the dulse flakes, shiitake mushroom, tamari and stock, reduce the heat to low and cook, covered, for 15 minutes or until the vegetables are just cooked. Add the cauliflower and peas and cook, covered, for another 5 minutes.

Place the kudzu in a small bowl with 1 tablespoon of water and mix until smooth.

Remove and discard the shiitake pieces. Add the kudzu to the pan and stir continuously until the ragoût comes to the boil and thickens. Mash, if required.

Corn and zucchini fritters

GLUTEN FREE
Makes 20

These are wonderful hot for breakfast, lunch or dinner and cool or cold for snacks. Made with left-over cooked quinoa, they are high in protein. They are especially delicious served with garden vegetable tomato sauce (see page 142), delicious avocado (see page 162) or any of the pestos (see pages 230–232).

  1 zucchini (courgette), about 250 g (9 oz)
  2 cobs of corn
  ½ onion, finely chopped, or 1–2 spring onions (scallions), finely sliced
  1 tablespoon maize flour (golden cornflour, see glossary)
  ½ cup cooked quinoa (see page 91)
  3 eggs, lightly beaten
  2 tablespoons finely chopped basil or coriander (cilantro) leaves
  olive oil, ghee (see page 107) or coconut oil, for frying

Grate the zucchini, then place it in a clean tea towel and roll up. Twist the ends of the tea towel, squeezing the juice from the zucchini, then place the flesh in a bowl.

If the corn cobs are young and fresh, cut the kernels from the cobs and add to the zucchini. If they are older or not as sweet, steam them until they are just cooked, then remove the kernels from the cob and cool before adding to the zucchini. Add the onion, maize flour, quinoa, eggs, herbs and a pinch each of sea salt and freshly ground black pepper and combine well.

Pour the fat of your choice into a large frying pan to cover the base well and place over medium heat. When the oil is hot, but not at all rippling or smoking (the oil is a good temperature if it lightly sizzles when the batter hits the pan), place tablespoonsful of mixture into the pan and cook for 3–4 minutes each side or until golden. (If the corn is already cooked, this may take less time.) Drain on paper towels. Repeat with the remaining mixture. Fritters will keep for up to 2 days in an airtight container in the fridge.

These fritters are incredibly forgiving and flexible—corn is not at all essential. When it's out of season, simply increase the amount of zucchini.

Baked cherry tomato, basil and olive fish parcels

GLUTEN FREE

Makes 2 adult serves and 1 toddler serve

A quick and delicious way to cook large fish is to bake the fillets. A sustainable larger fish local to me in Western Australia, for example, is mulloway. Tomatoes, basil and olives match the robust flavour of many larger Australian sustainable fish, and as a bonus, cook down to make a simple sauce.

> 200 g (7 oz) skinless fish fillets, bones removed, and cut into 2 adult and 1 toddler portion (see kitchen note)
> 10–12 ripe cherry tomatoes, halved, if large
> 10 basil leaves, roughly sliced
> 5 lemon slices
> 8–10 Kalamata olives, pitted and roughly chopped
> 30 g (1 oz) butter or 2 tablespoons ghee (see page 107)

Don't skip the butter, as it helps to absorb and utilise the omega-3 essential fatty acids in the fish. In winter, lime slices, coriander (cilantro), a little fresh ginger, mirin (Japanese rice wine) and tamari are great flavour additions to these fish parcels instead of the tomato, basil and olive.

Preheat the oven to 200°C (400°F/Gas 6).

Cut 3 sheets of baking paper, large enough to create a parcel around each piece of fish. Fold each piece of paper in half, then open it up again—the fold line will guide you in making the parcel. Place a piece of fish onto each piece of paper along the fold line and season to taste with sea salt and freshly ground black pepper.

Place the tomato, basil, lemon, olives and butter on top of the fish. For each parcel, fold the paper over, turn the edge inwards a couple of times and twist each end so that the twists hold the parcel together.

Place the 2 larger parcels on a baking tray and bake for 8 minutes, then add the smaller parcel. Cook for another 10 minutes, then remove and check if the fish is cooked—it should be opaque and flake easily. If not, reseal the parcels and return to the oven. Thin fillets may take less time, while thicker fillets may take longer.

 **KITCHEN NOTE**

An adult will eat a fillet weighing 60–100 g (2¼–3½ oz), depending on the density of the fish. A good amount for a toddler is about 30 g (1 oz).

Coconut and kaffir lime ceviche

Makes 2 toddler serves

Ceviche is a delicious and nutritious way to serve fish to young children—it makes for messy eating, but it's worth it. Instead of using heat to cook fish, the acidity of lime or lemon juice does the job for you. When your toddler is a little older, the ceviche is great served in a little lettuce cup.

    2 tablespoons lime juice
    3 kaffir lime leaves, torn
    1 teaspoon fish sauce
    125 ml (4 fl oz/½ cup) coconut milk
    3 teaspoons mirin (Japanese rice wine)
    1 teaspoon finely grated palm sugar (jaggery)
    100 g (3½ oz) skinless fish fillet (see kitchen note)

Place all the ingredients except the fish in a bowl, add a pinch of sea salt and combine well. Adjust the seasoning, as desired.

Run your fingers carefully over the fish and remove any protruding bones. Using a sharp knife, slice the flesh across the grain into 5 mm (¼ inch) thick slices. Add to the lime and coconut mixture, toss to combine well, then cover and refrigerate for 2–3 hours; the fish is ready when it looks opaque. Remove and discard the lime leaves. Spoon the fish and juices into small bowls.

 KITCHEN NOTE

Fish must be exceptionally fresh to make ceviche; if you are in any doubt whatsoever, cook the fish instead. Choose a sweet-flavoured and firm-fleshed fish. Avoid whiting which has too many bones, and many sustainable fish can be too strongly flavoured for ceviche. Black bream, red mullet or mulloway are all good choices.

Simple fish stew

GLUTEN FREE
Makes 2 adult serves and 1 toddler serve

This recipe is all about making a stock and stew in one, saving you lots of time, but still providing exceptional nourishment. It's simple but delicious, grounding and rich in gelatine, minerals and iodine.

Refrigerate any left-over broth (it will solidify in the fridge). The next day, reheat it and mix in a little cooked grain and some vegetables for a quick and nourishing meal for your toddler.

When choosing the fish carcass and head for the stock, choose a fish that is fairly mild in flavour and not too large (avoid strong-tasting fish like bonito and tailor).

Fish stock
1 fish carcass and head, about 250 g (9 oz)
1 flat-leaf (Italian) parsley sprig
1 bay leaf
1 thyme sprig
1 tablespoon ghee (see page 107) or butter
½ onion, finely diced
1 celery stalk, finely sliced
40 ml (1¼ fl oz) white wine

Fish stew
2–3 small potatoes, cut into 3 cm (1¼ inch) dice
1–2 carrots, finely diced
1 leek, white part only, thinly sliced and washed well
3 garlic cloves, peeled and left whole
1 lemon thyme sprig
250–300 g (9–10½ oz) fish fillets, skin on
6 basil leaves, thinly sliced
1 tablespoon fennel fronds
1 teaspoon mirin (Japanese rice wine), or to taste
1 teaspoon fish sauce

To make the fish stock Place the fish carcass and head, and the herbs, in the centre of a large piece of muslin, bring up the sides and tie with string to make a bag. Heat the fat of your choice in a heavy-based saucepan or cast-iron saucepan over medium heat. Add the onion and celery and season to taste with sea salt and freshly ground black pepper. Cook, stirring regularly, for 5–6 minutes or until the vegetables are just lightly coloured. Add the wine and simmer until nearly evaporated, then add 750 ml (26 fl oz/3 cups) of water and the bag of fish bones and herbs. Bring to the boil, then reduce the heat to low and simmer very gently for 1 hour to allow the gelatine and minerals to be released into the stock. Lift up the muslin bag and carefully squeeze as much liquid as you can from the bag into the pan, then discard.

To make the fish stew Add the potato, carrot, leek, garlic cloves and lemon thyme to the fish stock, cover and simmer gently for 15 minutes or until the vegetables are tender.

When the vegetables are tender, remove the garlic cloves, mash and return to the broth. Increase the heat to medium and simmer until the broth is reduced by one-third.

Wash the fish fillets well—this will remove any scales. Run your fingers over the fish and remove any protruding bones, then cut the flesh into large chunks. Add to the pan along with the basil, fennel, mirin and fish sauce and cook, uncovered, for 4–5 minutes or until the fish is just cooked. Taste, adjust the seasoning, as necessary.

When choosing the fish for the stew, look for a type that doesn't have a lot of small bones, such as red mullet or any of the bream family. Buy the fish whole, and ask the fishmonger to fillet it.

Fish and potato mash

GLUTEN FREE
Makes 2 adult serves and 1 toddler serve

This is a great recipe to use up any left-over fish. It is very loosely based on the traditional Provençal brandade, made with salted cod. It's delicious served with steamed vegetables or a small salad.

    200 g (7 oz) all-purpose potatoes, such as desiree, cut into chunks
    30 g (1 oz) butter or ghee (see page 107)
    1 teaspoon olive oil
    1 garlic clove, finely chopped
    130 g (4¾ oz) strong-tasting fish fillet, such as sea mullet, skin on,
        steamed until just cooked through
    1–2 teaspoons finely chopped herbs,
        such as fennel fronds, lemon thyme or dill
    ½ teaspoon lemon zest (optional)

Place the potatoes in a saucepan of cold, lightly salted water and bring to the boil. Simmer until tender, then drain and coarsely mash.

Place the butter, oil and garlic in a small frying pan over very low heat and cook for 1–2 minutes or until fragrant and soft. Ensure the heat is not too high— you do not want to brown the garlic.

Run your fingers carefully over the cooked fish and make sure there are no bones. Remove and discard the skin. Add to the mashed potato, along with the garlic mixture, herbs and lemon zest, if using, and combine until a rough mash forms. Season to taste with sea salt and freshly ground black pepper.

 VARIATION

Fish cakes Shape tablespoonsful of mash into patties. Fry in a little olive oil and ghee over medium heat for 2–3 minutes each side or until golden. Serve with a fried egg for a hearty, gluten-free meal.

Fish balls

Makes 14

Rolled in egg and arrowroot, then fried, these little fish balls are great to serve with garden vegetable tomato sauce (see page 142).

1 quantity fish and potato mash (see opposite)
1½ tablespoons true arrowroot
2 tablespoons yellow or white masa (maseca)
1 tablespoon coconut flour (see kitchen note)
1 egg, lightly beaten
coconut oil or olive oil, for frying

Shape about 3 teaspoons each of mash into small balls.

Place the arrowroot on a small plate and combine the masa and coconut flour on another plate.

Roll each ball in the arrowroot, dip in the egg, then roll in the masa and coconut flour mixture and place on a tray.

Pour enough oil into a large frying pan to cover the base about 1 cm (½ inch) deep and place over medium heat. When the oil is hot, but not smoking or rippling, add the balls, in batches, and cook, turning, for 5–6 minutes or until golden all over. Drain on paper towel and serve.

 KITCHEN NOTE

I've used masa and coconut flour to give a gluten-free result that is easily digested. If you find coconut flour hard to get, simply use 3 tablespoons of masa. Alternatively, you can use 3 tablespoons of finely ground sourdough breadcrumbs, although the fish balls may not be gluten free (depending on the bread).

Chicken fingers

Makes 8

Fried and battered chicken is always a favourite with the whole family and they're great finger food for young toddlers. This is the way I do them. These are best served fresh. If your little one can tolerate dairy, add a small amount of finely grated parmesan or pecorino to the breadcrumbs. You can double or adjust this recipe to suit your needs.

250 g (9 oz) skinless chicken breast fillet, cut into 8 long strips
250 g (9 oz/1 cup) yoghurt (see page 98)
squeeze of lemon juice
30 g (1 oz/¼ cup) true arrowroot, coconut flour or white spelt flour
80 g (2¾ oz/1 cup) fine sourdough breadcrumbs
¼ teaspoon each dried basil and dried thyme
1 teaspoon dulse flakes
1 egg, lightly beaten
coconut oil, for shallow-frying

Chicken is very often marinated in yoghurt or butter to soften and make the protein easier to digest. It will still be fine without, and you can omit this step if desired.

Place the chicken in a bowl with the yoghurt and lemon juice, combine well, cover and refrigerate for 1–2 hours.

Place the arrowroot or flour on a plate.

Combine the breadcrumbs, dried herbs and dulse flakes on another plate and add sea salt and freshly ground black pepper to taste.

Drain the marinade from the chicken, wiping it on the side of the bowl to remove the excess. Dust the chicken pieces in the arrowroot, then dip in the egg, coat in the breadcrumb mixture and place on a tray.

Pour enough coconut oil into a large frying pan to cover the base to about 1 cm (½ inch) deep and place over medium heat. When the oil is hot, but not smoking or rippling, add the chicken and cook for 2–3 minutes each side or until golden. Drain on paper towel and serve warm.

Chicken and vegetable coconut curry

GLUTEN FREE
Makes about 2 cups / 2–4 toddler serves

You can easily double this recipe for a delicious meal for the whole family. I've used Tuscan kale in this recipe because it's so rich in minerals, especially iron and calcium, but you could use any green vegetable—green beans, shelled and peeled broad (fava) beans, snow peas, peas or asparagus would all be good.

I've also added a little rolled amaranth or quinoa as a quick way to include complex carbohydrate and goodness. You could simply leave this out and serve with a little cooked grain (see page 89) instead.

For extra goodness, you can make this dish using chicken pieces on the bone, then shred the chicken before serving. Allow extra time for these to cook through.

2 teaspoons coconut oil
½ onion, finely diced
1 garlic clove
½–1 teaspoon finely grated ginger
1 teaspoon chopped coriander (cilantro) leaves and stems
80 g (2¾ oz) jap or butternut pumpkin, peeled, seeded and finely diced
½ small carrot, finely diced
130 g (4¾ oz) skinless chicken breast or thigh fillet,
    cut into small pieces
½ teaspoon sweet curry powder
1 kaffir lime leaf, torn into quarters
1 teaspoon dulse flakes
125 ml (4 fl oz/½ cup) chicken stock (see page 95)
125 ml (4 fl oz/½ cup) coconut milk
3–4 Tuscan black kale (cavolo nero) leaves, washed and thinly sliced
1 teaspoon rolled amaranth or quinoa

Heat the oil in a heavy-based saucepan or frying pan over low heat. Add the onion, garlic, ginger and coriander and cook, stirring occasionally, for 2–3 minutes, or until they have developed just a blush of colour.

Add the pumpkin, carrot, chicken, curry powder, lime leaf pieces, dulse flakes, stock, coconut milk and a pinch of sea salt. Cover with a lid and simmer gently for 10 minutes or until the vegetables are just soft.

Add the kale and rolled amaranth or quinoa and cook, uncovered, for another 8–10 minutes or until tender and the amaranth is cooked. Remove the lime leaf pieces and serve.

Sticky chicken and vegetable dinner

GLUTEN FREE (IF WHEAT-FREE TAMARI USED)
Makes 2–3 adult and 2 toddler serves

I've been making this for years as a faithful standby for a delicious and quick dinner. It's a very good example of why a large enamel-coated cast iron pot is such an excellent investment for your family's health and wellbeing. You can include any type of vegetables that are in season and you can add more or less, as desired. Whole cherry tomatoes would be a wonderful addition in summer. It is much cheaper to use a whole chicken and cut the pieces yourself, plus you're left with a carcass for making stock (see page 95).

3 small carrots
300 g (10½ oz) jap or butternut pumpkin, peeled and seeded
250 g (9 oz) baby potatoes (about 4–5), unpeeled and well scrubbed
2 tablespoons lemon thyme leaves
1½–2 kg (3 lb 5 oz–4 lb 8 oz) whole chicken
2 tablespoons olive oil
7 shallots (eschallots), peeled and left whole (or one large onion, peeled, halved and roughly sliced)
4–5 garlic cloves, peeled and left whole
1 tablespoon tamari
2 tablespoons stock (see pages 93–97) or water
60 ml (2 fl oz/¼ cup) mirin (Japanese rice wine)

½ cup green vegetables per person, such as green beans
     cut into 5 cm (2 inch) lengths, peas and shelled
     and peeled broad (fava) beans
3 cm (1¼ inch) knob ginger, peeled and finely grated

Preheat the oven to 165°C (320°F/Gas 3).

If the carrots are small, leave them as is. If larger, halve lengthways, then cut into 5 cm (2 inch) lengths. Cut the pumpkin into similar sizes; if using jap, make them a little bigger. If using large potatoes, cut into 4–5 cm (1½–2 inch) chunks.

Place the thyme leaves on a tray and combine with a good pinch each of sea salt and freshly ground black pepper.

Cut the thighs and legs from the chicken in one piece, then cut in half at the joint. Remove the wings and cut the breasts off the bone—you now have eight pieces of chicken. Reserve the carcass for stock. Place the chicken pieces, skin-side down onto the thyme-covered tray and press into the mixture well.

Place the oil in an enamel-coated cast-iron casserole pot over medium heat. When the oil is hot, but not rippling or smoking, add the chicken pieces, skin-side down, being careful as the oil will sizzle and spit a little. Cook without moving the pieces (or the skin will tear), for about 5 minutes or until golden. Remove the thighs and breasts when golden and place on a plate, then turn the wings and legs to brown the other side. When ready, remove and add to the other pieces. As space becomes available in the pot, add the shallots and garlic.

When all the chicken has browned, add the carrot, pumpkin and potato to the pot and cook, stirring regularly, for 5 minutes. Return the chicken pieces and any juices to the pot. Add the tamari, stock or water and 1 tablespoon mirin, cover with a lid and bake for 35–40 minutes or until the vegetables are just cooked through. Add the green vegetables 10 minutes before the end of the cooking time.

Remove from the oven, place the vegetables and chicken breasts on a tray and cover loosely with foil to keep warm. Add the remaining mirin and add the ginger to the pot. Bring to the boil over high heat, then reduce the heat to low and simmer, stirring occasionally, for 10 minutes or until the juices caramelise, thicken and reduce. Cut the chicken breasts into smaller portions and return, along with the vegetables, to the pot (this will also add a little more liquid) and serve. Shred the chicken and discard the bones before serving to young toddlers.

The material a cooking pot is made from can make a huge difference to how a recipe turns out. Larger pots used for stews are best made from enamel-coated cast iron. This material traps and diffuses heat better than anything else I know, and will result in exceptional flavour. Cast-iron can easily go from stovetop (for browning the meat) to oven and back to stovetop (for reducing the liquid), saving you lots of time and keeping the flavour in the one pot.

Lamb, oat and vegetable stew

WHEAT FREE (IF WHEAT-FREE TAMARI USED)
Makes 2 cups / 2–4 toddler serves

Lamb, a great source of zinc, makes a deeply nourishing stew for the cooler months. Lamb neck is a highly underrated cut—it's tender and makes for a mineral- and gelatine-rich broth. It's also a great way to include marrow, which is rich in vitamin A and minerals, especially iron, in your toddler's diet. You can include all sorts of root vegetables here—celeriac and swede are both excellent. If using turnip, go easy as its flavour can be overpowering.

I prefer to use an older sheep, hogget or mutton, which makes for a much more deeply flavoured stew.

1 tablespoon oat groats or rolled oats (see glossary)
1 teaspoon whey (see page 99) or lemon juice
2 teaspoons olive oil
500 g (1 lb 2 oz) lamb neck or 4–5 lamb neck chops
1 leek, white part only, thinly sliced and washed well
2–3 thyme sprigs
1 teaspoon finely chopped rosemary leaves
1 bay leaf
1 carrot, peeled and cut into thick slices
1 parsnip, peeled, core removed and cut into thick slices
2 celery stalks, thinly sliced
2 tablespoons white wine
1 tablespoon mirin (Japanese rice wine), or to taste
2 teaspoons tamari, or to taste
500 ml (17 fl oz/2 cups) stock (see pages 94–98)
1 tablespoon finely chopped flat-leaf (Italian) parsley leaves

Place the oats and whey or lemon juice and 125 ml (4 fl oz/½ cup) of water in a small bowl. Stir through, then allow to stand at room temperature for 6 hours or overnight. Drain and rinse oats.

Preheat the oven to 165°C (320°F/Gas 3).

Place the oil in an enamel-coated cast-iron casserole pot over medium heat. Add the lamb and cook until browned all over. Remove from the pot and set aside.

Reduce the heat to low, add the leek, herbs, carrot, parsnip, celery and a pinch each of sea salt and freshly ground black pepper and cook for 5–6 minutes or until the leek is soft. Add the wine, mirin and 1 teaspoon tamari and simmer until almost evaporated. Return the lamb to the pot along with the oats and stock. Cover with a lid and bake for 2 hours or until the lamb is tender and falling off the bone. Remove from the oven and check the seasoning—if it is too sweet, add the remaining tamari; if there is not enough depth of flavour, add a touch more mirin. Place the pot over high heat, bring to the boil and cook for 2–3 minutes or until the stew has reduced to desired consistency.

Remove the lamb and shred the meat off the bone. Scoop out the marrow and add back to the stew along with the meat. Sprinkle with parsley to serve.

Piccadillo

GLUTEN FREE

Makes 2 adult serves and 1 toddler serve

This is my version of a classic Mexican dish, which adds sweetness and fragrant spices to ground meat, traditionally pork. Any leftovers make a delicious filling for pupusas (see page 240).

These two dishes are great for using iron-rich minced beef; I like to add liver, which is even more iron-rich. Choose only the freshest organic liver. You can use strong-tasting cow liver or milder chicken liver. You only need a small portion and reduce the amount of minced meat accordingly. Trim the liver and soak in milk to soften the flavour—1 hour or so for chicken or up to 6 hours for beef.

2 tomatoes
500 ml (17 fl oz/2 cups) beef, lamb or chicken stock (see pages 95 and 97)
1 tablespoon olive oil
1 onion, finely chopped
2 garlic cloves, finely chopped
1 celery stalk, thinly sliced
200 g (7 oz) minced chuck steak (see side bar opposite)
¼ teaspoon ground cinnamon, or to taste
pinch of ground cloves
200 g (7 oz) jap or butternut pumpkin, peeled, seeded and finely diced
1 apple, peeled, core removed and finely diced
30 g (1 oz/¼ cup) sultanas
50 g (1¾ oz) organic liver (optional), trimmed, soaked, then finely chopped (see side bar)

Purée the tomatoes in a blender and add enough stock to make up 625 ml (21½ fl oz/2½ cups) of liquid. Heat the oil in a heavy-based saucepan over medium heat. Add the onion, garlic and celery and cook for 5–6 minutes or until the vegetables have a little colour. Add the beef, increase the heat to high and cook, breaking the beef up with a wooden spoon, for another minute or until lightly browned. Stir in the spices, pumpkin, apple, sultanas and tomato mixture and season to taste with salt and black pepper. Reduce the heat to low and simmer, stirring occasionally, for 30–40 minutes or until the vegetables are tender and the sauce has thickened. Skim off most of the fat (this rendered fat is full of flavour and can be saved for cooking). Add the liver, if using, in the last 10 minutes of cooking.

Meatballs

GLUTEN FREE / DAIRY FREE
Makes 2–3 adult serves and 2 toddlers serves

Meatlovers, and children especially, love this classic, which is delicious served with your choice of pasta (though remember to keep it minimal for a young child) and top with parmesan or pecorino cheese, as desired.

- 500 g (1 lb 2 oz) minced chuck steak (see side bar)
- ½ small onion, finely diced
- 1 tablespoon finely chopped basil
- 50 g (1¾ oz) fresh sourdough breadcrumbs
- 1–2 teaspoons dulse flakes
- 1 egg, lightly beaten
- 2 tablespoons olive oil
- 1 tablespoon balsamic vinegar
- 1 quantity garden vegetable tomato sauce (see page 142)
- 250 ml (9 fl oz/1 cup) chicken stock (see page 95)
- 100 g (3½ oz) organic liver (optional), trimmed, soaked, then finely chopped (see side bar opposite)

Place the beef, onion, basil, breadcrumbs, dulse flakes and egg in a bowl. Add a pinch each of sea salt and freshly ground black pepper and use your hands to combine the mixture well. Shape tablespoonsful into balls and place on a tray.

Heat the oil in a large heavy-based frying pan over medium heat. When the oil is hot, but not smoking or rippling, add the meatballs, in batches, and cook for 2–3 minutes each side or until browned, then transfer to a plate.

Drain off nearly all the excess fat in the pan, but leave a bit and all the delicious, sticky bits of meat on the base. Place the pan over medium heat, add the vinegar and stir well. Add the tomato sauce and stock, stir to combine well, then gently place the meatballs into the pan, tipping any juices from the plate into the sauce. Cover with a lid and cook over low heat for 10 minutes. Skim off most of the fat (this rendered fat is full of flavour and can be saved for cooking). Add the liver, stir gently and simmer for another 10–15 minutes or until the mixture is thick.

Most minced beef these days is made from topside, or some other cut that has little fat. I prefer mince made from chuck, with its fat intact—a good butcher will happily organise this for you. While you will end up with a fattier result, it's extremely nutrient-dense fat and valuable for young children. Cooking the meat in a bone stock adds valuable gelatine to help your toddler digest the protein.

Pot roast with many vegetables

GLUTEN FREE (IF WHEAT-FREE TAMARI USED)
Makes 3–4 adult serves and 1 toddler serve

A pot roast is traditionally a cheap and nourishing meal for the family. Including a bone stock in the sauce adds valuable gelatine to help digest the protein, plus it makes the meat exceptionally moist. This recipe may look like a bit of a hassle, but really it's incredibly easy and you should end up with left-over meat and sauce which is great to put into rolls for school lunches.

This pot roast is for the whole family. For a baby under 12 months, serve some of the vegetables mashed into the sauce —she may even like a chunk of meat to suck on. For a toddler, cut a little meat finely and serve with a large amount of vegetables and sauce.

1 kg (2 lb 4 oz) piece chuck steak
1 tablespoon olive oil
1 tablespoon roughly chopped thyme leaves
1 bay leaf
1 onion, roughly sliced
3–4 garlic cloves, peeled and left whole
4 carrots, 1 finely chopped, the others cut into large chunks
400 g (14 oz) tinned chopped tomatoes
500 ml (17 fl oz/2 cups) chicken, lamb or beef stock (see page 95–97)
1 tablespoon tamari
1–2 tablespoons molasses sugar or rapadura sugar, or to taste
1 teaspoon wholegrain mustard
½ teaspoon ground cumin
pinch ground cinnamon
800 g (1 lb 12 oz) desiree potatoes, larger potatoes cut into large chunks
350 g (12 oz) jap or butternut pumpkin, peeled, seeded
   and cut into large chunks
steamed green vegetables, such as peas, green beans, broccoli and
   brussels sprouts, tossed in butter (about ½ cup per adult), to serve

Preheat the oven to 160°C (315°F/Gas 2–3).

Season the meat with sea salt and freshly ground black pepper.

Heat the oil in an enamel-coated cast-iron casserole pot over medium heat. When hot, add the meat and brown on all sides. Remove and set aside.

Add the herbs, onion, garlic and finely chopped carrot to the pot, reduce the heat to low and cook for 6–8 minutes or until lightly coloured and caramelised. Return the meat to the pot, along with any juices, then add the tomatoes, stock, tamari, 1 tablespoon of sugar, mustard and spices. Mix through as best you can and bring to a gentle simmer. Cover with a lid and bake for 2 hours.

Add the potato, pumpkin and remaining carrot to the pot, cover and bake for another 1–1½ hours or until the vegetables are tender.

Remove the meat, potato, pumpkin and carrot chunks from the pot and set aside. Skim off any excess fat and mash the remaining vegetables and garlic into the sauce. Taste, and add a little more sugar, if required. Place the pot over high heat and cook at a rapid boil, stirring often, until reduced to a thick sauce. Return the potato, pumpkin and carrot to the pot and stir through. Slice the meat and return any juices to the pot. Serve the meat and vegetables with some sauce spooned over and the steamed greens on the side.

You can use a wide variety of root vegetables—parsnip, sweet potato, swede (rutabaga) are all good, but, if using turnip, go easy as it can overpower the flavour of the pot roast.

Cooking this pot roast in an enamel-coated cast-iron casserole will give the best results.

The pear-shaped day

PEAR-SHAPED DAYS HAPPEN OFTEN WITH TODDLERS. It may be that you're tired after a busy day, you've arrived home late and your toddler is stressed and hungry, or they are just not feeling their best. Here are my tips for those days and the recipes that follow are trusted standbys which work a treat for toddlers (and adults too!):

- *Stock in the freezer* A cup of stock by itself is a traditional way to nourish when someone is feeling unwell. Adding a small amount of coconut milk or oil to the broth will help also (see creamy coconut vegetable broth, page 139).

- *Traditional remedies* Working on the principle of opposites, there are some simple food preparations that can balance and soothe. Kudzu (kuzu) and miso—always use unpasteurised to utilise the beneficial bacteria— are two of the easiest to have on hand.

- *Emergency pasta* It doesn't hurt to include simple pasta in your toddler's diet. Both the following pasta recipes are quick and provide minerals and quality fats. Sprinkle over parmesan or wakame gomasio (see page 168).

- *Bread and toppings* Topping good bread with avocado provides nourishing and nutrient-dense goodness. A concentrated yeast extract spread, rich in vitamin B, such as Vegemite, is also ideal—there would be few Australians who have not grown up with this iconic spread. (However, check if it is made from genetically modified ingredients before using.) Unpasteurised genmai (brown rice) miso will give a similar flavour, is easily digested and, while not a vitamin source, behaves in a similar way (in that it is salty), which is generally what we crave with Vegemite.

- *Tasting plates* Toddlers love having a plate with lots of bits and pieces— my daughter's favourite way to eat salad was the tasting plate her Nonna used to make, arranged as Humpty Dumpty. Include small nutrient-dense bits, such as boiled egg, cheese, yoghurt (see page 98), labne (see page 99), olives, cooked and marinated lentils (see iron and energy! page 170), nuts (see page 104), dips and spreads (see page 162) and cooked meats.

Tamari kudzu drink

GLUTEN FREE (IF WHEAT-FREE TAMARI USED) / DAIRY FREE

Makes ½ cup / 1 toddler serve

½ teaspoon kudzu (kuzu)
¼ – ½ teaspoon tamari

Combine the kudzu and 125 ml (4 fl oz/½ cup) of water in a small saucepan, then cook, stirring continuously, over low heat until it boils and is thick. Add tamari to taste and serve in a mug or cup. Cool a little before serving.

Miso soup

GLUTEN FREE (IF WHEAT-FREE TAMARI USED) / DAIRY FREE

Makes 1 cup / 2 toddler serves

Ideal when one is feeling stressed and scattered. Never boil, or even heat, the soup too much once you've added the miso or you will destroy the beneficial bacteria.

2 cm (¾ inch) strip kombu
1 dried shiitake mushroom
1 thin slice ginger (optional)
1–2 teaspoons unpasteurised genmai (brown rice) miso (see glossary)
tamari and roughly chopped coriander (cilantro) leaves, to serve (optional)

Place the kombu, mushroom, ginger, if using, and 250 ml (9 fl oz/1 cup) of water in a small saucepan over low heat, cover and simmer for 15–20 minutes. Remove and discard the kombu and ginger, then remove the mushroom and squeeze out the liquid into the pan, or slice thinly and add to the pan, discarding the tough stem. Remove from the heat, stir in the miso and adjust to taste—you may like to add a little tamari. Sprinkle with coriander, if using. Cool a little before serving.

This warm drink is perfect when one has had too much sweetness and needs focusing—you will typically see this after toddlers have eaten refined sugar. Quick and easy to put together, this balancing broth is essentially a simplifed miso soup.

Jude's emergency pasta

Makes 1 cup

1 small dried shiitake mushroom, roughly broken into quarters
1 teaspoon dulse flakes
50 g (1¾ oz) pasta (farfalle is a good choice)
1 teaspoon butter, ghee (see page 107) or coconut oil
1 egg yolk
1 tablespoon finely grated parmesan or pecorino, or to taste
1–2 teaspoons thinly sliced basil or flat-leaf (Italian) parsley leaves

Place the mushroom pieces, dulse flakes, 500 ml (17 fl oz/2 cups) of water and a pinch of salt in a small saucepan and bring to the boil. Add the pasta and cook until al dente.

Meanwhile, place your fat of choice, egg yolk, parmesan and basil in a small bowl and combine well.

When the pasta is cooked, remove and discard the mushroom pieces. Add about 2 tablespoons of the pasta cooking water to the egg yolk mixture. Drain the pasta and return to the pan. Stir through the egg yolk mixture and cook, stirring continuously, over low heat for 2–3 minutes or until the sauce just begins to thicken. Spoon into a small bowl, top with extra parmesan, if desired, and serve.

Vanessa's emergency pasta

Makes 1 cup

2 small dried shiitake mushrooms
2 cm (¾ inch) strip kombu
1 teaspoon dulse flakes
50 g (1¾ oz) small pasta (spelt stelline is a good choice)
2 teaspoons butter, ghee (see page 107) or coconut oil, or to taste

Place the mushrooms, kombu, dulse flakes, 500 ml (17 fl oz/2 cups) of water and a pinch of sea salt in a small saucepan and bring to the boil. Add the pasta and cook until al dente. Drain and place in a small bowl. Remove and discard the kombu, then remove the mushroom and squeeze out the liquid into the pasta, or slice thinly and add to the pasta, discarding the tough stem. Toss the pasta with the fat of your choice to serve.

Creamy kudzu and tahini pudding

GLUTEN FREE / DAIRY FREE
Makes 2 cups / 4 toddler serves

This is a simple healing preparation for use on stressful days. The sweetness of the juice is expansive and the kudzu is soothing and calming.

1½ tablespoons kudzu (kuzu)
500 ml (17 fl oz/2 cups) good-quality fruit juice (pear or apricot are lovely)
½ teaspoon natural vanilla extract, or to taste
2 teaspoons–1 tablespoon unhulled tahini, or to taste

Place the kudzu and 60 ml (2 fl oz/¼ cup) of the juice in a small saucepan and mix to a smooth paste before adding the remaining juice. Place over low heat and simmer, stirring continuously, until it just begins to boil. It should no longer be chalky in colour and will have thickened. Remove from the heat immediately— it will continue to thicken as it cools. Stir in the vanilla and tahini to taste.

Pour into ramekins or one small dish, cool, then refrigerate for 30 minutes. This pudding will keep in the fridge for a couple of days.

If you like the pudding a little thicker, increase the amount of kudzu to 2 tablespoons.

Sweetness

CHILDREN FROM ONE TO THREE YEARS should gain all the nutrients they require from savoury foods, but, as they move from babyhood and the sweetness of breast milk, a small amount of real sweetness is a wholesome, healthy and delicious part of life. Such sweetness does not mean dessert is a typical part of a meal—rather it remains simple and uncomplicated, providing an accent to a toddler's weekly diet.

The simple and pure essence of ripe, seasonal fruit is one of the best ways to provide such deliciousness to a toddler, but don't overlook serving these with custard, yoghurt (see page 98), cream or the left-over rolled oat pudding (see page 160).

Keep serving portions small. Mini-muffin cups are a great size for baked goods, and make cookies to fit into your toddler's hands.

FRUIT JELLIES

Jelly is a wonderful thing for young and old alike. It's easy to make at home, meaning you can avoid the numerous chemical colours and flavours that are in commercial jellies—even the so-called 'natural' ones have them. You can make either a traditional jelly with gelatine, which provides great nutrition, or a vegetarian version using agar sea vegetable, which provides a wealth of minerals. Gelatine gives a smooth-textured jelly, but takes a long time to set, whereas agar sets as it cools, but has a coarser texture.

Agar-based jelly

GLUTEN FREE / DAIRY FREE
Makes 6 toddler serves

Agar dissolves best in high-pectin and low-acid juices. Simple juices such as apple, apricot and pear, with some strawberry or guava are all good choices. Avoid high-acid juices, such as grape and pineapple. I've included fruits in this jelly, but you can easily leave them out and have a simple jellied fruit juice.

500 ml (17 fl oz/2 cups) fruit juice (to suit the fruit you use)
1 teaspoon agar powder
400 g (14 oz) fruit (such as banana, stone fruit, fresh berries—all or any)

Place the juice in a small saucepan and whisk in the agar powder. Gently bring to the boil over low heat, then simmer, stirring frequently with a whisk or spoon to prevent the agar from sinking to the bottom, for 8 minutes. Remove from the heat and allow to cool slightly.

Cut any larger fruit into small pieces. Place in a 1 litre (35 fl oz/4 cup) capacity jelly mould or six 180 ml (6 fl oz) glasses or ramekins and pour the lightly cooled jelly over it. Cool slightly, cover and refrigerate for 30 minutes or until set. This jelly will keep in the fridge for up to 2 days.

Gelatine-based jelly

GLUTEN FREE / DAIRY FREE
Makes 6 toddler serves

500 ml (17 fl oz/2 cups) fruit juice (to suit the fruit you use)
3 teaspoons gelatine (see kitchen note)
400 g (14 oz) fruit (such as banana, stone fruit, fresh berries—all or any)

Place the juice in a small saucepan, bring to the boil then immediately remove from the heat. Add the gelatine to the hot liquid and stir through until it dissolves.

Cut any larger fruit into small pieces. Place in a 1 litre (35 fl oz/4 cup) capacity jelly mould or six 180 ml (6 fl oz) glasses or ramekins and pour over the lightly cooled jelly. Cool slightly, cover and refrigerate for 3–4 hours or until set. This jelly will keep in the fridge for up to 2 days.

 KITCHEN NOTE
I'm very fussy about the quality of the gelatine I use (see page 63 for more information). You'll need 1½ teaspoons of gelatine to set 1 cup of juice to a wobbly consistency, which is great for young toddlers. For a firmer set jelly, increase the gelatine to 2 teaspoons per cup of juice.

Adding kudzu will give agar jelly a smoother texture. Mix 1½ teaspoons kudzu with 1 tablespoon fruit juice. Once the agar has dissolved, whisk the kudzu mixture into the pan and bring to the boil, stirring constantly.

Almond, coconut milk and berry jellies

GLUTEN FREE / DAIRY FREE
Makes 6 toddler serves

230 g (8¼ oz/1½ cups) blanched almonds
250 ml (9 fl oz/1 cup) coconut milk
2 teaspoons natural vanilla extract
2–3 tablespoons maple syrup, or to taste
1½ teaspoons agar powder
2 teaspoons kudzu (kuzu)
200 g (7 oz) berries (whichever are in season)

Line a jug or bowl with 4 layers of muslin (cheesecloth) and use pegs to secure the sides. Place the blanched almonds, coconut milk and 560 ml (19¼ fl oz/2¼ cups) of water in a blender and process until the almonds are very finely chopped. Pour the mixture into the muslin-lined jug, gather up the sides of the muslin and squeeze the remaining liquid into the jug. You will need 750 ml (26 fl oz/3 cups) of almond milk, plus an extra 2 tablespoons—you may need to add a little water and squeeze some more.

Place the 750 ml (26 fl oz/3 cups) of almond milk in a saucepan, add the vanilla and 2 tablespoons of maple syrup. Taste and add the remaining maple syrup, if desired. Whisk in the agar powder. Gently bring to the boil over low heat, stirring frequently to disperse the agar powder evenly. Once the mixture comes to the boil, simmer for 8 minutes, stirring frequently with a whisk or spoon to prevent the agar from sinking to the bottom, then remove from the heat.

Place the kudzu in a small bowl with the extra 2 tablespoons of almond milk and mix until smooth. Whisk the kudzu mixture into the hot milk, return the pan to the heat and bring to the boil, stirring continuously. As soon as it boils, remove from the heat and allow to cool a little.

Divide the berries among six 185 ml (6 fl oz/¾ cup) capacity bowls or ramekins, then gently pour the slightly cooled milk mixture over them. Cool completely, then refrigerate for 1 hour or until set. This jelly will keep in the fridge for up to 2 days.

SWEET TREATS

From an apricot-laced biscuit that will fit into a little hand to a dreamy pure-fruit 'ice cream', you will find here a range of sweet treats perfect for a toddler. All use whole and natural sweeteners and are bursting with goodness and nutrient density.

Super toddler blueberry and coconut creamy popsicles

GLUTEN FREE
Makes 8

Packed with superfoods, these popsicles will turn your baby into a super toddler! Kefir milk or yoghurt provides beneficial bacteria, coconut cream offers quality fats and blueberries are packed with antioxidants—you don't need to be worried about the effects of these healthy frozen pops.

375 ml (13 fl oz/1½ cups) kefir milk (see page 100)
    or yoghurt (see page 98)
125 ml (4 fl oz/½ cup) coconut cream
1 banana
1 tablespoon honey
230 g (8¼ oz/1½ cups) frozen blueberries

Place the kefir milk or yoghurt, coconut cream, banana and honey in a blender and process until smooth and frothy. Pour half into a small jug and set aside.

Add the blueberries to the remaining mixture in the blender and process until smooth and fluffy.

Divide the plain banana and coconut milk mixture between 8 x 100 ml (3½ fl oz) popsicle moulds, then pour over the blueberry mixture. Place in the freezer until set. These popsicles will keep in the freezer for 4–5 days.

For a smoother texture, coconut cream is used here instead of coconut milk.

Super toddler chocolate and coconut fudge

Makes about 48 pieces

This recipe comes with a warning—it's very, very moreish. It's the most delicious way to include mineral-rich cocoa powder, healthful coconut oil (to boost the immune system), honey and nuts in your toddler's (and your) diet. Its only downside is that it doesn't travel well, as the coconut oil melts easily in warm conditions. I like to use almonds and macadamias for this recipe—soaked and lightly roasted, if possible (see page 104). If you can't manage this, simply blanch raw almonds to remove their skins.

  - 80 g (2¾ oz/½ cup) blanched almonds
  - 80 g (2¾ oz) desiccated coconut
  - 80 g (2¾ oz/½ cup) macadamia nuts
  - 250 ml (9 fl oz/1 cup) coconut oil (see kitchen note)
  - 250 ml (9 fl oz/1 cup) honey
  - 70 g (2½ oz) best quality cocoa powder (see glossary)
  - 1 teaspoon natural vanilla extract

You can easily halve this mixture, as it's not runny and will just set as you place it in the tin.

Line a 28 x 18 cm (11¼ x 7 inch) shallow baking tin (a lamington tin is perfect) with baking paper.

Place the almonds in a food processor and pulse once or twice, then add all the remaining ingredients and process until the nuts are finely chopped and the mixture has come together. Spoon into the prepared tin, pressing down to smooth the top. Cover with baking paper and refrigerate for 1–2 hours or until set. Cut into small pieces and store in an airtight container in the fridge for 2–3 weeks (although keeping it that long will require a great deal of restraint).

 KITCHEN NOTE
If the coconut oil is liquid, place it in the fridge to firm up a little before using—it works best when it is not too hard, but not too soft.

Pure fruit and coconut ice dream

GLUTEN FREE / DAIRY FREE
Makes 2 cups / 4–6 toddler serves

This is what my daughter first knew as 'ice cream', and even as an adult she still loves it. If your child can't tolerate dairy, this is a much better alternative to the many highly refined and processed non-dairy ice creams available.

It's always best to use banana as the base fruit, as it provides the important creaminess and sweetness. Any other ripe fruit can be used with the banana base.

2 small bananas
2 teaspoons lemon juice
1 mango (or any other fruit), chopped—you will need about
    280 g (10 oz) flesh
125 ml (4 fl oz/½ cup) coconut milk or cream

Roll the bananas in the lemon juice, place in a container and freeze.

Cut the mango into chunks, place in a container and freeze.

Chop the frozen banana and mango into smaller sized chunks. Place in a food processor with the coconut milk and process until the mixture resembles ice cream. (When you begin to process the fruit, it will look more like very small bits of frozen fruit. As it begins to thaw, it will cream up.) Serve immediately. You can also freeze this for up to 1 week.

Cashew nut cream

GLUTEN FREE / DAIRY FREE
Makes ¾ cup / 6 – 8 toddler serves

This is a delicious alternative for children who are intolerant to dairy and is great served with fruit.

115 g (4 oz/¾ cup) raw cashew nuts
125 ml (4 fl oz/½ cup) coconut milk
1 tablespoon maple syrup, or to taste
½ – 1 teaspoon natural vanilla extract, or to taste

Place the nuts and ½ teaspoon sea salt in a bowl and cover with water. Soak overnight at room temperature.

Strain the nuts and rinse well, then place in a blender with the remaining ingredients and process until very smooth. Adjust the consistency with more coconut milk or water, as desired, and adjust the sweetness with maple syrup and vanilla, as desired. This cream will keep in the fridge for a week or so.

Oat and spelt crackers

WHEAT FREE
Makes about 32

This is a simple, first biscuit for a young toddler. It is made from oats and spelt, both grains that are highly water-soluble, and the inclusion of buttermilk or yoghurt makes the digestion of the grains even easier. Serve with butter or avocado for a delicious snack. You can easily top these with seeds, such as sesame or poppy, even mixed herbs, or salt and pepper as your toddler gets older.

 160 g (5¾ oz/1¼ cups) white spelt flour, plus extra for dusting
 125 g (4½ oz/1 cup) oatmeal (see kitchen note, page 156)
 ½ teaspoon bicarbonate of (baking) soda
 1 tablespoon rapadura sugar
 125 g (4½ oz) cold unsalted butter, chopped
 150 ml (5 fl oz) buttermilk or 150 g (5 oz) yoghurt (see page 98)

Combine the flour, oatmeal, bicarbonate of soda, sugar and a pinch of sea salt in a bowl and whisk to break up any clumps. Using your fingertips, rub the butter into the flour until the mixture resembles fine breadcrumbs. (You can also do this in a food processor, then transfer the mixture to a large bowl.) Add the buttermilk or yoghurt. Using a butter knife, cut the buttermilk through the flour mixture until the dough just comes together into a ball. Shape into a disc, wrap in plastic wrap and refrigerate for 1–2 hours.

Preheat the oven to 180°C (350°F/Gas 4).

Roll out the chilled dough on a lightly floured surface until it is about 3 mm (⅛ inch) thick, then place on a baking tray and refrigerate for 5–10 minutes or until firm. Using a 4½ cm (1¾ inch) cookie cutter, stamp out rounds and place them on baking trays lined with baking paper. (In warm weather, chill in the fridge for 5–10 minutes before baking.)

Bake for 15–20 minutes or until lightly golden. Cool a little on the trays, then transfer to a wire rack to cool completely. Store in an airtight container for 2 weeks.

Oaty dried apricot biscuits

WHEAT FREE
Makes about 40

Another great, simple biscuit for a young toddler—made from oats and spelt, both grains that are highly water-soluble, and nice and firm for chewing. They are great to have on hand when out and about. For a very young toddler, you might also like to flatten these out into an oval shape, which is easier for a little hand to hold.

55 g (2 oz) dried apricots, roughly chopped
130 g (4¾ oz/1 cup) white spelt flour
60 g (2¼ oz) true arrowroot
100 g (3½ oz) oatmeal (see kitchen note, page 156)
45 g (1¾ oz/½ cup) desiccated coconut
¼ teaspoon baking powder
125 g (4½ oz) unsalted butter, melted and slightly cooled
80 ml (2½ fl oz/⅓ cup) maple syrup
80 ml (2½ fl oz/⅓ cup) rice syrup
1 teaspoon natural vanilla extract

Place the apricot and 80 ml (2½ fl oz/⅓ cup) of water in a small saucepan over low heat, cover and bring to the boil. Turn off the heat and allow to stand for 10 minutes, then mash to a rough purée.

Place the spelt flour, arrowroot, oatmeal, coconut and baking powder in a large bowl and combine well. Place the melted butter, syrups, vanilla and apricot purée in a small bowl and combine well. Add to the dry ingredients and gently mix together to form a dough, taking care not to overmix. Cover and refrigerate for 15–30 minutes.

Preheat the oven to 180°C (350°F/Gas 4).

Roll teaspoonsful of the dough into balls and place on baking trays lined with baking paper. Press down on the biscuits with a fork to slightly flatten. Bake for 15–30 minutes or until lightly golden on both sides. Transfer to wire racks to cool completely. Store in an airtight container for up to 2 weeks.

Everyday zucchini bread

Serves 8–10

A delicious, not too sweet bread, enriched with pumpkin seeds and dulse flakes for extra goodness. Serve with butter for a great morning or afternoon tea snack. As children get older, you can add nuts to this bread.

130 g (4¾ oz/1 cup) white spelt flour
165 g (5¾ oz/1 cup) wholemeal spelt flour
80 g (2¾ oz/½ cup) rapadura sugar
80 g (2¾ oz) sultanas
½ teaspoon ground cinnamon
2½ teaspoons baking powder
1 teaspoon dulse flakes
40 g (1½ oz) pumpkin seeds (pepitas), coarsely ground
300 g (10½ oz) zucchini (courgette)
1 egg
60 g (2¼ oz) unsalted butter or coconut oil, melted and slightly cooled
185 ml (6 fl oz/¾ cup milk) or 125 ml (4 fl oz/½ cup) coconut milk
      and 60 ml (2 fl oz/¼ cup) rice milk
1 teaspoon natural vanilla extract

Preheat the oven to 180°C (350°F/Gas 4).

Line a 1 litre (35 fl oz/4 cups) capacity loaf tin with baking paper.

Place the flours, sugar, sultanas, cinnamon, baking powder, dulse flakes and pumpkin seeds in a bowl and whisk through to break up any lumps.

Grate the zucchini, wrap it in a clean tea towel and wring to remove as much liquid as possible. Add the zucchini to the dry ingredients and mix through.

Whisk together the egg, melted fat of your choice, milk and vanilla. Add to the dry ingredients and gently mix together. Pour into the tin and bake for 50–60 minutes or until a skewer when inserted into the middle comes out clean. Cool a little in the tin before turning out to slice.

Jammy pecan and oat biscuits

WHEAT FREE / DAIRY FREE

Makes about 40

As your toddler gets older, nuts (but best to avoid peanuts) make a great addition to biscuits. This is a delicious, not too sweet biscuit for morning or afternoon tea.

150 g (5½ oz/1½ cups) rolled oats
110 g (3¾ oz) pecans
130 g (4¾ oz/1 cup) white spelt flour
¼ teaspoon baking powder
125 g (4½ oz) unsalted butter, ghee (see page 107) or coconut oil, melted and slightly cooled
80 ml (2½ fl oz/⅓ cup) rice syrup
80 ml (2½ fl oz/⅓ cup) maple syrup
1 teaspoon natural vanilla extract
160 g (5¾ oz/½ cup) good-quality jam

Preheat the oven to 180°C (350°F/Gas 4). Spread the oats on a baking tray and bake for 5 minutes or until lightly golden. Remove from the oven and immediately tip into a bowl to stop the cooking process.

Spread the pecans on the same baking tray and bake for 7–10 minutes or until lightly toasted, ensuring they don't burn.

Put the cooled oats in a food processor and grind to a coarse meal, then transfer to a mixing bowl. Coarsely grind the slightly cooled pecans and add to the oats. Add the flour and baking powder and whisk through to combine.

Combine the melted fat of your choice, syrups and vanilla in a jug, then add to the dry ingredients and stir until the dough comes together. Roll 2½ teaspoons each of the dough into balls and place on baking trays lined with baking paper. (As your child gets older, you can make the biscuits bigger.) Flatten them slightly with the palm of your hand, then, using the end of a wooden spoon or your little finger, make small indentations in the balls. Place ½ teaspoon of jam in the indentations, then bake for 15 minutes or until light golden. Cool on the trays for 10 minutes, then transfer to a wire rack to cool completely. Store in an airtight container for up to 5 days.

 KITCHEN NOTE

You can use any jam for these cookies, but keep in mind that those sweetened with sugar will run and caramelise more than jam sweetened with fruit juice. Use a simple, unsweetened fruit purée (see peach purée, page 120) for the most delicious result. If using, unsweetened fruit purée, increase the amount added to the uncooked biscuit to 1 teaspoon, as it will reduce down in the oven, becoming similar to a soft fruit leather.

TOWARDS
INDEPENDENCE

3–7 YEARS

*No longer a toddler,
the three-year-old hurtles towards
independence, testing their
boundaries wherever possible.
Good food makes a huge difference
to children during these years.*

Building on wholesome foundations

PHYSICALLY, YOUNG CHILDREN ARE STILL GROWING, although this growth will come more in spurts and their hunger will fluctuate to match. But just as importantly they are still developing intellectually, socially and emotionally. Delicious, nutrient-dense food plays a large role in this development.

While their digestive system is far more mature than that of a baby or toddler, it's still a good idea to take care with the amount of fibre and bulk included in their diet—you'll notice some recipes use white basmati rice rather than brown, and quite a few cakes use white spelt flour. Both of these are still exceptionally nourishing—in our zealousness we can easily overload a child's digestive system with too many whole flours and grains, nuts and seeds.

> During these years, it is the immune system that requires the most support—quality fats, coconut and stocks are some of your best allies in this area.

The recipes in this chapter are also suitable for children up to the age of ten, although you will need to adjust the portion sizes accordingly.

What to eat becomes more difficult as your child spends more time away from the home. School lunches are notoriously difficult—it's natural for children to come home with half-eaten lunches. Temperature, food being damaged as it moves around in the bag, playing with friends—all these things affect a child's desire to eat. While it is always important to provide delicious and wholesome options, I suggest you place emphasis on breakfast, afternoon tea and dinner, bookending the hours at school. This way you can be assured that your child is getting the best possible nourishment, and it does relieve some of the pressure to provide a 'healthy' lunchbox.

Building on what the child has seen and heard as a baby and toddler, a four-year-old now begins to become an even more active participant in the family food culture. Cooking, shopping, visiting the farmers' market, growing food, eating together as a family and extended family, setting the table—all are incredibly valuable ways to hold, ground, enrich and nourish your child in body and soul. These activities will help your child know their place in the world—I can't emphasise this enough. With grounded stability and security, and a strong sense of belonging, they can go out into the world to become all they can possibly be.

Breakfast

WITHOUT DOUBT, BREAKFAST IS THE MOST IMPORTANT MEAL of the day, especially for young children heading to kindergarten or school. It not only provides fuel for doing and being, but signals to the body that food is at hand, kick-starting the metabolism—an essential aspect in maintaining a healthy weight.

Honey ambrosia

GLUTEN FREE / DAIRY FREE
Makes about 520 g (1 lb 2½ oz/2 cups)

This is really just a simple thing to have on hand, ready to drizzle a little on a bowl of yoghurt (see page 98) or labne (see page 99) to add deliciousness and a bit of density.

40 g (1½ oz/⅓ cup) raisins
20 g (¾ oz) dried apricots or peaches
30 g (1 oz) blanched almonds
30 g (1 oz) pecans
400 g (14 oz) raw honey (runny is best)

Roughly chop the dried fruit and nuts and place in a bowl. Gently stir through the honey and store in a sealed, clean glass jar in the fridge. It will keep for up to 2 weeks.

What you serve for breakfast should take into account what will be eaten for lunch, afternoon tea and dinner. Carbohydrate for breakfast (porridge), morning tea (cookie), lunch (sandwich), afternoon tea (cake or biscuit) and a grain-based dinner is not a good idea; while this example may be exaggerated, I commonly see carbohydrate is most often relied upon. Remember that the higher the protein and fat, the more sustaining the food will be.

Gluten-free muesli

GLUTEN FREE / DAIRY FREE
Makes about 420 g (15 oz/3 cups)

With no highly refined puffed or crisped grains or bran and plenty of nuts, seeds and dried fruits, this is an excellent muesli for young children and adults alike. If you have time, soak and lightly roast your nuts and seeds to make them more digestible (see page 104).

Serve with plenty of yoghurt (see page 98) or kefir milk (see page 100) to aid digestion. For a dairy-free accompaniment, substitute with coconut milk.

95 g (3¼ oz/1 cup) rolled amaranth
100 g (3½ oz/1 cup) rolled quinoa
30 g (1 oz/¼ cup) pumpkin seeds (pepitas)
40 g (1½ oz/¼ cup) sesame seeds
40–80 g (1½ oz–2¾ oz/¼–½ cup) blanched almonds or macadamia nuts, lightly roasted and roughly chopped
35 g (1¼ oz/¼ cup) currants or sultanas
60 g (2¼ oz) dried fruit, finely chopped, if necessary

Combine all the ingredients in a large bowl. Store in an airtight container in a cool, dark place or in the fridge. It will keep for up to 4 weeks.

Gluten-free muesli, Bircher style

GLUTEN FREE / CAN BE DAIRY FREE
Makes 1–2 child serves

Muesli is always best served bircher style—soaked overnight to break down the grain. The addition of grated apple, or fruit with its skin on, also increases the enzymatic reaction, resulting in a far more digestible grain. Only make this in small portions, as it is best eaten right away and does not keep well.

65 g (2½ oz/½ cup) gluten-free muesli (see opposite)
60 g (2¼ oz/¼ cup) yoghurt (see page 98)
¼ apple, skin on
1–2 tablespoons blueberries or other fruit
yoghurt or coconut milk and maple syrup or honey, to serve

Place the muesli in a small bowl with the yoghurt and 60 ml (2 fl oz/¼ cup) of water. Grate the apple directly into the bowl, stir gently to combine, cover with a plate and refrigerate overnight.

Add the blueberries, a small dollop of extra yoghurt or coconut milk and drizzle with sweetener, as desired. Serve immediately or within 3 hours.

 VARIATION

Dairy-free Soak the grains with coconut milk and add 1 teaspoon of whey (see page 99) instead of the yoghurt.

Cinnamon and coconut toasted oat muesli

WHEAT FREE
Makes 5 cups

This is the next best option to soaking your muesli overnight and represents a ready-to-eat breakfast cereal. It does take a bit of time, but the result is a highly digestible and nourishing breakfast cereal. I've used hazelnuts and figs in this recipe, but you can use any nut, seed or dried fruit. Serve with yoghurt, as desired.

300 g (10½ oz/3 cups) rolled oats
185 g (6½ oz/¾ cup) yoghurt (see page 98) or kefir milk (see page 100)
125 ml (4 fl oz/½ cup) coconut oil, melted
60 ml (2 fl oz/¼ cup) maple syrup
60 ml (2 fl oz/¼ cup) rice syrup
½–1 teaspoon ground cinnamon
½ teaspoon ground cardamom
1 teaspoon natural vanilla extract
140 g (5 oz/1 cup) hazelnuts, lightly roasted, skins rubbed off,
    and roughly chopped
125 g (4½ oz/1 cup) sultanas
95 g (3¼ oz) dried figs, finely chopped

It's very important to use natural yoghurt or one which has no milk solids to soak the rolled oats.

I like to serve this muesli with poached summer fruit (see page 227) or poached winter fruit (see page 228) and a bit of their poaching liquid depending on the season. These make a dry breakfast cereal much easier to digest.

Place the oats, yoghurt, coconut oil and 250 ml (9 fl oz/1 cup) of water in a bowl and mix together well. Cover with a clean tea towel and refrigerate for 24 hours. In winter you can leave this out at room temperature.

Preheat the oven to 90°C (195°F/Gas ¼).

Place the maple and rice syrups, cinnamon, cardamom and vanilla in a small saucepan and stir over low heat until runny. Add to the oats and mix well. Spread onto a baking tray in an even layer.

Bake, gently stirring the mixture every 30 minutes, for 2 hours. Increase the heat to 150°C (300°F/Gas 2) and bake for another 40 minutes to 1 hour or until toasted to your liking. Stir every 10 or so minutes, exposing any underneath layers to the heat. If your oven has a hot spot, rotate the tray as well.

Remove from the oven and cool, then place in a bowl with the hazelnuts and dried fruit and combine well. Store in an airtight container in a cool, dark place. It will keep for up to 4 weeks.

Baked oatmeal

WHEAT FREE
Makes 4–6 child serves

This is a delicious and comforting way to have oats and could happily double as a dessert after a bowl of soup. It does take some time to cook—but is well worth it, and would be perfect weekend fare.

45 g (1¾ oz/¼ cup) oat groats (see glossary)
75 g (2¾ oz/¾ cup) rolled oats
2 teaspoons whey (see page 99) or 1 teaspoon lemon juice
1 tablespoon melted butter, plus extra, for greasing
250 ml (9 fl oz/1 cup) full-cream (whole) milk
2 eggs
30 g (1 oz/¼ cup) sultanas, or any chopped dried fruit
2 tablespoons rapadura sugar or maple syrup
½–1 teaspoon ground cinnamon
1 large granny smith apple, peeled, cored and chopped into small pieces
yoghurt (see page 98) and stewed fruit, to serve (optional)

Process the oat kernels in a food processor until coarsely ground. Place in a bowl along with the rolled oats, whey and 500 ml (17 fl oz/2 cups) of water and combine well. Cover and allow to stand at room temperature overnight, or in the fridge if the weather is warm.

Preheat the oven to 170°C (325°F/Gas 3). Lightly grease a 24 cm (9½ inch) square, 1¼ litre (44 fl oz/5 cup) capacity baking dish.

Whisk together the melted butter, milk and eggs. Add to the oat mixture with the dried fruit, sugar, cinnamon and apple and mix together well. Pour into the greased dish and bake for 1¾–2 hours or until just set. Serve as is, or with yoghurt and stewed fruit.

It's important to keep the oven temperature low for this recipe so the eggs don't curdle. Baked oatmeal is also delicious with pear or blueberries in place of apples.

Power breakfast quinoa

GLUTEN FREE (IF WHEAT-FREE TAMARI USED)
Makes 2 adult and 2 child serves

I love quinoa for breakfast—it's such a high-protein grain, so it keeps you going much longer than many of the others. This is an incredibly easy and flexible savoury risotto, served topped with yoghurt or labne and wakame gomasio.

100 g (3½ oz/½ cup) quinoa
1 teaspoon whey (see page 99) or lemon juice
2 teaspoons butter or ghee (see page 107)
2 teaspoons coconut oil
1 celery stalk, finely diced
1 carrot, finely diced
½ teaspoon dried basil
½ teaspoon dried thyme
1 teaspoon dulse flakes
185 ml (6 fl oz/¾ cup) chicken or vegetable stock (see pages 94–95),
    or 250 ml (9 fl oz/1 cup), if the grain is unsoaked
½ cup green vegetables (see side bar)
1 teaspoon tamari
1–2 tablespoons coriander (cilantro) leaves, roughly chopped
yoghurt (see page 98) or labne (see page 99)
    and wakame gomasio (see page 168), to serve

For the green vegetables, try finely diced zucchini (courgettes) in summer; broccoli cut into small florets or beans; or thinly sliced Tuscan black kale (cavolo nero) in winter; or green peas or roughly chopped asparagus in spring. Instead of yoghurt, try topping with a fried or poached egg.

Place the quinoa, whey or lemon juice and 250 ml (9 fl oz/1 cup) of water in a small bowl and combine well. Cover with a tea towel and stand overnight at room temperature, or in the fridge if the weather is very hot. Drain.

Melt the butter and coconut oil in a saucepan over medium heat. Add the celery, carrot, basil, thyme and dulse flakes and cook for 5 minutes or until lightly coloured. Add the quinoa and stock and bring to the boil, then cover with a lid, reduce the heat to low and simmer gently for 15 minutes. Add the green vegetables and cook, covered, for another 10 minutes or until just tender. Season to taste with tamari, then stir in the coriander. Top with yoghurt and wakame gomasio.

Nessie's cheesy vegetable scrambled eggs

GLUTEN FREE
Makes 2 child serves

One of the quickest breakfasts around, this is how my daughter makes scrambled eggs—with as little fuss, and as few dishes to wash, as possible. You can easily add this to a wrap for a breakfast on the go or scoop it into a cup, with a spoon for eating in the car. Other vegetables work just as well—English spinach, green peas, broad (fava) beans and asparagus are great vegetables to use in spring. Most herbs work well, too—chives and flat-leaf (Italian) parsley especially. When your child is going through a growth spurt, you may need to increase the number of eggs to three.

    1 tablespoon butter, ghee (see page 107) or coconut oil
    1 small zucchini (courgette), finely diced
    100 g (3½ oz/½ cup) corn kernels
    3–4 cherry tomatoes, halved
    2 eggs, lightly beaten
    20 g (¾ oz) feta cheese, cut into small chunks
    a few basil leaves, or other herbs, thinly sliced
    sprinkle of dulse flakes (optional)

Melt your fat of choice in a small frying pan over medium heat. Add the zucchini, and cook for 3 minutes, then add the corn and tomato and cook for another 2–3 minutes. Reduce the heat to low and add the eggs, cheese, basil and dulse flakes, if using, and a pinch of freshly ground black pepper. Stir gently until the eggs are softly scrambled, then remove from the heat a little before they are done to your liking—they will keep cooking when taken off the heat. Taste and adjust with sea salt, as desired—the feta is often salty enough.

Tombolas

Makes 6

Far sturdier than a frittata, tombolas are a great grab-and-go breakfast.

The beauty of the tombola is that just about any uncooked vegetable can be used—cauliflower and broccoli are especially good. Leaves, such as spinach and Tuscan black kale (cavolo nero), however, are best wilted and squeezed of any liquid before using, and cabbage should be cooked. Zucchini (courgette) should be grated and wrapped in a tea towel and wrung to remove as much liquid as possible, too. A little grated parmesan or cheddar will enrich the flavour, as will herbs of your liking.

35 g (1¼ oz/¼ cup) white spelt flour
185 ml (6 fl oz/¾ cup) milk
30 g (1 oz) butter, melted
1 teaspoon dulse flakes
3 eggs
45 g (1¾ oz/½ cup) grated peeled carrot
30 g (1 oz/½ cup) finely chopped broccoli
80 g (2¾ oz/½ cup) finely chopped capsicum (pepper)
60 g (2¼ oz/½ cup) finely chopped cauliflower
1–2 tablespoons roughly chopped herbs, such as flat-leaf (Italian) parsley, basil and coriander (cilantro), depending on the season (optional)
1 tablespoon finely grated pecorino or parmesan, or 1–2 tablespoons cheddar (optional)

Preheat the oven to 180°C (350°F/Gas 4). Line six holes of a muffin tin with baking paper, folding the paper over a little to fit the shape; don't cut the paper to fit or the juices will seep through.

Place the flour, milk, butter, dulse flakes, eggs and a pinch of sea salt and freshly ground black pepper in a large bowl and whisk together well. Add the vegetables and herbs and cheese, if using. Ladle the mixture into the muffin holes.

Bake for 30 minutes or until puffed and lightly golden. Let them sit for 5 minutes in the tin, then turn out onto a wire rack. Gently peel off the paper, if serving immediately, or cool completely in the paper, then peel off. Store in an airtight container in the fridge for up to 2 days.

 VARIATION

Dairy-free Replace the milk with 125 ml (4 fl oz/½ cup) oat milk and 60 ml (2 fl oz/¼ cup) coconut milk, and the butter with olive oil.

Poached summer fruit

GLUTEN FREE / DAIRY FREE
Makes 2 adult and 2–3 child serves

Poached summer fruits, especially stone fruit and berries, make a delicious and moist addition to a breakfast. They also make a wonderful snack or dessert, served simply with yoghurt (see page 98), labne (see page 99), cream, kefir cream (see page 102) or custard.

    4 peaches, quartered
    4 apricots, halved
    ½–2 tablespoons raw (demerara) sugar, or to taste
    1 vanilla bean, halved lengthways, or 1 teaspoon natural vanilla extract

Place the fruit in a saucepan with ½ tablespoon of sugar, the vanilla bean or extract and 125 ml (4 fl oz/½ cup) of water. Cover and cook over low heat for 10–15 minutes or until the fruit starts to release its juices. Taste for sweetness and add more sugar, as required. Increase the heat a little and simmer for another 5 minutes or until the fruit is just soft. If using a vanilla bean, run the tip of a small sharp knife down the bean and scrape the seeds back into the fruit, then gently stir through the fruit. Serve warm or chilled. Poached fruit will keep in the fridge for up to 1 week.

When poaching I use a couple of tricks. First, choose your sweetener—I like raw (demerara) sugar, because it lets the flavour of the fruit come through, but maple syrup is my other favourite. Start with just a little, adding more if needed—different fruits will require very different amounts of sweetening. Also, add only the tiniest amount of liquid to protect the fruit from burning before it sweats out its juices—this will give you a better-flavoured result. Add vanilla extract and rose essence for flavour.

Poached winter fruit

GLUTEN FREE / DAIRY FREE
Makes 2 adult and 2–3 child serves

Organic, sulphur-free dried fruits are expensive, but it's easy to mix them with traditional winter fruits to extend their delicious flavour. They are also rich in iron.

- 10 dried apricot halves
- 7 dried peach segments
- 6 pitted prunes
- 4 dried figs
- 1 cinnamon stick
- 1 orange
- 125 ml (4 fl oz/½ cup) grape, apple or pear juice
- 1 vanilla bean, halved lengthways, 1 teaspoon natural vanilla extract, or 1 teaspoon vanilla bean paste
- 2 small pears, peeled, cores removed and quartered
- 2 small apples, peeled, cores removed and quartered
- 1 tablespoon rapadura sugar or honey, or to taste

Put the dried fruit and cinnamon stick into a saucepan. Using a vegetable peeler, remove the peel from half of the orange (avoiding the white pith) and add to the pan. Juice the orange, pour into a measuring jug and add enough water to give 250 ml (9 fl oz/1 cup) of liquid. Add to the pan along with the grape juice. If using a vanilla bean, add it to the pan (if using vanilla extract or paste, add it a little later).

Cover with a lid, bring to a gentle boil, then simmer for 5 minutes. Add the pear and apple and add just enough water to barely cover—about 185 ml (6 fl oz/¾ cup). Cover and continue to simmer for 5–6 minutes or until the fruit is just soft—take care not to overcook. Discard the orange peel. Test for sweetness and add sugar, as desired. If using vanilla extract or paste, stir it in now. If using the vanilla bean, remove it and set it aside on a plate.

Increase the heat and cook at a rapid boil for 2 minutes to reduce the liquid, taking care not to stir the fruit too much or break it up. When the liquid has reduced, discard the cinnamon stick. If using a vanilla bean, run the tip of a small sharp knife down the bean and scrape the seeds back into the fruit, then gently stir through the fruit. Taste again and adjust the sweetness, as desired. Poached fruit will keep in the fridge for up to 1 week.

Poached berries

GLUTEN FREE / DAIRY FREE
Makes about 1 cup

When I see organic strawberries or any organic berries discounted because some are a bit old and dodgy, I buy them for poaching. They are fabulous with the basmati rice pudding (page 271), on pancakes or with yoghurt (see page 98).

125 g (4½ oz/1 cup) berries, any green leaves removed, larger strawberries halved or quartered and washed
1 teaspoon raw (demerara) sugar, plus extra, if required

Place the berries and sugar in a small saucepan with 1 tablespoon of water. Cover with a lid and cook over very low heat for 8–10 minutes or until the juices have been released from the berries. Increase the heat and cook for a further 5 minutes. Taste and add more sugar, as desired.

You can also use any frozen berries for this recipe. Use exactly the same method; they will take about 2 minutes extra cooking time before they begin to sweat out their juices.

Dips and spreads, breads and pastry

EVERYTHING IN THIS SECTION HAS BEEN designed primarily for its ability to be packed and travel well. Here you'll find more dips and pâtés (in addition to those in *Developing Complexity, 1–3 Years*, see pages 150–215) for crudités, or to fill a sandwich, a delicious gluten-free bread, and slices and pies that are held together with pastry and fit easily into a small hand.

Classic basil pesto

GLUTEN FREE
Makes 1 cup

I admit I cannot write a book without including pesto. As far as I'm concerned, a house is not a home without pesto—it's a brilliant way to include vitamins and minerals from leafy greens. The olive oil and the fat from the pine nuts ensure all the goodness is bioavailable, and it can redeem almost anything. You can easily replace a portion of the basil with flat-leaf (Italian) parsley or young rocket (arugula).

2 large handfuls basil leaves
50 g (1¾ oz/½ cup) finely grated parmesan
40 g (1½ oz/¼ cup) pine nuts
3 garlic cloves, crushed
80 ml (2½ fl oz/⅓ cup) olive oil, plus a little extra, to seal

Place all the ingredients in a food processor and process until well combined. Try not to pulse for too long—pesto should be chunky, not a smooth, homogeneous blend. Place in a small airtight container and pour a little extra oil over to cover the top and prevent the pesto from oxidising. It will keep in the fridge for up to 2 weeks.

Pumpkin seed and coriander pesto

GLUTEN FREE / CAN BE DAIRY FREE IF NO CHEESE USED
Makes about 1 cup

In winter and spring, when basil is not available, my garden is bursting with coriander. Pumpkin seeds are a great way to add a little more omega-3 essential fatty acids to your child's diet and they pair well with coriander.

  130 g (4¾ oz/1 cup) good-quality pumpkin seeds (pepitas)
  2–3 tablespoons lemon or lime juice, or to taste
  2 garlic cloves, crushed
  1 large handful coriander (cilantro) leaves, roughly chopped
  60 ml (2 fl oz/¼ cup) olive oil, plus a little extra, to seal
      (see kitchen note)
  1–2 teaspoons white (shiro) miso (see glossary) or 2 tablespoons
      finely grated parmesan or pecorino

Lightly toast the pumpkin seeds in a dry frying pan over medium heat, shaking the pan from time to time, until they begin to pop and swell. Take care not to burn them. Transfer to a plate and cool.

Place the cooled pumpkin seeds, 2 tablespoons lemon juice and the remaining ingredients in a food processor. Pulse until you have a smoothish paste. Pumpkin seeds can be a little tough, so it may take a bit longer than regular pesto. Adjust the flavour, adding more lemon juice, if necessary. Season to taste with sea salt and freshly ground black pepper. Place in a small airtight container and pour a little extra oil over to cover the top and prevent the pesto from oxidising. It will keep in the fridge for up to 5 days.

🍵 KITCHEN NOTE

Do make sure that the olive oil is fruity and full. Any harsh flavours will show up in the end result—an olive oil pressed with lemon or lime would be perfect. If using an infused oil, omit the lemon or lime juice and replace with a little water.

Dairy-free basil pesto

GLUTEN FREE / DAIRY FREE

Makes ⅔ cup

100 g (3½ oz/⅔ cup) pine nuts
3 large handfuls basil leaves
2 teaspoons white (shiro) miso (see glossary)
2 garlic cloves, crushed
1 tablespoon lemon juice
100 ml (3½ fl oz) olive oil, plus a little extra, to seal

Place all the ingredients in a food processor and pulse until well combined. Try not to pulse for too long—it should be well combined, but slightly chunky. Place in a small airtight container, and pour a little extra oil over to cover the top and prevent the pesto from oxidising. It will keep in the fridge for up to 5 days.

Lime and coriander hummus

GLUTEN FREE / DAIRY FREE
Makes 2 cups

I've avoided a hummus recipe in my previous books, believing that there are already many good recipes for this staple. However, I've been swayed with this one, which is delicious in winter when coriander and limes are at their peak. It won't be anywhere near as tasty if made with commercial coriander, so why not buy a few seeds, throw them in the ground and grow your own—you'll be rewarded with the best coriander you've ever tasted.

165 g (5¾ oz/¾ cup) dried chickpeas
1 tablespoon whey (see page 99) or 2 teaspoons lemon juice
5 cm (2 inch) strip kombu
60 ml (2 fl oz/¼ cup) lime juice
2–3 garlic cloves, crushed
135 g (4¾ oz/½ cup) unhulled tahini
2–3 tablespoons olive oil
1 good handful coriander (cilantro) leaves and stems, roughly chopped

You can easily make this with tinned chickpeas, but it will be much cheaper, more nourishing and tastier to cook them from scratch.

Place the chickpeas, whey or lemon juice and 2 litres (70 fl oz/8 cups) of water in a large bowl. Cover with a clean tea towel and allow to stand at room temperature overnight, or in the fridge if the weather is warm.

Drain and rinse the chickpeas well, place in a large saucepan with the kombu and enough water to cover them by about 10 cm (4 inches). Bring to the boil, then reduce the heat and simmer for 2–3 hours or until the chickpeas are very soft. Remove the scum and foam as they cook and top up with extra water, if needed.

Drain the chickpeas, reserving 2 tablespoons of the cooking water. Allow the chickpeas to cool slightly, then place in a food processor with the remaining ingredients. Season to taste, then process until smooth. Check for taste, adding more garlic, lime juice, sea salt, freshly cracked black pepper or cooking liquid, as needed. It will keep in an airtight container in the fridge for 4 days.

Lentil and walnut pâté

GLUTEN FREE / DAIRY FREE
Makes 3 cups / 10 slices

A hearty and sustaining vegetarian pâté that keeps well and freezes brilliantly. You can serve it as is, form it into balls and roll them in chopped flat-leaf (Italian) parsley, or spoon and press into a dish for slicing. A lovely cool-weather pâté to make when walnuts are in season.

125 g (4½ oz/⅔ cup) brown or green lentils, picked over and rinsed
1 bay leaf
200 g (7 oz/2 cups) walnuts
1 tablespoon olive oil
1 red onion, finely diced
3 teaspoons dried basil
3 teaspoons minced garlic
3 teaspoons mirin (Japanese rice wine)
¼ – ½ teaspoon umeboshi paste
1 tablespoon white (shiro) miso (see glossary)

Walnuts burn easily—even when they are lightly browned they can be overdone and bitter. Make sure that the walnuts are absolutely fresh and not at all rancid.

Preheat the oven to 180°C (350°F/Gas 4).

Place the lentils and bay leaf in a saucepan and cover with enough water to reach about 2 cm (¾ inch) above the lentils. Place over medium heat and bring to the boil, then reduce the heat to low and simmer for 30–40 minutes or until the lentils are tender. Drain and set aside.

Meanwhile, place the walnuts on a baking tray and bake for 10 minutes or until just aromatic.

Heat the oil in a small frying pan over low heat, add the onion, dried basil and garlic and cook for 10 minutes or until soft and cooked but not coloured, then remove from the heat.

Transfer the onion mixture to a food processor along with all of the remaining ingredients and process until slightly chunky. Check for taste and add a little more mirin or umeboshi paste, if necessary. Spoon into a bowl or small terrine and serve.

If you would like a firmer pâté for slicing, place it in the fridge for 1–2 hours to firm up a little. Pâté will keep in an airtight container in the fridge for up to 3 days.

 **KITCHEN NOTE**

I've made this about 500 times, and only recently had a disaster. I'd used conventional lentils, and they had very little flavour. It was a good reminder of just how much difference organic ingredients make.

Creamy chicken mayonnaise sandwich filling

GLUTEN FREE
Makes enough for 2 sandwiches

This simple and delicious sandwich filling is nutrient dense and wonderfully versatile—my mum used to add a few roasted almonds for extra crunch. If I have pesto in the fridge, I like to swirl some of that in it as well. Finely chopped cucumber makes a delicious addition in summer with a little lemon zest. This filling works well with lots of lettuce in the sandwich.

- 100 g (3½ oz) skinless chicken breast fillet, or 4 chicken tenderloins
- 60 ml (2 fl oz/¼ cup) coconut milk
- 60 ml (2 fl oz/¼ cup) mayonnaise (see page 166)
- 60 g (2¼ oz/½ cup) thinly sliced celery
- 1 teaspoon finely snipped chives
- 1 tablespoon finely chopped herbs, such as basil,
    flat-leaf (Italian) parsley or chervil

Place the chicken and coconut milk in a small saucepan and pour in enough water to just cover the chicken. Bring to a simmer over medium heat, then reduce the heat to low and simmer gently for another 6 minutes. Remove from the heat and allow the chicken to stand in the liquid until cool.

Place the remaining ingredients in a bowl, season to taste with sea salt and freshly ground black pepper and combine well. Drain, then finely chop the chicken, add to the bowl and combine well. The filling will keep in an airtight container in the fridge for up to 2 days.

Rustic tray-baked vegetable tart

WHEAT FREE
Makes 8 slices

You can use so many vegetables in this rustic tart—roasted or grilled pumpkin, sweet potato, capsicum (pepper), eggplant (aubergine) and fennel are especially good. Olives and good-quality salami or sausage also make great additions.

This was a big hit in our house, and I wish I had worked it out when my daughter was younger. It's very easy to make—you can use pretty much whatever is on hand (including leftovers). It makes a sturdy slice for lunches, keeps for 2–3 days in the fridge, still tastes delicious when reheated and freezes well.

Barley and spelt pastry
65 g (2½ oz/½ cup) barley flour
130 g (4¾ oz/1 cup) white spelt flour
1 teaspoon dulse flakes
125 g (4½ oz) cold butter, chopped, plus extra for greasing

Vegetable filling
1 cup blended garden vegetable tomato sauce (see page 142)
1 tablespoon olive oil
½ onion, finely diced
1 zucchini (courgette), quartered lengthways and thinly sliced
1 garlic clove, finely chopped
1 teaspoon dried basil
¼ – ½ teaspoon dried oregano
6–8 Tuscan black kale (cavolo nero) leaves, roughly chopped

Savoury topping
250 g (9 oz/1 cup) sour cream
125 g (4½ oz/½ cup) Greek-style yoghurt
50 g (1¾ oz/½ cup) grated parmesan or pecorino
2 egg yolks

To make the barley and spelt pastry Place the flours, dulse flakes and a pinch of sea salt in a bowl. Using your fingertips, rub in the butter until the mixture resembles fine breadcrumbs. Do not overwork it or it will become tough. Using a butter knife, gradually 'cut' 60 ml (2 fl oz/¼ cup) of chilled water into the mixture. Use only as much water as you need—some white spelt flours will absorb more liquid than others. Once the mixture looks moist, shape into a disc (but don't work it too much), wrap in plastic wrap and chill for 20 minutes or until cold to the touch.

To make the vegetable filling Place the sauce in a small saucepan and simmer over low heat until reduced to ¾ cup. Set aside.

Heat the oil in a large frying pan over medium heat. Add the onion and cook for 3–4 minutes. Add the zucchini, increase the heat slightly and cook for another 3–5 minutes or until the zucchini is lightly coloured but not mushy. Add the garlic and dried herbs and cook for another minute. Transfer to a bowl and set aside.

Add the kale and 1 tablespoon of water to the pan, cover and cook for 2–3 minutes or until wilted. Remove the lid, increase the heat to high and simmer until all the liquid has evaporated. Add to the zucchini mixture and combine well.

To make the savoury topping Place all the ingredients in a small bowl, season to taste with sea salt and freshly ground black pepper and whisk together well.

To assemble Preheat the oven to 200°C (400°F/Gas 6). Lightly grease a shallow baking tray, 25 x 28 x 1½ cm (10 x 11¼ x ⅝ inch) with the extra butter. Lightly dust a surface and a rolling pin. Roll the pastry out once or twice, then run a palette knife underneath to move the pastry, lightly dust the rolling surface with a little more flour and turn the pastry over. Lightly dust the pastry with flour and roll out again. Repeat until the pastry is 3 mm (⅛ inch) thick and 26 x 29 cm (10½ x 11½ inch) in size. Because barley flour is low in gluten, the pastry will be brittle—you'll need to roll the pastry onto your rolling pin, then unroll it over the tray. Gently push it into the tray, trim the edges and prick the base with a fork. Place in the freezer for 5–10 minutes or until the pastry is very firm and cold to the touch.

Remove the tray from the freezer and place a sheet of baking paper over the pastry. Fill with baking beads or dried beans and bake for 10 minutes, then remove the paper and beads. Reduce the heat to 180°C (350°F/Gas 4) and bake for another 8–10 minutes or until the pastry is golden and dry. Remove the tart shell from the oven and increase the temperature to 190°C (375°F/Gas 5).

Spread the sauce over the base of the tart, top with the vegetable mixture, then carefully spread the savoury topping over to cover the vegetables evenly. Bake for 25–30 minutes or until the top is light golden. Remove from the oven and let cool a little in the tray before slicing. The tart will firm as it cools.

Alternatively, put the flours, dulse flakes and butter in a food processor, pulse once or twice until the mixture resembles small breadcrumbs, then turn into a bowl and add the water.

Coconut, lentil and vegetable pocket pies

GLUTEN FREE (IF WHEAT-FREE TAMARI USED) / DAIRY FREE
Makes 8

I love pocket pies—they're the perfect food for packing and travelling. The filling is an easy, delicious and very flexible little number and will make more than is needed. It will keep in the fridge for up to 2 days, and can be served warm with buttered toast or a cooked grain. You can also warm it in a frying pan, make a little well in the centre and cook an egg in it.

Pocket pie pastry
260 g (9¼ oz/2 cups) white spelt flour (see kitchen note, page 240)
125 ml (4 fl oz/½ cup) coconut oil, well chilled and cut into cubes
1½ teaspoons apple cider vinegar
50 g (1¾ oz/½ cup) wakame gomasio (see page 168) or sesame seeds

Coconut, lentil and vegetable filling
1 tablespoon small green or black lentils, picked over and rinsed
1 tablespoon coconut oil
½ onion, finely chopped
large pinch ground cumin
1 teaspoon dulse flakes
1 garlic clove, finely chopped
60 g (2¼ oz) carrot, finley diced
60 g (2¼ oz) orange sweet potato, finely diced
125 ml (4 fl oz/½ cup) coconut milk
1 cob of corn, kernels cut off (the cob can be kept for stock)
75 g (2¾ oz/1 cup) finely chopped Tuscan black kale (cavolo nero)
    or cabbage leaves
1 teaspoon tamari
1 egg, lightly beaten, for brushing

A little squeeze of lime and some chopped coriander (cilantro) leaves, makes a delicious addition to the vegetable filling. Piccadillo (see page 196) makes a delicious meat filling for these pies—just make sure it's cold before using.

To make the pastry Place the flour in a bowl and grate the cold coconut oil into the flour. Using your fingertips, rub the oil into the flour as quickly as possible (the heat from your hands will melt it very quickly) until the mixture resembles fine breadcrumbs. Mix together 100 ml (3½ fl oz) of chilled water and the vinegar and add to the flour mixture with the wakame gomasio or sesame seeds. Using a butter knife, 'cut' the liquid into the flour mixture. You may need to add another tablespoon of chilled water—some white spelt flours will absorb more liquid than others. Once the mixture looks moist, shape into a disc (but don't work it too much), wrap in plastic wrap and refrigerate for 20 minutes or until cold to the touch.

To make the coconut, lentil and vegetable filling Place the lentils in a small saucepan with 250 ml (9 fl oz/1 cup) of water and cook over low heat for 30–35 minutes or until just soft. Drain and set aside.

Heat the oil in a frying pan over medium heat. Add the onion and cumin and cook, stirring occasionally, for 1–2 minutes. Add the dulse flakes, garlic, carrot, sweet potato, coconut milk and sea salt and freshly ground black pepper to taste and stir through. Cover, reduce the heat to low and cook for 10 minutes or until the vegetables are just cooked through. Stir in the corn, kale, lentils and tamari, cover and cook for another 5 minutes. Transfer to a bowl and cool.

To assemble Preheat the oven to 180°C (350°F/Gas 4). Cut the chilled pastry in half and roll out one-half at a time. Lightly dust a surface and a heavy, decent-sized rolling pin with as little flour as possible. Roll the pastry once or twice, then run a palette knife underneath, move the pastry firmly and quickly, lightly dust the rolling area with a little more flour and turn the dough over. Lightly sprinkle the surface of the pastry with flour and swiftly rub over. Repeat this process until you have a 3 mm (⅛ inch) thick, 23 cm (9 inch) square, then trim the edges to neaten. Cut into 4 pieces, then repeat with the remaining piece of pastry, so you will have 8 squares of pastry.

Place 1 heaped tablespoon of cooled filling in the centre of each piece of pastry. Using a palette knife or spatula, carefully fold the pastry over to cover the filling to make a rectangle. Transfer to a baking paper-lined oven tray, press the tines of a fork along the edges to seal well and brush the tops with egg. Bake for 35 minutes or until golden. Cool a little before serving.

Alternatively, put the flours, dulse flakes and coconut oil in a food processor, pulse once or twice until the mixture resembles small breadcrumbs, then turn into a bowl and add the water.

 KITCHEN NOTE

*It is very important that at least 130 g (4¾ oz/1 cup) of the spelt flour
has as little germ and bran as possible. This will give you a moist and
flexible pastry. Too much wholemeal will give you a dry and unattractive
pastry that won't hold together well. You will need to assess the white
spelt flour available to you. If it looks almost like a light wholemeal,
I'd suggest you sift enough spelt flour (to catch the germ and bran)
to give you 130 g (4¾ oz/1 cup) of a fine white spelt flour.*

Coconut, lentil and vegetable pupusas

GLUTEN FREE / DAIRY FREE
Makes 8

Similar to thick stuffed flat bread, pupusas originate from El Salvador and are
made from masa harina (dried maseca). When cut, they will open up to make a
little pocket.

    180 g (6¼ oz/1½ cups) masa harina (see kitchen note)
    1 quantity coconut, lentil and vegetable filling (see page 238), chilled
    2 tablespoons cheese, such as grated cheddar, soft goat's cheese,
        or labne (see page 99, optional)

Place the masa harina in a bowl and pour in 310 ml (10¾ fl oz/1¼ cups) of warm
water. Stir vigorously with a wooden spoon until the mixture comes together.
Cover and set aside to cool.

Divide the cooled dough into eight portions (keeping them covered to avoid
drying out). Place one ball of dough in the palm of your hand and use your other
hand to form the shape of a small but flattish bird's nest. The diameter of the
base should be about 7 cm (2¾ inches) with the sides of the nest about 1½–2 cm
(⅝–¾ inch) high and 5 mm (¼ inch) thick.

Place a tablespoon of filling, and 1 teaspoon of cheese, if using, on the base,
then gently and slowly press the sides over the filling. Place the pupusa, seam-side
up or down, on a piece of baking paper and gently press it out until it reaches

8–10 cm (3¼–4 inches) round, taking care that the filling does not spill out. Repeat with the remaining dough and filling. At this stage the pupusas can be placed on a baking tray lined with baking paper, covered with plastic wrap and refrigerated for up to 2 days.

Heat a cast-iron frying pan or chargrill plate over high heat and cook the pupusas for 2–3 minutes each side or until they have brown spots on the pastry. No fat is added to the pan, and the hotter the pan, the better.

Cooked pupusas keep well for a day or so, covered, in the fridge, but are best lightly warmed or brought to room temperature before eating. Cooked pupusas also freeze fabulously. To reheat, wrap the frozen pupusas in foil and place in a moderate oven for 10–15 minutes or until heated through.

🐦 KITCHEN NOTE

Masa (maseca) is a special flour made from corn (maize) that has been soaked in lime (an alkaline, not the citrus). This ensures the bound vitamin B3 is released and balances the proteins, so it is nutritionally sound. It is wonderfully versatile and an excellent and easy option for those with gluten-free requirements. When dried it is called masa harina.

🐦 VARIATION

Bean pupusas Fill the pastry with a little cooked mashed beans or bean pot pies filling (see page 254) instead of the coconut, lentil and vegetable filling. Serve with a simple salad: finely chopped lettuce, tomatoes, avocado, cucumber and a squeeze of lime juice.

Quinoa corn bread

GLUTEN FREE / DAIRY FREE
Makes a 20 cm (8 inch) square 'loaf'

This is my adaptation of a recipe by brilliant natural foods chef Myra Kornfeld. It offers a nutrient-dense, delicious gluten-free slice that, while not exactly a bread, is wonderful when you have gluten and dairy restrictions. It would be delicious served with the pocket pie coconut, lentil and vegetable filling (see page 238).

The polenta can be coarse or finely ground, but for better flavour and nutrition, look for polenta that has the germ intact.

coconut or olive oil, for greasing
110 g (3¾ oz/¾ cup) polenta (see side bar)
80 g (2¾ oz/½ cup) quinoa flour
60 g (2¼ oz/½ cup) true arrowroot
½ teaspoon bicarbonate of (baking) soda
1 teaspoon baking powder
1 tablespoon rapadura sugar
2 tablespoons apple cider vinegar
100 ml (3½ fl oz) coconut, macadamia or olive oil
250 ml (9 fl oz/1 cup) rice or oat milk
¼ quantity cooked quinoa (see page 91), slightly cooled

Preheat the oven to 190°C (375°F/Gas 5). Lightly grease a 20 cm (8 inch) square cake tin with oil.

Place the polenta, quinoa flour, true arrowroot, bicarbonate of soda, baking powder, sugar and a pinch of sea salt in a bowl. Whisk through to evenly distribute the ingredients.

Place the vinegar, oil and milk in a separate bowl and whisk together. Add the cooked quinoa and whisk to combine well. Add to the dry ingredients and whisk until just combined.

Pour the mixture into the tin and bake for 25–30 minutes or until a skewer inserted into the middle comes out clean. Turn out and serve immediately or cool on a wire rack. The bread will keep in an airtight container for up to 5 days. In the warmer weather, it is best kept in a cool place.

Lunchboxes

THERE ARE MANY CHALLENGES A PARENT FACES as a child moves out into the world, and creating a 'healthy' lunchbox is certainly one of them. My best advice to you is to stop trying to make the perfect, complete, wonderful lunchbox. There are too many variables that will impact on what (and how) your child will eat, to place so much nutritional pressure on the lunchbox. Rather, look at the lunchbox as part of the overall eating pattern for the day, and as mentioned previously, I suggest you place more emphasis on breakfast, afternoon tea and dinner—bookending the hours at school. I also suggest you don't get too stressed with the order in which your child eats what you have provided—we are all individuals.

When preparing your child's lunchbox, consider the weather. Cooked fruit in winter may be an ideal option for some children, and a warm soup in a wide-mouthed thermos will be far more nourishing than cold food on a cold day.

With regards to cold meat, this traditionally came from the left-over roast or meat cooked for lunches, rather than deli meat. It is not only much cheaper this way, but avoids the highly processed commercial products that pose as meat but are a source of artificial colours, nitrates, additives and preservatives. Left-over roasts also offer the opportunity for left-over gravy—rich in gelatine, gravy makes a delicious addition to the meat and aids digestion.

Where possible, I've kept nuts out of the equation.

LUNCHBOX BASICS

There are lots of basic foods that go well in a child's lunchbox. It's a good idea to supplement these basic items with foods depending on what kind of breakfast they've had.

FRUIT

- Whole or cut fresh seasonal fruit with sweet labne (see page 99), yoghurt (see page 98), coconut cream or kefir cream (see page 102). In winter, some children may prefer lightly stewed fruit, such as poached winter fruit (see page 228).
- Fruit purée (see page 118) swirled into yoghurt, sweetened labne, coconut cream or kefir cream.

VEGETABLES

- A selection of vegetables (salad or dipping sticks) with a small serve of fat-based dip, such as dressing, mayonnaise (see page 166) or delicious avocado (see page 162).
- A small salad, such as warm potato, green bean, roasted beetroot and egg salad (see page 172) or iron and energy! (see page 170).

PROTEIN-BASED LUNCH FOODS

After a grain-based breakfast, your child's lunchbox should be light on complex carbohydrate and should rely on protein and fat as primary fuel, in addition to a selection of the basics. Many of the protein suggestions, eggs, meat and fish, are animal-based as these are some of the most nourishing protein sources for young children. Don't forget to include a cool pack in the lunchbox to keep food fresh.

PROTEIN

- cold meats
- cold sausage
- chicken fingers (see page 190)
- tombolas (see pages 156 and 226)
- boiled egg
- egg and olive spread (see page 165)
- fish balls (see page 189)
- labne (see page 99)
- lentil and walnut pâté (see page 234)
- vegetable and nut pâté (see page 163)

SWEETNESS

- 1 cookie or slice of cake

COMPLEX CARBOHYDRATE-BASED
LUNCH FOODS

After a protein-based breakfast, focus on lunchbox foods that are high in complex carbohydrate, in addition to a selection of the basics. I've included a number of suggestions for quality gluten-free lunches that are not based on highly refined gluten-free bread products. Don't forget to include a cool pack in the lunchbox to keep food fresh.

COMPLEX CARBOHYDRATE
- coconut, lentil and vegtable pupusas (gluten free, see page 240)
- coconut, lentil and vegetable pocket pies (see page 238)
- sandwich or wrap (see page below)
- quinoa corn bread (gluten free, see page 242)
- bright and happy quinoa salad (with or without nuts, gluten free, (see page 252)
- rustic tray-baked vegetable tart (see page 236)
- corn and zucchini fritters (gluten free, see page 183)
- sweet potato patties with peach salsa and raita (gluten free, see page 180)
- chard, mushroom and rice bake (gluten free, see page 256)

SWEETNESS
- dried apricot, date and coconut balls (see page 278)
- fruit leather

SANDWICHES AND WRAPS

Bread should be sourdough for ease of digestion, but often this can be too heavy for a sandwich. Excellent options include breads made from sprouted grain flour— these are highly digestible breads and often quite soft. I have included some fillings that have nuts, and while they may not make it into a school lunch, they will be good options for weekend sandwich times.

SPREADS

These are especially important when the filling is not soft and moist (for example, with roasted meat).

- butter
- mayonnaise (dairy free, see page 166)
- delicious avocado (see page 162)
- pesto (see pages 230–232)
- mashed roasted pumpkin or sweet potato (with unhulled tahini added)
- unhulled tahini

GOOD CHEESES

- cheddars
- soft cheeses, such as cottage, quark, labne (see page 99) and feta
- goat's or sheep's cheese

GREAT FILLINGS

- liver pâté (see page 138)
- sardine pâté (see page 137)
- egg and olive spread (see page 165)
- curried egg (made with mayonnaise, see page 166)
- labne (see page 99) or delicious avocado (see page 162) and vegetable and nut pâté (see page 163)
- feta and lentil and walnut pâté (see page 234)
- lime and coriander hummus (see page 233) and delicious avocado (see page 162) and salad
- funky bright green broad bean dip (see page 164)
- roasted vegetables
- creamy chicken mayonnaise sandwich filling (see page 235)
- cold meats, such as pot roast with many vegetables (see page 198) or Nonna's roasted rack of lamb with mashed potato and gravy (see page 148)

Hearty meals

HERE IS A BROAD SELECTION OF MEALS THAT WORK for lunch or dinner. Many have afternoon tea in mind—children may not always eat what is in their lunchbox, or it's difficult to transport some meals, such as soup. The meals are all nutrient dense, easy to digest and will not only nourish your growing child, but the whole family.

Sweet and sour bowl

GLUTEN FREE (IF WHEAT-FREE TAMARI USED) / DAIRY FREE
Makes 2 adult and 1 child serves

You can count on 50 g (1¾ oz/¼ cup) uncooked rice serving two older children when cooked.

All you need is this simple sauce to make a delicious meal out of what is essentially vegetables and grain. You can use any grain that appeals to you—I've suggested Thai red jasmine rice, which is such a funky colour.

100 g (3½ oz/½ cup) long-grain Thai red jasmine rice or brown rice
80 g (2¾ oz) broccoli or broccolini, cut into long florets
1 teaspoon whey (see page 99) or lemon juice
2 teaspoons coconut oil
1 carrot, peeled and cut into julienne
7–8 asparagus spears, woody ends discarded, spears
    cut on the diagonal into quarters
½ red capsicum (pepper), cut into thin strips
8–10 snow peas, topped and tailed, and cut in half on the diagonal
1–2 tablespoons coriander (cilantro) leaves

Sweet and sour sauce
2 teaspoons kudzu (kuzu) or cornflour (cornstarch)
125 ml (4 fl oz/½ cup) pineapple juice
125 ml (4 fl oz/½ cup) rice syrup, plus 1 tablespoon extra
1½ tablespoons brown rice vinegar

1 tablespoon tamari
¼ teaspoon toasted sesame oil

Place the rice, whey or lemon juice and 250 ml (9 fl oz/1 cup) of water in a small bowl and combine well. Cover with a tea towel and allow to stand for 6 hours or overnight at room temperature, or in the fridge if the weather is very warm.

Rinse the rice and drain well. Pat dry with a tea towel, then place in a small saucepan with 170 ml (5½ fl oz/⅔ cup) of water. (If the rice is unsoaked, add 185ml (6 fl oz/¾ cup) of water and a pinch of salt.) Cover with a lid and bring to the boil over medium heat. As soon as it comes to the boil, turn the heat down to low and cook for 40–45 minutes. Check if there is any water left by tipping the pan on an angle about 5 minutes before the end of cooking time. If so, continue to cook until there is no water left. When the rice is ready, small steam holes should appear on the surface. Remove from the heat, place a clean tea towel under the lid to absorb any steam and allow to stand for 5 minutes or until you are ready to serve.

To make the sweet and sour sauce Place the kudzu and pineapple juice in a small saucepan and mix to a smooth paste. Add the remaining ingredients, and bring just to the boil over medium heat, stirring continuously. Remove the pan from the heat as soon as you see bubbles forming. Kudzu continues to thicken as it cools. (This sauce keeps in the fridge for up to 1 week.)

When you are ready to serve, cook the broccoli in lightly salted boiling water until just tender, then drain.

Heat the oil in a frying pan over medium–high heat and when it is hot, but not smoking or rippling, add the carrot and cook, stirring every now and then, for 2 minutes. Add the asparagus and cook for another 2–3 minutes, then reduce the heat to low and add the capsicum and snow peas and cook for a few seconds. Add the broccoli and coriander and toss to combine.

Divide the rice among serving bowls, top with the vegetables and drizzle with a little warm sweet and sour sauce.

 KITCHEN NOTE

The sweet and sour sauce should be nice and flowing. If you'd like to make it thicker, and thus better for coating and dipping, increase the kudzu to 3 teaspoons.

Barley minestrone

WHEAT FREE / DAIRY FREE
Makes 4 adult and 2 child serves

This is a rough and tumble version of a minestrone. Pearl barley provides wholegrain goodness and a lovely starchy creaminess to this hard-working stew. It does take a while to cook—barley reveals its creamy deliciousness to those who are patient. It's a well-balanced lunch dish—not too much carbohydrate, but just enough to anchor and ground the vegetables. Enjoy it fresh from the fridge after a day or so, or freeze it—it behaves well and still tastes good. Add a little yoghurt to aid digestion, and pesto (see pages 230–232) or parmesan, if desired. It also makes a great breakfast.

100 g (3½ oz/½ cup) dried borlotti (cranberry) beans
2 tablespoons pearl barley
2 teaspoons whey (see page 99) or lemon juice
1½ tablespoons olive oil
1 onion, finely diced
1 teaspoon dried basil
½ teaspoon dried oregano
2 garlic cloves, finely chopped
5 cm (2 inch) strip kombu
1 dried shiitake mushroom, quartered
1¼ litres (44 fl oz/5 cups) stock (see pages 94–98) or water
1 large carrot, finely diced
3 celery stalks, thinly sliced
100 g (3½ oz) orange sweet potato, peeled and finely diced
400 g (14 oz) tinned chopped tomatoes
55 g (2 oz) Tuscan black kale (cavolo nero) or cabbage leaves, thinly sliced
40 g (1½ oz) zucchini (courgette) finely diced
    or green beans cut into 1 cm (½ inch) lengths
2–3 teaspoons mirin (Japanese rice wine), or to taste
2–3 teaspoons tamari, or to taste

Place the borlotti beans, half the whey or lemon juice and 1 litre (35 fl oz/4 cups) of water in a bowl and stir through. Place the pearl barley, remaining whey or lemon juice and 125 ml (4 fl oz/½ cup) of water in another bowl and stir through. Cover both with a clean tea towel and allow to stand at room temperature overnight, or in the fridge if the weather is warm. Drain the beans and barley and rinse well.

Place the oil in a large saucepan over low heat. Add the onion and dried herbs and cook for 3–4 minutes, then stir in the garlic and cook for another minute. Add the drained beans and barley, kombu, mushroom and stock or water. Cover with a lid, slightly ajar, and simmer gently for 1 hour. Add the carrot, celery, sweet potato and tomato and continue to simmer for another 2 hours.

Remove the lid and gently stir the minestrone, breaking up any remaining bits of kombu into the soup. Add the kale and zucchini, 2 teaspoons each of mirin and tamari and simmer for another 15 minutes or until the green vegetables are cooked. Taste and adjust with the remaining mirin and tamari, as needed.

Bright and happy quinoa salad

GLUTEN FREE (IF WHEAT-FREE TAMARI USED) / DAIRY FREE
Makes 2–3 adult and 2 child serves

It's hard to measure
a small amount of
arame—many home
scales don't register
such small weights.
What you will pick up
with a small pinch
will be ample—too
much can be a little
overwhelming.

Most vegetables
can be used in this
salad—spring onion
(scallion), fresh peas
and lightly steamed
broccoli florets are
all good.

The main quantity
of sesame oil in the
salad dressing is not
toasted—it should
be a lovely light
colour, with a
subtle fragrance
of sesame.

This has a bright flavour and you'll be happy because it's simple to make. It's an exceptionally nutrient-dense but not too heavy salad—perfect to pack in a lunchbox or to serve with some fish or meat for dinner. I do like to use all the dressing—it makes it deliciously moist, but you can hold back a little, if desired. It gets better as it sits in the fridge.

pinch arame sea vegetable
½ quantity cooked quinoa (see page 91)
80 g (2¾ oz/½ cup) peeled and grated carrot
½ cob of corn, kernels removed and lightly steamed
¼ red capsicum (pepper), finely diced
2 tablespoons coriander (cilantro) leaves, roughly chopped
1–2 teaspoons wakame gomasio (see page 168)
40 g (1½ oz/¼ cup) lightly roasted cashew nuts, chopped

Aromatic dressing
2 tablespoons lemon juice
2 tablespoons natural sesame oil (see side bar)
2 drops toasted sesame oil
½ teaspoon finely grated ginger
2–3 drops tamari, or to taste
1 teaspoon honey

To make the aromatic dressing Place all the ingredients in a small bowl and stir until well combined and the honey is dissolved. Check for taste and add the remaining tamari, if required.

Place the arame in a small bowl with 250 ml (9 fl oz/1 cup) of water and stand for 15 minutes. Drain, then roughly chop and place in a large bowl. Add the remaining salad ingredients, pour over the dressing and toss together.

Potato and sweet potato pizzettes

GLUTEN FREE
Makes about 12

Who doesn't love pizza? These are so quick and easy to put together and they make for a perfect afternoon tea or weekend lunch.

    200 g (7 oz) large potato, well scrubbed and
        cut into 8 mm – 1 cm (⅜ – ½ inch) thick slices
    140 g (5 oz) orange sweet potato, cut into 8 mm–1 cm
        (⅜ – ½ inch) thick slices
    olive oil, for brushing
    60 g (2¼ oz/¼ cup) pizza sauce (see side bar)
    6 Kalamata olives, pitted and quartered
    1 – 2 slices fresh or tinned pineapple in natural juices, cut into small pieces
    1 slice organic, nitrate-free ham, or naturally-cured salami,
        cut into small pieces (optional)
    40 g (1½ oz) grated cheddar or mozzarella, cut into small pieces

Preheat the oven to 165°C (320°F/Gas 3). Brush both sides of the potato and sweet potato slices with oil and arrange in a single layer on baking trays lined with baking paper. Bake for 15–20 minutes or until just cooked and lightly golden. Do not overcook them or they will fall apart when held later on. (You can cook them a couple of hours ahead, if desired.)

Increase the temperature to 190°C (375°F/Gas 5). Top each slice with 1 teaspoon sauce, a couple of pieces of olive, pineapple and ham, and the cheese. Bake for 6–10 minutes or until the cheese is melted and lightly golden. Allow to cool a little before serving.

 KITCHEN NOTE

It's best to choose nice, plump potatoes and sweet potatoes for these—large enough to produce a slice with a diameter of about 6–7 cm (2½–2¾ inch).

When I'm short on time I use an organic, tinned pizza sauce. You could, however, use the garden vegetable tomato sauce (see page 142), enrich it with a few more herbs, and reduce it down so it is nice and thick. Alternatively, you can use pesto (see pages 230–232) as a base instead of the tomato sauce—it is especially good on these potato pizzettes.

Bean pot pies

WHEAT FREE

Makes 4 adult and 2 older (or 4 younger) child serves

This is really a cheat's version of lasagne, but without all the pasta. Rather, the carbohydrate comes from the more complex beans. It's brilliant for afternoon tea when children are ravenous. They're incredibly easy to make and when baked, freeze well.

1 eggplant (aubergine), cut into 1½ cm (⅝ inch) thick slices
olive oil, for brushing, plus 2 teaspoons extra
2 teaspoons dried basil
1 tablespoon butter
1 red onion, finely diced
2 Swiss brown mushrooms, cut into small chunks
2–3 garlic cloves, finely chopped
1 teaspoon dulse flakes
2 celery stalks, thinly sliced
1 large carrot, finely diced
100 g (3½ oz) orange sweet potato, finely diced
280 g (10 oz) cooked beans (borlotti [cranberry], pinto
    or cannellini [white] are good, see page 84)
400 g (14 oz) tinned chopped tomatoes
250 ml (9 fl oz/1 cup) vegetable stock (see page 94)

Creamy topping
40 g (1½ oz) butter
50 g (1¾ oz) white spelt flour
750 ml (26 fl oz/3 cups) milk
30 g (1 oz/1¼ cup) grated cheddar, plus extra, for sprinkling

Preheat the oven to 180°C (350°F/Gas 4). If the eggplant is very young, freshly picked and has few seeds, cut it into thick slices. (If the eggplant is older, cut it into thick slices, place in a sieve placed over a bowl, sprinkle generously with sea salt and toss to coat. Stand for 30 minutes, then rinse well, pat dry on a clean tea towel. Brush both sides generously with oil and place in a single layer on a baking tray. Sprinkle with half of the dried basil and season to taste with sea salt and freshly ground black pepper. Bake for 20–25 minutes or until the eggplant is golden, then coarsely chop.

Heat the extra oil and butter in a heavy-based saucepan over medium–high heat. Add the onion and mushrooms and cook, stirring occasionally, for 5–6 minutes or until the mushrooms are lightly browned—there should be no liquid in the pan. Add the garlic, remaining dried basil, dulse flakes and celery, season to taste with salt and pepper and stir to combine well. Reduce the heat to low and cook, stirring, for 2 minutes. Add the carrot, sweet potato, beans, tomato, stock and eggplant, cover and simmer gently for 25 minutes or until the vegetables are just cooked through. Increase the heat to medium and cook, uncovered, for another 10 minutes or until the mixture has reduced and thickened.

To make the creamy topping Melt the butter in a small saucepan over low heat. Remove from the heat, add the flour and mix with a wooden spoon until a smooth paste forms. Whisking continuously, gradually add the milk and whisk until smooth. Return to the heat, then whisk continuously until the mixture just comes to a gentle boil and is thick and smooth. (Heavy boiling will cause the milk to split.) Remove from the heat immediately, add the cheese and stir in until melted and smooth. Season to taste with salt and pepper.

To assemble Place six 250 ml (9 fl oz/1 cup) capacity ramekins on a baking tray and divide the bean mixture between them. Top with the creamy topping and sprinkle a little extra cheese over. Bake for 20–25 minutes or until golden and bubbling. Allow to cool a little before serving.

 KITCHEN NOTE
You can also prepare this in one large dish, but it will take about 50 minutes to cook.

Chard, mushroom and rice bake

GLUTEN FREE

Makes 2 adult and 2 older (or 4 younger) child serves

This is the dish I was making as I wrote my introduction to my previous book, *Coming Home to Eat: Wholefood for the Family*. I've been cooking it for years and it was a favourite of my daughter Nessie's as she was growing up. This has the addition of the high-protein grain, amaranth. When served with a dessert, it makes a simple and sustaining dinner; it packs well in a lunchbox; can be warmed gently for breakfast; and keeps well in the fridge for a couple of days.

55 g (2 oz/¼ cup) medium-grain brown rice
1 teaspoon amaranth
1 teaspoon whey (see page 99) or lemon juice
1 tablespoon olive oil
2 teaspoons butter or ghee (see page 107)
1 onion, thinly sliced
150 g (5½ oz) Swiss brown or button mushrooms, roughly chopped
2 garlic cloves, finely chopped
300 g (10½ oz) rainbow chard or silverbeet, thick stems discarded, leaves
    washed and shredded
50 g (1¾ oz/½ cup) grated parmesan or pecorino
250 g (9 oz/1 cup) ricotta, crumbled
2 eggs, lightly beaten
1 tomato, thinly sliced
40 g (1½ oz/¼ cup) pine nuts, roughly chopped

Place the rice, amaranth, whey or lemon juice and 125 ml (4 fl oz/½ cup) of water in a small bowl and stir to combine. Cover with a tea towel and allow to stand for 6 hours or overnight at room temperature or in the fridge, if the weather is very warm.

There is no need to drain the grains, because amaranth is so fine. Simply transfer the grains and soaking water into a small saucepan. Cover, bring to the boil, then reduce the heat to very low and cook for 45–50 minutes. Check it at about 40 minutes and, if you're absolutely sure there's not enough water, add a touch more. When cooked, turn out into a large bowl.

Preheat the oven to 180°C (350°F/Gas 4).

Heat the oil and butter or ghee in a large frying pan over medium–high heat. Add the onion and mushrooms and cook, stirring occasionally, for 5 minutes or until the mushrooms are lightly browned and there is no liquid in the pan. Add the garlic and stir for another minute. Add the mixture to the grains.

Place the rainbow chard and 1 tablespoon of water in the same frying pan and cook over low heat, turning a few times until wilted. Give the chard a squeeze with some tongs and drain off any liquid. Add to the grains. Allow to cool for a few minutes, then add the parmesan, ricotta and eggs, season to taste with sea salt and freshly ground black pepper and combine well.

Spoon the mixture into an 8 x 28 x 4 cm (3¼ x 11¼ x 1½ inch) loaf tin or a 1¼ litre (44 fl oz/5 cup) capacity baking dish and pat the top to smooth. Arrange the tomato slices on top and sprinkle with the pine nuts.

Bake for 1–1¼ hours or until the centre is set and firm to the touch. It will ooze and bubble around the sides a little—this is fine. Allow to cool a little before serving.

 KITCHEN NOTE

You can bake this in any ovenproof dish, but a loaf-shaped dish makes it great for slicing. A cast-iron loaf tin is ideal. No matter what dish you use, the fundamental rule is: the deeper the dish, the longer it will take to cook.

Fish fingers with tartare sauce

DAIRY FREE
Makes about ½ cup tartare sauce / 2 older (or 4 younger) child serves

This is such a delicious way to have fish, and it's quick to prepare. I have to confess to a weakness for gherkins—they often made an appearance in my lunchbox when I was younger. Unfortunately, most gherkins today are made with refined sugar, colour and a large number of additives, but you can find brands that keep them simple, without colours and additives, even though they still use white sugar. The tartare sauce is also delicious with the addition of a finely chopped hard-boiled egg, and makes a brilliant dip for raw vegetables.

> 2 red mullet fillets, skin on (about 165 g/5¾ oz in total)
> 1½ tablespoons true arrowroot
> 40 g (1½ oz/½ cup) fresh sourdough breadcrumbs
> 1 teaspoon dulse flakes
> 1 tablespoon coconut flour
> 1 egg, lightly beaten
> coconut oil, for frying
>
> *Tartare sauce*
> 2 tablespoons mayonnaise (see page 166)
> 1 teaspoon finely chopped gherkins
> 1 teaspoon finely chopped capers
> 2–3 teaspoons lemon or lime juice
> 1–2 teaspoons finely chopped herbs, such as
>   flat-leaf (Italian) parsley, dill or mint
> 1–2 drops agave nectar (optional)

To make the tartare sauce Combine all the ingredients together in a bowl, then adjust the seasoning with sea salt and freshly ground black pepper, as desired. Refrigerate until ready to serve. The tartare sauce will keep in the fridge, covered, for up to 1 week.

Run your fingers carefully over the fish fillets and remove any protruding bones. Cut each fillet into four pieces or sizes to your liking.

Place the arrowroot in a shallow bowl. Mix together the breadcrumbs, dulse flakes, coconut flour and a pinch of sea salt in another shallow bowl.

Dust the fish pieces in the arrowroot, then dip in the egg, allowing the excess to drip off, then coat in the breadcrumb mixture.

Place enough oil in the base of a small frying pan to coat the base generously. When it is hot, but not smoking or rippling, cook the fish pieces, in batches, making sure not to overcrowd the pan, for 2–3 minutes each side. The cooking time will depend on how thick the fillets are. Serve with the tartare sauce.

🫖 KITCHEN NOTE

The best heat for frying the fish depends a lot on the thickness of the fish. If the fillets are very thin, the heat will need to be higher, to ensure the coating is golden by the time the fish is cooked. If they are thicker, the heat can be lower, as the coating will have more time in which to brown. If the heat is too low, the coating will be soggy, rather than lovely, crisp and golden.

Fish tacos or burritos

Makes 2 adult and 2 child serves

Don't be afraid of strong flavours—even when children are very young, they love them. This is a quick and easy meal to put together, and a great way to use strongly flavoured, sustainable fish that are high in omega-3 essential fatty acids.

3–4 skinless fish fillets (about 330 g/11¾ oz in total, see kitchen note)
2 teaspoons ground cumin
1 teaspoon paprika
chilli powder, to taste
2 teaspoons oregano leaves
2 garlic cloves, finely chopped
juice of 1 lemon
1–2 tablespoons olive oil, plus extra, for shallow-frying
corn tortillas or taco shells, sour cream or yoghurt (see page 98), shredded
    iceberg lettuce and delicious avocado (see page 162), to serve

Salsa
2 tomatoes, finely diced
large handful coriander (cilantro) leaves, finely chopped
juice of ½–1 lime
1 long red chilli, seeded and finely sliced (optional)

To make the salsa Place the tomato, coriander and the juice of ½ a lime in a bowl and toss together. Add more lime juice, as desired, and season to taste with sea salt and freshly ground black pepper. Refrigerate until required. Serve the chilli on the side for the adults.

Run your fingers carefully over the fish fillets and remove any protruding bones. Cut the fish into good-sized chunks and place in a non-metallic bowl.

Place the spices, oregano and garlic in a bowl, add salt and pepper to taste and combine well. Add to the fish, along with the lemon juice and oil.

Massage the fish with the mixture, rubbing it into the flesh gently but thoroughly. Cover and refrigerate for 30 minutes to 1 hour.

Just before cooking the fish, if using tortillas, wrap in a clean tea towel. If using taco shells, preheat the oven to 180°C (350°F/Gas 4), place taco shells on a baking tray and bake for 5 minutes or until heated through.

Place the extra oil in a large frying pan over medium heat. When it is hot, but not smoking, add the fish and cook for 2–3 minutes each side or until the fish is cooked through. Drain on paper towels.

Place the fish, salsa, tortillas or tacos, sour cream or yoghurt, shredded lettuce and avocado in separate bowls on the table and let the family assemble their own tacos or burritos. For younger children, provide a little of everything on their plate.

 **KITCHEN NOTE**

I like to use sea mullet for this, as the marinade dulls its strong flavour. A fillet weighs about 235 g (8½ oz), and should feed one adult, although some may prefer two. Younger children will manage about one-quarter of a fillet and older children half to one. Flathead is also excellent in this recipe.

Navarin of lamb shank with apple and peas

WHEAT FREE
Makes 2 adult and 1–2 child serves

Navarin is just a classy name for a casserole, although to me it always means one made with spring vegetables. It's also generally made with diced lamb shoulder— however, the shank, with all its gelatinous sinew, will give you a glossier and more nutrient-dense sauce.

- 2 teaspoons butter
- 1 teaspoon olive oil
- 1 large lamb shank or 2 smaller shanks
  (about 800 g/1 lb 12 oz, see kitchen note)
- 1 onion, sliced
- 1 carrot, cut into 1 cm (½ inch) thick slices
- 1 teaspoon rapadura sugar
- 1 tablespoon white spelt flour
- 1 tablespoon tomato paste (concentrated purée)
- 3 garlic cloves, peeled and left whole
- 3 thyme sprigs
- 2 bay leaves
- 2 teaspoons apple cider vinegar, or to taste
- 1 litre (35 fl oz/4 cups) chicken or vegetable stock (see pages 94–95)
- 8 young carrots (if using larger carrots,
  peel and cut into 1½ cm/⅝ inch thick slices)
- 8 baby potatoes, left whole
- 1 good handful young green beans, topped and tailed and, if long, halved
- 1 teaspoon apple juice concentrate, or to taste
- 1 tablespoon roughly chopped mint leaves
- 150 g (5½ oz/1 cup) fresh or frozen peas

Preheat the oven to 180°C (350°F/Gas 4).

Heat the butter and oil in a large cast-iron casserole pot over medium–high heat. Season the lamb shank with sea salt and freshly ground black pepper and cook until lightly browned all over. Remove the lamb and set aside.

Reduce the heat to medium, add the onion and sliced carrot and cook, stirring occasionally, for a few minutes or until lightly coloured. Stir in the sugar, flour, tomato paste, garlic, herbs and vinegar. Gradually stir in enough stock to make a thick paste, then add the remaining stock.

Return the lamb to the pot, cover and bake for 2½ hours or until the meat is tender and almost falling off the bone. Remove the lamb and set aside.

Strain the liquid through a fine sieve placed over a heatproof bowl and discard the solids. Using a spoon, remove any fat from the top of the liquid, then return the liquid to the pot. Return the lamb to the pot, along with the young carrots and potatoes, cover and bake for 30–35 minutes. Remove the lamb and set aside.

Place the pot over medium–high heat, add the green beans, apple juice concentrate and mint (if using frozen peas, add them now, too) and simmer for 5 minutes, removing any fat that pools on the top. Meanwhile, shred the meat from the bone.

At this stage, taste and adjust the flavours of the sauce—you may need a little more apple juice concentrate, a drop or two of apple cider vinegar, or a little extra salt and pepper. When the sauce has reduced to your desired thickness (remember, you have yet to add the meat back), add the fresh peas and return the meat to the pot and continue to cook for a minute or so, or until the peas are just ready. The sauce should be very thick and glossy.

 KITCHEN NOTE

Many butchers cut the sinewy end off the shank, leaving just the meaty top bit and a clean end bone. This won't give you the kind of gelatinous, deeply nourishing sauce you're looking for. Ask your butcher to leave on as much of the sinew as possible.

Keema pie

Makes 8 pot pies or 1 large pie

One of my favourite dishes when I was young was Mum's lamb curry, which she made with apples and sultanas—this is my take on that dish. Keema simply means 'minced', although it generally refers to minced lamb. I use hogget or mutton rather than lamb, as I believe they give a better flavour. This dish gets better the next day; it also freezes well, unbaked.

2 teaspoons coconut oil
1 small onion, finely chopped
1 garlic clove, finely grated
1 heaped teaspoon finely grated ginger
500 g (1 lb 2 oz) minced hogget or mutton
¼ – ½ teaspoon sweet curry spice powder
¼ teaspoon each garam masala, ground cumin and ground coriander
¼ – ½ teaspoon chilli powder (see kitchen notes)
pinch ground cinnamon
2 tablespoons tomato paste (concentrated purée)
1 teaspoon pomegranate molasses (see kitchen notes)
1 red or green apple, unpeeled and grated
1 tablespoon currants or sultanas
100 g (3½ oz) jap pumpkin, peeled, seeded and finely diced
1 carrot, finely diced
1 celery stalk, thinly sliced
250 ml (9 fl oz/1 cup) chicken stock (see page 95)
80 g (2¾ oz/½ cup) fresh or frozen peas
¼ – ½ teaspoon rapadura sugar, or to taste

Mashed potato topping
500 g (1 lb 2 oz) all-purpose potatoes, such as desiree, chopped
30 g (1 oz) butter
2 tablespoons milk
80 – 125 ml (2½ – 4 fl oz/⅓ – ½ cup) cream

Place the oil, onion, garlic and ginger in a large heavy-based saucepan over low heat and cook, stirring occasionally, for 5–6 minutes or until the onion is lightly coloured. Increase the heat to high, add the hogget or mutton, spices and a pinch of sea salt, and cook, breaking the mince up with a wooden spoon as you go, for 5 minutes or until lightly browned. Add the tomato paste, pomegranate molasses, apple, currants or sultanas, pumpkin, carrot, celery and stock and stir to combine. Reduce the heat to low, cover and simmer gently for 35–45 minutes or until the vegetables are cooked through.

Skim off any fat and discard (if your meat is grass fed, this will be valuable fat to keep and use, see *Drippings and rendered fats*, page 58). Add the peas and simmer, uncovered, for another 5–6 minutes or until the mixture has reduced and thickened a little. Taste and add the sugar, if required. Skim off any further fat.

To make the mashed potato topping Place the potato in a large saucepan of cold, lightly salted water. Bring to the boil, then simmer until very tender. Drain, then return the potato to the pan and shake over low heat for 1–2 minutes to remove excess moisture. Add the butter and milk, season to taste with salt and pepper and mash until smooth. Set aside.

To assemble Preheat the oven to 200°C (400°F/Gas 6). Divide the hogget or lamb mixture between eight 185 ml (6 fl oz) ramekins or a 1½ litre (52 fl oz/ 6 cup) capacity ovenproof dish, top with the mashed potato topping and run a fork over to give a rough appearance. Spoon the cream over the top and bake for 15–20 minutes or until golden. Allow to cool a little before serving.

 KITCHEN NOTES

- *Chilli powder is used here to give colour, plus a deep and fragrant undertone with just a little warmth. Avoid the ones you commonly find in the supermarket labelled 'chilli powder' as they are usually cayenne —which is a chilli with no flavour and a bitey heat. You need a proper dried chilli for this dish—look for a New Mexico or ancho chilli and grind it yourself.*

- *Pomegranate molasses gives the most delicious sweet and sour undertone to this dish, but you can replace it with tamarind purée.*

Apple, lemon, rosemary and mint gelée

GLUTEN FREE
Makes 185 ml (6 fl oz/¾ cup)

This is my interpretation of the traditional gelled mint sauce served with roasted or grilled lamb. It is rounder in flavour and not as sweet as the generic mint sauce—and very, very good. Because it's made with gelatine, it aids protein digestion.

    250 ml (9 fl oz/1 cup) apple juice
    13 mint leaves
    6 rosemary leaves
    1 tablespoon lemon juice
    1 tablespoon rapadura sugar
    2¼ teaspoons Bernard Jensen gelatine (see page 63)

Place the apple juice and herbs in a small saucepan and bring to the boil over medium heat. Simmer for 6–8 minutes or until reduced by one-quarter, then remove from the heat.

Strain through a sieve into a heatproof bowl. Reserve the herbs and return the liquid to the pan over low heat. Add the lemon juice and sugar and stir until the sugar is dissolved. Bring back to the boil, then remove from the heat immediately and pour into a heatproof bowl. Add the gelatine and stir until dissolved. Finely chop the reserved herbs and add to the mixture.

Allow the mixture to cool, then refrigerate for 3–5 hours or until set. As the jelly just begins to set and becomes slushy, stir gently to distribute the herbs evenly throughout. The gelée will keep, covered, in the fridge for up to 10 days.

Chicken noodle soup to heal all ills

GLUTEN FREE (IF WHEAT-FREE TAMARI USED) / DAIRY FREE
Makes 1 litre (35 fl oz/4 cups) / makes 4–6 child serves

It's such a bonus having good chicken stock in the freezer. This is my version of the classic soup—it is perfect for school-aged children, with coconut oil, shiitake mushroom and chicken fat to boost the immune system.

1 tablespoon coconut oil
1 small leek, white part only, thinly sliced and washed well
2 garlic cloves, finely chopped
2 celery stalks, finely sliced
1 carrot, finely diced
½ teaspoon dried thyme or 1 teaspoon fresh thyme leaves
½ teaspoon dried sage or 1 teaspoon chopped sage leaves
1 large or 2 small dried shiitake mushrooms, quartered
1 litre (35 fl oz/4 cups) chicken stock (see page 95)
2 chicken wings
1 teaspoon dulse flakes
40 g (1½ oz/¼ cup) peas
4–5 dark green leaves, washed and thinly sliced (see side bar)
50 g (1¾ oz) pasta (see side bar)
1–2 teaspoons mirin (Japanese rice wine), or to taste
1–2 teaspoons tamari, or to taste
1 tablespoon finely chopped flat-leaf (Italian) parsley

Place the oil in a large heavy-based saucepan over low–medium heat. Add the leek, garlic, celery, carrot and herbs and cook, stirring frequently, for 5 minutes. Add the mushroom, stock and chicken wings, cover with a lid and bring to the boil. Reduce the heat to low and simmer for 40 minutes to 1 hour. Remove the chicken wings and place on a plate to cool. Add the dulse flakes, peas, green leaves and pasta to the pan and cook for another 10 minutes or until the pasta is just cooked. Shred as much meat as possible from the chicken wings and stir through the soup. Taste and adjust with the mirin and tamari. Add the parsley and serve.

Dark leaves, such as collard greens, Tuscan black kale (cavolo nero) or the dark, outer leaves of cos lettuce, are great additions.

Use whatever pasta appeals; if using long pasta, I suggest breaking it up a little. I prefer to use alphabet pasta.

Pesto chicken and vegetable pilaf

Makes 2 adult and 2 child serves

This is such an easy and flexible meal to put together. You can use whatever vegetables are in season (fennel is delicious)—just remember to add the hardier ones first, and the lighter, quick-cooking ones towards the end. I've used a whole chicken as it's much cheaper to cut the pieces yourself—plus you get a carcass for stock. You can easily make this into a vegetarian meal by leaving out the chicken entirely and replacing the chicken stock with vegetable stock; begin by sautéing your vegetables in the warm coconut oil and ghee. This is also delicious served with yoghurt. Any leftovers make a great lunch the next day or stuffing for vegetables.

1½ kg (3 lb 5 oz) whole chicken
2 teaspoons coconut oil
2 teaspoons ghee (see page 107)
1 onion, finely diced
2–3 garlic cloves, finely chopped
2 carrots, finely diced
2 celery stalks, thinly sliced
½ red capsicum (pepper), finely diced
10 or so basil leaves, roughly chopped, or ½ teaspoon dried basil leaves
½ teaspoon dried oregano
1 teaspoon dulse flakes
200 g (7 oz/1 cup) basmati rice, rinsed well
500 ml (17 fl oz/2 cups) chicken stock (see page 95)
60 g (2¼ oz/¼ cup) pesto (see pages 230–232),
    plus extra to serve (optional)
70 g (2½ oz) green beans, topped and tailed and
    cut into 2 cm (¾ inch) lengths, or peas
5–6 Tuscan black kale (cavolo nero) leaves, finely shredded
40 g (1½ oz/¼ cup) pine nuts, lightly roasted
25 g (1 oz/¼ cup) finely grated parmesan or pecorino

Preheat the oven to 180°C (350°F/Gas 4).

Cut the thighs and legs from the chicken in one piece, then remove the 2 breasts. To separate the thigh and leg, cut at the joint. Reserve a breast for another dish and the wings and carcass to make stock. Sprinkle the remaining 5 chicken pieces with sea salt and freshly ground black pepper.

Place the oil and ghee in a large, shallow, heatproof casserole dish over medium heat. When the oil is hot, but not rippling or smoking, add the chicken pieces, skin-side down, and cook for 5 minutes or until golden. Try not to move the chicken during this time, as lifting it too early before the skin is golden can tear it. Remove the thighs and breast when golden and place on a plate. Turn the legs to brown the other side, removing when ready.

Reduce the heat to low, add the onion, garlic, carrot, celery, capsicum, herbs and dulse flakes and cook for 5 minutes or until the vegetables have developed a little colour. Stir in the rice, then add the stock.

Rub the pesto over the chicken and place on top of the rice and vegetables. Bring to the boil, then cover and bake for 25 minutes. Gently stir in the green beans and kale, cover and bake for another 10 minutes or until the green vegetables are just tender. Remove the chicken and cut the breast meat into three pieces. Divide the chicken and rice among serving bowls, sprinkle with the pine nuts and parmesan and serve with extra pesto, if desired.

KITCHEN NOTES
- *A large, shallow cast-iron dish that you can use on top of the stove and in the oven is perfect for this pilaf.*
- *I grow my own Tuscan black kale (cavolo nero)—if you use the larger-leafed curly kale, remember to reduce the number of leaves.*

Sweetness

A LITTLE SOMETHING DELICIOUS AND SWEET IN A LUNCHBOX, for afternoon tea or dessert, is a powerful thing. Our current attitudes give healthy food, cakes and biscuits a pretty hard time—we have some very skewed ideas of what healthy sweetness is. I remember one of my cookery students who had made beautiful, organic muffins using whole unrefined flours, a small amount of whole sweetener, fruit, good fats and nuts. She received a note from her child's school asking her not to provide this 'bad' food again and listing acceptable alternatives. I can tell you that her muffin was vastly superior to most of the options suggested, many of which were highly refined and processed.

The recipes in this section are all made with unrefined sweeteners and flours, and with quality fats. I've mostly used spelt flour, as it behaves much the same as wheat flour but is more easily tolerated and digested. I've stuck to white spelt where possible, as it gives a lighter biscuit or cake, and I think in our overzealousness, we can overload a young child with fibre.

When using white spelt, you'll need to use your common sense, as spelt flours vary enormously. All start off as wholemeal, and are then sifted to remove some of the bran and germ—this varies from brand to brand; some may be lovely and light (predominantly endosperm) and some quite hefty, with a large amount of bran and germ still present (they almost look like a light wholemeal). I generally like to use 50 per cent white spelt, and 50 per cent wholemeal spelt when I bake. But if my white spelt is almost a light wholemeal, I will use 100 per cent of that and not include any wholemeal in the mix.

With regard to the fat in baking, I've most commonly used butter as it provides the best crumb to a cake and is exceptionally nourishing. If you prefer, you can replace it with macadamia, almond or coconut oil—if using coconut oil, a cake will be more crumbly when cool; a biscuit will be fine, though (see page 58).

This section goes beyond fruit—for while fruit can be an exceptionally healthy and delicious sweet snack, it is only that when it is ripe and in season. It's not always appropriate for every body type either—cold fruit on a cold day is not a good or nourishing food for everyone.

DESKERTS

Wholesome and delicious desserts can and do go beyond simple stewed or baked fruits. Most of the following recipes have fruit as the star ingredient.

Basmati rice pudding

GLUTEN FREE

Makes 2 adult and 2 child serves

This is a much lighter version of the traditional rice pudding and is perfect for young children. You can replace some of the milk with cream for a richer pudding, and use a wide variety of dried fruits. It keeps well, and makes a great breakfast.

butter, for greasing
80 g (2¾ oz/⅓ cup) basmati rice, unwashed
1 tablespoon sultanas
1 tablespoon finely chopped dried apricots or peaches
375 ml (13 fl oz/1½) cups milk
2 tablespoons maple syrup
1 teaspoon natural vanilla extract
pinch ground cardamom
large pinch ground ginger
large pinch ground cinnamon
poached (see pages 227–229) or baked fruit, to serve

Preheat the oven to 180°C (350°F/Gas 4).

Lightly grease a 15 x 15 x 5 cm (6 x 6 x 2 inch), 750 ml (26 fl oz/3 cup) capacity ceramic baking dish. Sprinkle the rice over the base of the dish, followed by the dried fruit. Place the milk, maple syrup, vanilla and ground cardamom and ginger in a bowl and whisk together. Pour over the rice and sprinkle with the cinnamon. Bake for 40–45 minutes or until the pudding is just firm. Check after 20 minutes—if the top of the pudding is lifting up (the milk will form a skin), then reduce the heat a little. Allow to cool for 10 minutes before serving with poached or baked fruit.

Because I like to serve this with poached fruit , this recipe makes only small puddings.

Quick and simple fruit sponge pudding

WHEAT FREE / DAIRY FREE
Makes 4–6 child serves

I grew up with this old-fashioned pudding and return to it frequently when I want something delicious, quick and light. Use whatever fruit is in season—this version is for apple and berries, but any stewed fruits will work, just substitute the same weight. The important thing here is that the stewed fruits must not be too wet, and to my mind, not overly sweetened, as you have the sweetness in the sponge to consider. My brilliant friend Jeanie bought delicious plums at the farmers' market, chopped them up, sweetened and stewed them, adding a drop or two of pure rose oil. They would be perfect for this pudding. Serve with yoghurt (see page 98), sweetened labne (page 99), cream or coconut cream, if desired.

2 eggs
50 g (1¾ oz) golden caster (superfine) sugar
45 g (1¾ oz) white spelt flour

Fruit base
280 g (10 oz) apples (about 2), peeled, core removed and finely diced
300 g (10½ oz) berries (any or a mix is fine)
1–2 tablespoons maple syrup
1 teaspoon natural vanilla extract
softened butter, for greasing

To make the fruit base Place the fruit, maple syrup and vanilla in a saucepan over low heat. Cover and cook for about 10 minutes or until the fruit has begun to sweat out juices. Remove the lid, increase the heat to medium and cook for another 7–8 minutes or until the juices have reduced and the fruit is tender but still holding its shape. Pour into a lightly greased 23 x 16 x 4 cm (9 x 6¼ x 1½ inch), 1¼ litre (44 fl oz/5 cup) capacity ovenproof baking dish.

Preheat the oven to 180°C (350°F/Gas 4).

Using electric beaters, whisk the eggs and sugar together until thick, pale and doubled in size. When the beaters are lifted, the mixture should hold a trail. Sieve the flour over the egg mixture and use a spatula to fold through.

Pour the batter over the fruit base and bake for 20–30 minutes or until the sponge is golden and springs back when gently touched in the middle with your fingertip. Serve immediately.

 KITCHEN NOTE

It's good to use a baking dish that gives you an even, not-too-deep layer of fruit—the base of the dish should not be narrower than the top. A larger and shallower dish is better than a smaller and deeper dish. You could also easily bake smaller puddings in individual ramekins.

Apple and blueberry crumble bake

WHEAT FREE
Makes 8 good slices

A crumble is one of my favourite ways to have something a little sweet. In this recipe a sturdy pastry supports the filling and gives you a gorgeous slice for a lunchbox, or a wholesome afternoon tea. This is also delicious served hot, with cream.

800 g (1 lb 12 oz) cooking apples, such as granny smith or golden
    delicious, peeled, core removed and cut into chunks
155 g (5½ oz/1 cup) fresh or frozen blueberries
1 teaspoon cornflour (cornstarch), kudzu (kuzu) or true arrowroot
1 teaspoon lemon zest
60 g (2¼ oz/½ cup) white spelt flour
50 g (1¾ oz/½ cup) rolled oats
1 teaspoon ground cinnamon
90 g (3¼ oz/½ cup) rapadura sugar
25 g (1 oz/¼ cup) shredded coconut or 80 g (2¾ oz/½ cup) roughly
    chopped unsalted macadamia nuts
80 g (2¾ oz) cold unsalted butter, chopped

Pastry
100 g (3½ oz/¾ cup) white spelt flour, plus extra for dusting
125 g (4½ oz/¾ cup) wholemeal spelt flour
1 tablespoon golden caster (superfine) sugar
125 g (4½ oz) cold unsalted butter, chopped, plus extra for greasing
½ teaspoon natural vanilla extract

To make the pastry Place the flours and sugar in a bowl and whisk together. Using your fingertips, rub the butter into the flour until the mixture resembles fine breadcrumbs. (You can also use a food processor to do this, then transfer the dough to a bowl.) It is important not to overwork the pastry or it will become tough. Combine the vanilla with 2 tablespoons of chilled water, then, using a butter knife, 'cut' the water into the flour mixture. Use only as much water as you need—some white spelt flours will absorb more liquid than others. Once the mixture looks evenly moist, shape into a disc (don't work it too much), wrap in plastic wrap and chill for 20 minutes, or until cold to the touch.

Place the apple in a saucepan with 60 ml (2 fl oz/¼ cup) of water over medium heat. Cover and cook for 5–6 minutes or until soft but not mushy. Remove from the heat, uncover and allow to stand for a few minutes to cool slightly before adding the berries, cornflour and lemon zest. (If using kudzu, grind to a fine powder before adding.) Stir through gently and set filling aside.

Place the flour, oats, cinnamon, sugar and coconut in a bowl. (If using macadamia nuts, these are to be spread over the crumble just before baking.) Using your fingertips, rub the butter into the mixture until it resembles chunky breadcrumbs. Set crumble topping aside in a cool place.

To assemble Preheat the oven to 190°C (375°F/Gas 5). Lightly grease a 28 x 18 x 4 cm (11¼ x 7 x 1½ inch) baking tin with butter. Lightly dust a surface and rolling pin with as little flour as possible. Roll the pastry out once or twice, then run a palette knife underneath, move the pastry, lightly dust the rolling surface with a little more flour and turn the dough over. Lightly dust the pastry with flour and roll out again. Repeat until the pastry is 3 mm (⅛ inch) thick and will fit the base and sides of the tin. To line the tin, swiftly fold the pastry into four (so it looks like a rectangle) and place one point at the centre of your tin. Unfold and gently fit the pastry into the tin. Trim the edges—they don't need to come up to the top—prick the base of the pastry with a fork and place the tin in the freezer for 5 minutes or so or until the pastry is very firm and cold to the touch.

Place a sheet of baking paper over the pastry, fill with dried beans or pastry weights and bake for 10 minutes. Remove the baking paper and beans, reduce the temperature to 180°C (350°F/Gas 4) and bake for another 8–10 minutes or until dry and light golden.

Spoon the fruit filling into the tart shell and top evenly with the crumble mixture (if using macadamia nuts, sprinkle them on top). Bake for 30 minutes or until the juices are bubbling up the sides and the top is golden. (Check after 20 minutes, and, if the juices are still watery, increase the heat a little for the last 10 minutes.)

Passionfruit, orange and lemon flummery I

GLUTEN FREE / DAIRY FREE
Makes 4–6 child serves

Flummery is a seriously old-fashioned dessert, one of my all time favourites, and brilliant for children. I've given you two versions: this one without gelatine and the next one with. Nutritionally, both have their strengths, but I prefer the performance of this agar-based one. It sets in a fraction of the time and maintains the set out of the fridge—the gelatine-based flummery will start to melt in warmer weather.

125 g (4½ oz/½ cup) passionfruit pulp (from about 6 passionfruit)
185 ml (6 fl oz/¾ cup) orange juice, strained
125 ml (4 fl oz/½ cup) lemon juice, strained
125 ml (4 fl oz/½ cup) agave nectar, or to taste
250 ml (9 fl oz/1 cup) coconut milk
1½ teaspoons agar powder
1 tablespoon kudzu (kuzu) or cornflour (cornstarch)

Strain the passionfruit pulp through a sieve placed over a bowl. Press down with a large spoon to extract as much juice as possible. You will need 80 ml (2½ fl oz/⅓ cup) strained juice. Transfer the passionfruit juice to a saucepan and add the orange and lemon juices, agave nectar and coconut milk, then whisk in the agar powder. Bring to the boil over low heat, stirring frequently to stop the agar from sinking to the bottom and sticking. From the time it comes to the boil, simmer gently, stirring frequently, for 8 minutes. Remove from the heat.

Place the kudzu in a small bowl, add 1 tablespoon of water and mix until smooth. Whisk this into the hot mixture, return the pan to the heat and bring to the boil, stirring continuously. As soon as the mixture comes to the boil, remove from the heat. Pour into a large bowl and stand in a cool place until it looks as if it is starting to set—you want it to still be a little slushy, but have body.

Using an electric beater, beat the mixture at high speed for 10 minutes or until thick and creamy. If it does not thicken, it may need to be chilled in the fridge before continuing. Ladle the mixture into 4–6 ramekins or glasses and refrigerate for 30 minutes or until set. The flummery will keep, covered, in the fridge for up to 4 days.

Passionfruit, orange and lemon flummery II

GLUTEN FREE / DAIRY FREE

Makes 4–6 child serves

125 g (4½ oz/½ cup) passionfruit pulp (from about 6 passionfruit)
1 tablespoon kudzu (kuzu) or cornflour (cornstarch)
185 ml (6 fl oz/¾ cup) orange juice, strained
125 ml (4 fl oz/½ cup) lemon juice, strained
125 ml (4 fl oz/½ cup) agave nectar, or to taste
250 ml (9 fl oz/1 cup) coconut milk
1 tablespoon Bernard Jensen gelatine (see page 63)

Strain the passionfruit pulp through a sieve placed over a bowl. Press down with a large spoon to extract as much juice as possible. You will need 80 ml (2½ fl oz/⅓ cup) strained juice. Transfer the passionfruit juice to a small saucepan, add the kudzu and mix until smooth. Whisk in the remaining ingredients, then place over medium heat and bring to the boil, stirring continuously.

Pour into a large bowl, cool, then refrigerate until it begins to set around the edge and looks very slushy.

Using an electric beater, beat at high speed for 10 minutes or until the mixture is thick and creamy. If it does not thicken, it may need to be chilled in the fridge before continuing. Ladle the mixture into 4–6 ramekins and refrigerate for 3–4 hours or overnight. The flummery will keep, covered, in the fridge for up to 4 days.

CAKES, SLICES AND SWEETS

The following recipes are all simple, down-to-earth treats for everyday use. Because nuts are banned from most schools, I've kept them out of the recipes, but please feel free to add, as desired—they will enrich both the flavour and the nutritional content.

Dried apricot, date and coconut balls

GLUTEN FREE
Makes 22 small balls

This is such a nutrient-dense snack, has no sugar other than what the fruit itself brings, and the dried apricot is rich in iron. The coconut provides a huge amount of immune-boosting lauric acid and energy.

95 g (3¼ oz/¾ cup) dried apricots, roughly chopped
55 g (2 oz/¼ cup) fresh dates, pitted and roughly chopped
185 g (6½ oz/1 cup) coconut butter (spread) (see page 59)
1 tablespoon coconut oil, melted, if required
25 g (1 oz/¼ cup) desiccated coconut

Process the apricots in a food processor until they are finely chopped and beginning to come together. Add the dates and pulse a couple of times, then add the coconut butter and process until combined. Scrape down the sides, if needed and continue to pulse. If the mix does not come together, add the coconut oil and pulse again.

Roll the mixture into small balls, then roll in the coconut and place on a tray lined with baking paper. Leave for 30 minutes to set at room temperature, or in the fridge, if the weather is warm. The balls will keep in an airtight container for up to 2 weeks. Store them in the fridge in hot weather.

Some coconut oils call themselves 'butter'—usually in brackets after the word oil. You can't replace a true coconut butter with oil in this recipe, because it would just melt at body temperature, making the balls fall apart when you pick them up to eat them.

Banana, oat and dried fruit lunchbox slice

WHEAT FREE / DAIRY FREE
Makes 16 slices

This is a delicious, not-too-sweet treat. It's gorgeously chewy. It has a lot of moist fruit in it, so make sure to store it in a cool place or in the fridge when the weather is hot.

1 cup finely chopped dried fruit, including dried figs, apricots and raisins
150 g (5½ oz/1½ cups) rolled oats
130 g (4¾ oz/1 cup) white spelt flour
45 g (1¾ oz/½ cup) desiccated coconut
¼ teaspoon baking powder
350 g (12 oz) bananas (about 2), roughly mashed
125 g (4½ oz) unsalted butter, melted, plus extra for greasing
1 teaspoon natural vanilla extract
60 ml (2 fl oz/¼ cup) rice syrup
60 ml (2 fl oz/¼ cup) maple syrup

Preheat the oven to 180°C (350°F/Gas 4).

Lightly grease a 20 cm (8 inch) square slice tin and line with baking paper.

Place the dried fruit in a small saucepan with 60 ml (2 fl oz/¼ cup) of water. Cover and bring to a gentle boil over low–medium heat. Cook for 1 minute, then remove from the heat and allow to stand for 10 minutes, stirring the fruit occasionally to ensure it is plump and all the water has been absorbed.

Spread the oats on a baking tray and bake for 5 minutes. Remove from the oven and immediately tip into a bowl to stop the cooking process. Add the flour, coconut and baking powder and whisk through to combine. Place the banana, butter, vanilla and syrups in a large bowl, add the dried fruit and combine. Add to the dry ingredients and combine well—you may need to use your hands to press the mixture together. Spoon into the tin, spreading evenly. Bake for 40 minutes or until golden, turning the tin around halfway through cooking. Cool in the tin before slicing. The slice will keep for 3–4 days in an airtight container.

Berry jam and coconut slice

WHEAT FREE
Makes 16 slices

As adults, we often don't want something 'wholesome and wholemeal' for a sweet treat, and this is equally true of children. Too much fibre in a wholegrain flour can also overload their immature digestive system. Traditionally, this slice is made with jam, which I find far too sweet—I prefer it to be fruitier. You can make the filling, as I've suggested here, or substitute with 1 cup not-too-sweet, good-quality fruit spread. Because the jams I make myself are chunky and low-sugar, I will often use those also. Just make sure to spread it thick. Personally, I love this with the macadamia nuts on top, but for school it's just as good without.

Fruity filling
500 g (1 lb 2 oz) fresh or frozen berries
80 ml (2½ fl oz/⅓ cup) maple syrup
1 tablespoon rose water or a couple of drops of pure rose oil

Pastry base
90 g (3¼ oz) unsalted butter, softened
55 g (2 oz/¼ cup) golden caster (superfine) sugar
1 egg
1 teaspoon natural vanilla extract
130 g (4¾ oz/1 cup) white spelt flour

Coconut and macadamia nut topping
2 eggs, lightly beaten
90 g (3¼ oz/1 cup) desiccated coconut
135 g (4¾ oz/1 cup) macadamia nuts, finely chopped
1½ tablespoons golden caster (superfine) sugar

To make the fruity filling Place the berries, maple syrup and rose water in a wide saucepan. Bring to the boil over high heat and cook until the berries have reduced to the consistency of runny jam. Avoid stirring, as you will break down the berries; rather, just give the pan a shake from time to time. Set aside to cool.

Preheat the oven to 180°C (350°F/Gas 4). Grease and line the base of a 20 cm (8 inch) square slice tin with baking paper.

To make the pastry base Using electric beaters, beat the butter and sugar until light and fluffy. Add the egg and vanilla and beat until well combined. Stir in the flour until the mixture comes together. Press the pastry into the base of the tin and bake for 10–15 minutes or until just lightly golden.

To make the coconut and macadamia nut topping While the pastry is baking, place the eggs, coconut, nuts and sugar in a bowl and combine well. Set aside.

To assemble When the base is ready, remove from the oven and gently spoon the berry mixture (or fruit spread) over the top. Gently spread over the topping (I do this by hand) and lightly press it down. Bake for another 10–15 minutes or until lightly golden. Cool in the tin for 15 minutes, then cut into slices and transfer to a wire rack to cool completely. The slice will keep in an airtight container for 2–3 days.

Drop scones

WHEAT FREE
Makes 14

Drop scones are one of my fondest memories of living in New Orleans many years ago. They are generally a little sweeter and have more fat than Australian scones. Served warm with loads of delicious fresh fruit in season, whipped or kefir cream or sweet labne, they are a delicious dessert after a protein-based or salad meal. When baked, they freeze well. You don't need to worry about thawing them before warming in the oven.

130 g (4¾ oz/1 cup) white spelt flour, plus extra flour for dusting
165 g (5¾ oz/1 cup) wholemeal spelt flour
2 tablespoons rapadura sugar
2 teaspoons baking powder
½ teaspoon bicarbonate of (baking) soda
¼–½ teaspoon ground cinnamon
80 ml (2½ fl oz/⅓ cup) coconut oil, chilled
1 tablespoon apple cider vinegar
250 ml (9 fl oz/1 cup) rice milk
½–1 cup fresh fruit, per drop scone, sliced, to serve
maple syrup, whipped or kefir cream (see page 102)
    or sweet labne (see page 99), to serve

Preheat the oven to 200°C (400°F/Gas 6).

Place the flours, sugar, baking powder, bicarbonate of soda and cinnamon in a large bowl. Whisk through to distribute the ingredients evenly. Grate the cold coconut oil into the flour, then, using your fingertips, rub the oil into the flour as quickly as possible (the heat from your hands will melt it rapidly) until the mixture resembles fine breadcrumbs. Alternatively, use a food processor, then transfer the mixture to a bowl.

Combine the vinegar and all but 1 tablespoon of rice milk. Add to the dry ingredients and lightly combine, do not overmix or you will get heavy scones. If the mixture looks dry, add the remaining milk (the dough needs to be very moist).

Turn the dough out onto a lightly floured surface. Using lightly floured hands, shape the dough into a 3 cm (1¼ inch) thick rectangle about 18 x 20 cm (7 x 8 inch). Lightly flour a knife and cut the dough into 14 pieces (the dough should be moist and sticky enough to cling a little to the knife). Using a palette knife, pick the pieces up as best you can (don't worry if they fall out of shape a little—they're not proper scones) and place on a baking tray lined with baking paper.

Bake for 10–15 minutes or until lightly golden and cooked inside. Cool a little on the tray, then turn out onto a wire rack or eat immediately. Split the warm drop scones in half, top with the fruit sweetened with a little maple syrup, and cream or labne. Drop scones are best eaten on the day of baking but will keep for up to 2 days in an airtight container.

Carrot, banana and coconut muffins

WHEAT FREE

Makes 12 muffins / 24 mini-muffins

Simple muffins to put together, these are enriched with seeds and coconut. Banana provides extra sweetness, but you could also use grated apple or pear, skin and all.

130 g (4¾ oz/1 cup) white spelt flour
165 g (5¾ oz/1 cup) wholemeal spelt flour
90 g (3¼ oz/½ cup) rapadura sugar
2½ teaspoons baking powder
½ teaspoon ground cinnamon
45 g (1¾ oz/½ cup) desiccated coconut
1 teaspoon dulse flakes
60 g (2¼ oz/½ cup) pecans or walnuts, roughly ground
30 g (1 oz/¼ cup) sunflower seeds, roughly ground
30 g (1 oz/¼ cup) pumpkin seeds (pepitas), roughly ground
155 g (5½ oz/1 cup) grated carrot
1 banana, cut into small pieces
60 g (2¼ oz/½ cup) sultanas
90 g (3¼ oz) unsalted butter, melted and cooled
1 egg
125 ml (4 fl oz/½ cup) coconut milk
125 g (4½ oz/½ cup) yoghurt (see page 98) or kefir milk (see page 100)
1 teaspoon natural vanilla extract

You can replace 2 tablespoons of wholemeal spelt flour with 2 tablespoons of coconut flour, for added deliciousness.

Preheat the oven to 180°C (350°F/Gas 4). Line the muffin tin with cupcake papers or baking paper cut into squares and pleated to fit.

Place the flours, sugar, baking powder, cinnamon, dessicated coconut, dulse flakes, nuts and seeds in a bowl and whisk through to distribute evenly. Add the carrot, banana and sultanas and gently mix through to evenly distribute.

Place the butter, egg, coconut milk, yoghurt and vanilla in a bowl and beat until just combined. Add to the dry ingredients and mix through, taking care not to overwork the mixture. Allow to stand for 1–2 minutes to absorb some of the liquid.

Spoon the batter into the muffin tins and bake for 30–35 minutes for medium size muffins, and 15–20 minutes for mini-muffins. Cool for 5 minutes in the tins, then turn out and cool on wire racks. Muffins will keep for 2–3 days in an airtight container. You can also freeze baked muffins, then thaw and warm through in a low oven to serve.

◗ VARIATIONS

There are lots of ways to change this recipe to suit your dietary restrictions:

- *Dairy free* Replace the butter with 100 ml (3½ fl oz) macadamia oil or melted coconut oil. Replace the yoghurt with 60 ml (2 fl oz/¼ cup) each rice and coconut milk plus 1 teaspoon apple cider vinegar.
- *Egg free* Add 2 more tablespoons liquid—coconut milk or yoghurt.
- *Gluten free* Replace the flours with 280 g (10 oz/1½ cups) brown rice flour and 40 g (1½ oz/¼ cup) amaranth flour. You will also need to increase your liquids a little—by about 2 tablespoons. If making these egg free also, you will need to use an egg replacement to ensure the mix binds together.
- *Nut free* Omit the nuts and increase seeds to 60 g (2¼ oz/½ cup) each.

Banana, pineapple and coconut cake
with cream cheese frosting

WHEAT FREE
Makes 1 cake / 12 muffins

Banana adds natural sweetness and is an all-round brilliant choice for baking. Again, I've baked this on a large tray, which makes it easy for cutting and slicing, but you can also bake as a cake or muffins.

I like this cake with the addition of 70 g (2½ oz/½ cup) lightly toasted, chopped macadamia nuts. Because most schools don't allow nuts, I've used pineapple instead. Please add macadamias if you'd prefer, even with the pineapple.
If making muffins, they could simply be sprinkled on top with a little coconut, cinnamon and rapadura sugar.

130 g (4¾ oz/1 cup) white spelt flour
165 g (5¾ oz/1 cup) wholemeal spelt flour
½–1 teaspoon ground cinnamon
1½ teaspoons baking powder
45 g (1¾ oz/½ cup) desiccated coconut
2 eggs
180 g (6¼ oz/1 cup) rapadura sugar
125 ml (4 fl oz/½ cup) melted coconut oil or butter,
     plus extra for greasing
1 teaspoon natural vanilla extract
460 g (1 lb ½ oz) ripe bananas (about 3–4), roughly mashed
110 g (3¾ oz/⅔ cup) fresh or tinned pineapple in natural juices,
     drained and cut into small pieces
125 g (4½ oz/½ cup) yoghurt (see page 98)

Cream cheese frosting
250 g (9 oz/1 cup) cream cheese
120 g (4¼ oz) chilled coconut milk (see kitchen notes)
60 ml (2 fl oz/¼ cup) maple syrup
1 teaspoon lime zest
1 teaspoon natural vanilla extract or vanilla bean paste

Preheat the oven to 175°C (340°F/Gas 3–4). Grease a 20 x 30 cm (8 x 12 inch) baking tray and line the base with baking paper.

Place the flours, cinnamon, baking powder and desiccated coconut in a bowl, and whisk through to break up any lumps and distribute the ingredients evenly.

Place the eggs, sugar and coconut oil in a large bowl and, using electric beaters, beat well until light and thick. Stir in the vanilla extract, banana and pineapple, then add the flour mixture and yoghurt and mix together gently until the flour mixture is incorporated. Spoon the batter into the tin.

Bake for 30 minutes or until a skewer inserted into the middle comes out clean. Cool in the tin for 15 minutes before turning out onto a wire rack to cool completely.

To make the cream cheese frosting Place all the ingredients in a bowl, and using electric beaters, beat until creamy and smooth. Cover and place in the fridge to firm a little before using, but take care not to leave it too long or it will be too hard. If this happens, just leave it out at room temperature until it returns to the desired consistency. When the cake has cooled, ice with frosting.

 KITCHEN NOTES

- *To chill the coconut milk, place a tin of coconut milk in the fridge or freezer until the creamy part of the milk has firmed up—there will be a clear separation of solid milk (cream) and watery liquid. Spoon this solid portion from the can until you have 120 g (4¼ oz). The remainder can be kept and used for smoothies. Bear in mind that the coconut milk must be full strength (not 'light'), and not stabilised.*
- *A 22 cm (8½ inch) cake (baked in a springform cake tin) will cook in 40–45 minutes; muffins in 25–30 minutes; and mini-muffins in 15 minutes.*

Apple and fig tray bake

Makes 24 slices

Not much beats a simple apple cake. I've baked this in a large tray, which makes it easy for cutting and slicing. You can just as easily use this mixture to make muffins or a round cake. For extra deliciousness, sprinkle the top with chopped pecans before baking.

500 g (1 lb 2 oz) red or green apples (about 4), peeled, cores removed and finely diced
3–5 dried figs, finely chopped
130 g (4¾ oz/1 cup) white spelt flour
165 g (5¾ oz/1 cup) wholemeal spelt flour
large pinch ground nutmeg
2½ teaspoons baking powder
2 teaspoons ground cinnamon
125 g (4½ oz) unsalted butter, melted and cooled
180 g (6¼ oz/1 cup) rapadura sugar, plus 1 teaspoon extra
1 teaspoon natural vanilla extract
2 large eggs
125 g (4½ oz/½ cup) yoghurt (see page 98) or kefir milk (see page 100)
120 g (4¼ oz/1 cup) pecans, walnuts or hazelnuts, roughly chopped (optional)

Preheat the oven to 180°C (350°F/Gas 4). Grease a 20 x 30 cm (8 x 12 inch) baking tray and line the base with baking paper.

Place one-quarter of the apple in a small saucepan with 2 tablespoons of water. Cover and simmer over low heat for 3–5 minutes or until well cooked. Remove from the heat, roughly mash, then stir in the dried figs. Set aside to cool.

Place the flours, nutmeg, baking powder and 1 teaspoon of cinnamon in a bowl and whisk through to distribute the ingredients evenly and break up any lumps. Stir in the remaining apple.

Place the butter and sugar in a bowl, and using electric beaters, whisk until light and fluffy. Add the vanilla and eggs, one at a time, beating well after each addition, until thick and creamy. Add to the flour mixture along with the cooled stewed fruit and yoghurt and stir until just combined. Take care not to overwork the mixture. Spoon the batter into the tin. Combine the extra teaspoon of sugar and remaining cinnamon and sprinkle over the top, and the nuts, if using.

Bake for 30 minutes or until a skewer inserted in the middle comes out clean. Cool a little in the tin before slicing.

 KITCHEN NOTE

If you wish to make a cake, bake in a 22 cm (8½ inch) springform cake tin in a preheated 180°C (350°F/Gas 4) oven for 1 hour.

CELEBRATIONS

*Our children are a gift and a blessing.
We are reminded of this as we
celebrate a christening or naming
ceremony, and subsequently
each birthday.*

Joy and delight

IN THE BEGINNING OF THIS BOOK, I talked about how everything we do in the early years of a child's life affects their ability to understand and experience life.

However, experiencing a life is far more than learning to read, add and write; indeed, Thomas Aquinas would say that 'Joy, is a human's noblest act'—I have to agree.

When we celebrate, we invite joy into our lives. At baby's first and second birthdays, the celebration and the foods eaten will be orientated more towards the adults. From three onwards, though, the food focus shifts towards what the child will enjoy—and there is no reason this food has to include refined or sugar- and additive-laden options. There is an enormous misperception that these are treat foods, which is a hangover from the days when fizzy drinks and sweet treats were to be enjoyed every now and then. But back then, they were still real—slightly refined, but real. This is not the case today and by gracing these foods with the aura of 'treat', you enhance their status and desirability in a child's eye. You certainly don't need the manufactured colours in drinks and lollies to delight children—nature's palette is vast and beautiful.

Celebration cakes

NOTHING DEFINES A CELEBRATION MORE THAN A CAKE. When it comes to a christening or birthday cake, I like to relax the rules a little and choose lighter ingredients than usual, but as little refined as possible. A heavy, dense wholemeal cake is not necessarily a healthier cake and can often be overwhelming for young children. From a good base you can build or create cakes that are limited only by your imagination—my daughter always had a firm idea of what she wanted, from a meat-eating dinosaur cake (which says something about the fact I wouldn't let her have meat when she was little, I'm sure!) to a Lost City of Gold cake (from a TV cartoon series) and, when she was a little older, a cake based on the wedding cakes I used to make with a white chocolate butter cream. It's a beautiful feeling to know she remembers those cakes to this day and that cakes for celebration and birthdays have become part of her food culture.

The basic cake recipes that follow will provide a sturdy crumb for cutting and building—for example a butterfly or frog—yet also make a delicious cake or cupcakes. They keep and freeze well. I've used spelt, as its gluten structure and good water-solubility makes it easier to digest. When making a cake the day before, allow it to cool completely before wrapping well and storing it in an airtight container (as much as I dislike it, plastic wrap is perfect for this job). When making a cake further ahead, cool and wrap it, as described, and freeze it. Allow it to thaw in the fridge before you use it.

Remember that oven temperature has a huge impact on baking a good cake. If your oven is fan-forced, you may need to reduce the temperature by 20°C (68°F) or so lower than indicated in the recipes. My fan-forced oven bakes these cakes at 150°C (300°F/Gas 2) and 140°C (275°F/Gas 1) for the genoise patty cakes.

Genoise sponge cake

WHEAT FREE
Serves 8–12

This basic cake is well worth perfecting and is best described as a sturdy sponge. If making the day before, place in an airtight container or wrap once it is cool. If your child is gluten free, this is one of the rare occasions I would suggest you buy and use a gluten-free flour mix—while they're not the most nourishing of mixes, it will give you a soft and light cake.

 4 eggs, at room temperature
 100 g (3½ oz/½ cup) golden caster (superfine) sugar
 1 teaspoon natural vanilla extract
 130 g (4¾ oz/1 cup) white spelt flour (see kitchen notes)
 40 g (1½ oz) unsalted butter, melted and cooled

Preheat the oven to 180°C (350°F/Gas 4). Grease and line the base and side of a 22 cm (8½ inch) round cake tin with baking paper.

Using electric beaters, whisk the eggs and sugar until thick and creamy and tripled in volume. The mixture is ready when you can lift the beaters and the mixture falls back into the bowl in a ribbon that rests on the surface for about 10 seconds. Add the vanilla during the last moments of whisking.

Sift one-third of the flour over the mixture and gently fold through—I like to use a whisk. Stop as soon as the flour looks incorporated. Fold in the remaining flour in two more additions, holding back 1 tablespoon. You won't be using this flour and can return it to the packet.

Place the butter in a small bowl, then gently fold in about 1 cup of batter. Add this back to the cake mixture and gently fold through. Take care not to overmix. Pour into the prepared cake tin.

Bake for 20–25 minutes or until the centre springs back when lightly touched and the cake is coming away from the sides. If the cake is browning too quickly and not ready, reduce the oven temperature and continue cooking.

Allow to cool completely in the tin, then turn out onto a wire rack.

Ice with your choice of icing or frosting, as desired (see pages 305–308). The cake will keep for 2 days in an airtight container and freezes brilliantly.

🫖 KITCHEN NOTES

- *Even if you have a lovely white spelt flour with no bran and germ, weigh the amount of flour needed rather than relying on the cup measurement. This is because the weight of white spelt flours varies between brands—1 cup could actually weigh 140 g (5 oz), which would be too heavy for this recipe. Remember, you will still need to hold back 1 tablespoon from your flour once weighed.*

- *However, if your white spelt flour looks more like a light wholemeal, I recommend sifting 165 g (5¾ oz/1¼ cups) in a fine sieve. This will catch most of the germ and bran, which you can discard. Measure 130 g (4¾ oz/1 cup) from this sifted flour. Remember, you will still need to hold back 1 tablespoon from your flour once weighed.*

- *This recipe makes one 22 cm (8½ inch) round cake, which will relax to 3½ cm (1¼ inches) when cooled. Cut in half horizontally, this is a good depth for a child's cake.*

- *This recipe makes one 20 cm (8 inch) round cake, which will relax to 5 cm (2 inches) when cooled. It will take 30–35 minutes to cook.*

- *This recipe makes one 27 x 18 x 4 cm (10¾ x 7 x 1½ inch) rectangular cake, which will relax to about 3 cm (1¼ inches) when cooled and is good for layering.*

- *To make a three-tiered 22 cm (8½ inch) round cake, you will need to double the mixture and divide it between three 22 cm (8½ inch) cake tins.*

- *This recipe makes 10–12 cupcakes. Bake for 25–30 minutes. Cupcakes (and patty cakes) also need to cool completely before turning out.*

- *Half of this recipe makes 12 small patty cakes for jelly cakes (see page 312). Spoon about 1 generous tablespoon of batter into patty cake tins and bake for 20 minutes.*

Classic butter cake

WHEAT FREE
Serves 8–12

This is my version of a classic butter cake, using white spelt flour and a reduced amount of a less-refined sugar. It's a very good cake and will give you a moist yet sturdy crumb, which will last very well. This is the kind of cake to keep in a tin, ready for lunches or afternoon teas. You could flavour the cake with citrus zest.

260 g (9¼ oz/2 cups) white spelt flour (see kitchen notes)
1½ teaspoons baking powder
250 g (9 oz) unsalted butter, softened, plus extra for greasing
170 g (6 oz) golden caster (superfine) or golden raw (demerara) sugar
4 eggs, at room temperature
2 teaspoons natural vanilla extract
60–125 ml (2–4 fl oz/¼–½ cup) milk

Preheat the oven to 170°C (325°F/Gas 3). Grease the base and side of a 22 cm (8½ inch) round cake tin and line with baking paper.

Sift the flour and baking powder into a bowl and set aside.

Using electric beaters, beat the butter and sugar until pale, light and fluffy. Add the eggs, one at a time, beating well after each addition. If the mix begins to split and look curdled, it is because it has become too cold to incorporate the eggs. A good trick is to place the mixing bowl in a little warm water for a few minutes —this will soften the butter again and allow it to absorb the eggs. Add the vanilla and beat well.

Add the sifted flour mixture and 60 ml (2 fl oz/¼ cup) of milk and gently beat in—if using electric beaters, begin very slowly to prevent the flour going everywhere. Beat until smooth and the flour and milk are well incorporated. Only add the extra milk if the mix is very heavy (this will generally be because of the presence of bran and germ from the flour). Spoon into the tin.

It is very important that the butter is soft—the consistency should be similar to that of a face cream. The main technique used to raise the cake in this recipe is by beating air into the butter and sugar, and for this you need a soft (but not melted) butter. I use an unrefined golden caster sugar for this cake, but you could also use the slightly larger grained unrefined golden raw sugar.

Bake for 1 hour or until a skewer inserted into the middle comes out clean. Cool in the tin for 30 minutes, then transfer to a wire rack to cool completely. It will shrink a little and deflate which is normal.

Ice with your choice of icing or frosting, as desired (see pages 305–308). The un-iced cake will keep in an airtight container for up to 5 days.

🫖 KITCHEN NOTES

- *Even if you have a lovely white spelt flour with no bran and germ, weigh the amount of flour needed rather than relying on the cup measurement. This is because the weight of white spelt flours varies between brands—1 cup could actually weigh 140 g (5 oz), which would be too heavy for this recipe.*

- *However, if your white spelt flour looks more like a light wholemeal, I recommend sifting 325 g (11½ oz/2½ cups) in a fine sieve. This will catch most of the germ and bran, which you can discard. Measure 260 g (9¼ oz/2 cups) from this sifted flour.*

- *This recipe makes one 22 cm (8½ inch) round cake. Cut in half horizontally, this is a good depth for a child's cake.*

- *This recipe makes 9–12 cupcakes. Bake for 25–30 minutes.*

Vanilla and coconut cupcakes

WHEAT FREE / CAN BE DAIRY FREE / EGG FREE

Makes 12

This is the recipe I turn to when a dairy- and egg-free cake is needed—it will give you a well-textured and moist crumb. It's extremely flexible and keeps and freezes well. If your child can tolerate butter or ghee, I'd suggest using those—it will be more nourishing. The creamy chocolate and coconut frosting (see page 308) is a perfect dairy-free match for this cake, and looks especially pretty when used on cupcakes.

195 g (7 oz/1½ cups) white spelt flour (see kitchen notes)
1 teaspoon baking powder
¾ teaspoon bicarbonate of (baking) soda
45 g (1¾ oz/½ cup) desiccated coconut
2 teaspoons apple cider vinegar
2 teaspoons natural vanilla extract
185 ml (6 fl oz/¾ cup) maple syrup
125 ml (4 fl oz/½ cup) coconut milk
60 ml (2 fl oz/¼ cup) rice milk
80 ml (2½ fl oz/⅓ cup) almond oil, macadamia nut oil, melted butter
or ghee (see page 107), plus extra, for greasing

Preheat the oven to 180°C (350°F/Gas 4). Lightly grease a 12-hole muffin tin.

Sift the flour, baking powder and bicarbonate of soda into a bowl, add the desiccated coconut and whisk through.

In a separate bowl, place the vinegar, vanilla, maple syrup, coconut and rice milks and almond oil and mix together. Add to the dry ingredients and mix until just combined. Allow to stand for 1–2 minutes—the mixture will look wet but will firm up as it stands. Spoon into the muffin tin.

Bake for 25–30 minutes or until a skewer inserted into one of the muffins comes out clean. Cool in the tin for 20 minutes, before transferring to a wire rack to cool completely.

Ice with your choice of icing or frosting, as desired (see pages 305–308). The un-iced cupcakes will keep for 3 days in an airtight container. In warmer weather, they should be stored in the fridge.

KITCHEN NOTES

- *Even if you have a lovely white spelt flour with no bran and germ, weigh the amount of flour needed rather than relying on the cup measurement. This is because the weight of white spelt flours varies between brands—1½ cups could actually weigh 210 g (7½ oz), which would be too heavy for this recipe.*

- *I prefer to use a white spelt here, but the recipe will cope even if the white spelt has a little bit of germ and bran in it. It will be slightly heavier and the crumb won't be as fine. For a better crumb or if your white spelt flour looks quite hefty, almost like a light wholemeal, I suggest sifting 260 g (9¼ oz/2 cups) flour in a fine sieve. This will catch most of the germ and bran, which you can discard. Measure 195 g (7 oz/1½ cups) from the sifted flour.*

- *This recipe makes about 12 cupcakes or 20 mini cupcakes.*

- *This recipe makes one 20 cm (8 inch) round cake. Once cut in half and iced, this will give you a lovely tall cake.*

- *To make a three-tiered 20 cm (8 inch) round cake, you will need to double the mixture and divide it between three 20 cm (8 inch) cake tins.*

- *To make a 24 cm (9½ inch) round cake, you will need to double the mixture. Cut in half and iced, this will give you a lovely tall cake.*

VARIATIONS

- *Nut free* Replace the almond oil with melted butter or ghee. You can also use coconut oil—the cake will be lovely while still fresh, but the crumb will toughen and constrict a little when it has sat for some time or been refrigerated.

- *Adding an egg* This firms up the crumb and makes the cake more sturdy for building—if you are making, for example, a themed cake, such as a train. Replace the rice milk with 1 egg.

Chocolate and coconut cupcakes

WHEAT FREE / CAN BE DAIRY FREE / EGG FREE
Makes 8–12

This variation of the vanilla and coconut cupcakes (see page 298) is ideal for chocolate lovers.

130 g (4¾ oz/1 cup) white spelt flour, plus 1½ tablespoons, extra
    (see kitchen notes)
40 g (1½ oz) unsweetened Dutch-processed cocoa powder
¾ teaspoon bicarbonate of (baking) soda
45 g (1¾ oz/½ cup) desiccated coconut
2 teaspoons apple cider vinegar
2 teaspoons natural vanilla extract
185 ml (6 fl oz/¾ cup) maple syrup
125 ml (4 fl oz/½ cup) coconut milk
80 ml (2½ fl oz/⅓ cup) almond oil, macadamia oil,
    melted butter or ghee (see page 107)
30 g (1 oz/¼ cup) fresh or frozen raspberries
    (if frozen, thawed, drained and juice discarded)

Preheat the oven to 180°C (350°F/Gas 4). Lightly grease a 12-hole muffin tin.

Sift the flour, cocoa and bicarbonate of soda into a bowl. Add the desiccated coconut and whisk through to distribute evenly.

In a separate bowl, place the vinegar, vanilla, maple syrup, coconut milk and almond oil and mix together. Add to the dry ingredients and mix until just combined, then gently fold the raspberries through. Allow to stand for 1–2 minutes—the mixture will look wet but will firm up as it stands. Spoon into the muffin tin.

Bake for 25–30 minutes or until a skewer inserted into one of the muffins comes out clean. Cool in the tin for 20 minutes, before transferring to a wire rack to cool completely. Ice with your choice of icing or frosting, as desired (see pages 305–308). The un-iced cupcakes will keep for 3 days in an airtight container. In warmer weather, they should be stored in the fridge.

KITCHEN NOTES

- *Even if you have a lovely white spelt flour with no bran and germ, weigh the amount of flour needed rather than relying on the cup measurement. This is because the weight of white spelt flours varies between brands—1 cup could actually weigh 140 g (5 oz), which would be too heavy for this recipe.*

- *I prefer to use a white spelt here, but the recipe will cope even if the white spelt has a little bit of germ and bran in it. It will be slightly heavier and the crumb won't be as fine. For a better crumb or if your white spelt flour looks quite hefty, almost like a light wholemeal, I suggest sifting 165 g (5¾ oz/1¼ cups) flour in a fine sieve. This will catch most of the germ and bran, which you can discard. Measure 130 g (4¾ oz/1 cup) from the sifted flour.*

- *This recipe makes about 12 cupcakes or 20 mini cupcakes.*

- *This recipe makes one 20 cm (8 inch) round cake. Once cut in half and iced, this will give you a lovely tall cake.*

- *To make a three-tiered 20 cm (8 inch) round cake, you will need to double the mixture and divide it between three 20 cm (8 inch) cake tins.*

- *To make a 24 cm (9½ inch) round cake, you will need to double the mixture. Cut in half and iced, this will give you a lovely tall cake.*

VARIATIONS

- *Nut free* Replace the almond oil with melted butter or ghee. You can also use coconut oil—the cake will be lovely while still fresh, but the crumb will toughen and constrict a little when it has sat for some time or been in the fridge.

- *Adding an egg* This will firm up the crumb and make the cake sturdier. Replace the raspberries with 1 egg.

Gluten-free chocolate cake

Serves 8–12

This is a beautifully moist but sturdy chocolate cake. It will keep and freeze well.

160 g (5¾ oz/1 cup) brown rice flour
30 g (1 oz/¼ cup) true arrowroot
90 g (3¼ oz/½ cup) desiccated coconut
40 g (1½ oz) unsweetened Dutch-processed cocoa powder (see glossary)
¾ teaspoon bicarbonate of (baking) soda
2 teaspoons apple cider vinegar
2 teaspoons natural vanilla extract
185 ml (6 fl oz/¾ cup) maple syrup
125 ml (4 fl oz/½ cup) coconut milk
1 egg
80 ml (2½ fl oz/⅓ cup) melted butter or ghee (see page 107),
    plus extra, for greasing

Preheat the oven to 180°C (350°F/Gas 4). Grease the base and side of a 20 cm (8 inch) round cake tin and line with baking paper.

Place the rice flour, arrowroot and desiccated coconut in a bowl. Sift the cocoa and bicarbonate of soda into the bowl, then whisk through to combine.

Place the vinegar, vanilla, maple syrup, coconut milk and egg in a bowl and whisk to combine well. Add to the dry ingredients and stir until just combined. Allow to stand for 1–2 minutes—the mixture will look wet but will firm up as it stands. Pour into the prepared tin.

Bake for 35–40 minutes or until a skewer inserted into the middle comes out clean. Cool in tin for 20 minutes, before transferring to a wire rack to cool completely. Ice with your choice of icing or frosting, as desired (see pages 305–308). The un-iced cake will keep for 3 days in an airtight container. In warmer weather, this should be stored in the fridge.

⬡ *This recipe makes one 20 cm (8 inch) round cake. Once cut in half and iced, this will give you a lovely tall cake.*

⬡ *This recipes makes one 20 x 20 x 4 cm (8 x 8 x 1½ inch) square cake—this will relax to 2½ cm (1 inch) when cooled and is good for layering.*

⬡ *This recipe makes 9–12 cupcakes and about 20 mini cupcakes. Bake cupcakes for 30 minutes and mini cupcakes for 15–20 minutes.*

⬡ *To make a three-tiered 20 cm (8 inch) round cake, you will need to double the mixture and divide it between three 20 cm (8 inch) cake tins.*

⬡ *To make a 24 cm (9½ inch) round cake, you will need to double the mixture. Cut in half and iced, this will give you a lovely tall cake.*

🫖 VARIATIONS

⬡ *Egg free* You can omit the egg in this recipe, but the batter won't be as sturdy. It will make beautiful cupcakes, though. Replace the egg with 30 g (1 oz/¼ cup) raspberries—if frozen, thaw, drain and discard the juice. Fold the raspberries through the batter before pouring into the cake tin.

⬡ *Dairy free* You can replace the melted butter or ghee with almond or macadamia nut oil. You can also use coconut oil—the cake will be lovely while still fresh, but the crumb will toughen and constrict a little after sitting or if it has been in the fridge.

⬡ *Princess cake* Raspberries are the most beautiful match with this cake. For a stunning and delicious celebration cake, halve the cake horizontally, spread crème fraîche over the base and top with fresh raspberries (or raspberry jam). Sandwich with the other half and ice the side and top with raspberry buttercream (see page 307). You will need 1 quantity of buttercream for this. If making cupcakes, pipe the buttercream over, or split the cupcakes to make butterfly cakes and fill with the buttercream.

Passionfruit cake

Serves 8–12

Passionfruit is a beautiful match for the genoise sponge cake, giving it a luscious but light flavour and colour.

90 g (3¼ oz/⅓ cup) passionfruit pulp (from about 7 small passionfruit)
2 tablespoons golden caster (superfine) sugar or maple syrup, or to taste
1 genoise sponge cake (see page 294)
1 quantity passionfruit buttercream (see page 307)

Place the passionfruit pulp in a small saucepan and taste before adding any sweetener—some passionfruit will be sweeter than others. Add the sweetener to taste and simmer over low heat for 5–6 minutes to dissolve the sugar and reduce a little. Take care not to reduce the mixture too much. Set aside to cool. The jam will thicken as it cools.

To assemble When the sponge cake is perfectly cool, you will need to assess it. If the top is uneven with a noticeable dome, use a serrated knife to carefully cut the top off to give an even surface. (These extra bits never go to waste and are a yummy treat.)

Halve the cake horizontally. Remove the top half and set it aside. Place the bottom half on a cake stand and, using a palette knife, spread with the jam. Top with ⅔ cup of the buttercream and, using a clean palette knife, spread it over evenly. Gently sandwich with the other cake half. Spread a thin layer of buttercream around the side and over the top of the cake. This is your base icing layer (or crumb coat) and provides an even surface for the rest of the icing. Place in the fridge to chill.

When the icing layer is firm, finish icing the cake with the buttercream.

ICINGS AND FROSTINGS

Icings and frostings dress up a cake and they also add moistness. The following use either maple syrup or golden icing sugar which provides less sweet, yet still delicious, results. Using golden icing sugar will tint the icing a soft beige, which can make colouring difficult. I use natural fruit and vegetable-based commercial food colourings, but you can also make your own. They tend to tint the icing softly rather than giving the opaque, bright colours you may be used to, but there are other ways you can bring colour into a cake, such as using ribbons and paper.

All the recipes in this section will ice or frost 12 cupcakes, or one 20–22 cm (8–8½ inch) round or square cake. If you need extra to fill a cake, or to ice a larger cake, double the recipe.

Quick and simple butter icing

GLUTEN FREE

This is a classic butter icing—quick to make, and always delivers great results. If you want a less sugary icing, try the better buttercream (see page 306).

    125 g (4½ oz) unsalted butter, softened (see kitchen note)
    560 g (1 lb 4 oz/3 cups) golden icing (confectioner's) sugar, sifted
    60 ml (2 fl oz/¼ cup) milk
    1 teaspoon natural vanilla extract
    1 teaspoon lemon juice

Beat the butter, icing sugar and milk using electric beaters on low speed until the mixture comes together. Increase the speed to medium and beat for 3–4 minutes or until the mixture is smooth, thick and creamy. Add the vanilla, lemon juice and flavouring, if desired, and beat until smooth.

 KITCHEN NOTE
- *The butter must be very soft, with the texture of face cream—this will enable you to achieve a light result. Because this icing has a butter base, it is very flexible. You can incorporate flavours into it, such as raspberry purée, lemon, citrus zest, rose water and passionfruit.*

 VARIATION
- Replace the cow's milk with coconut milk.

Better buttercream

GLUTEN FREE

This is the icing I turn to for special occasions as it always gives a reliable, delicious result. It has a beautiful cream colour, and is incredibly flexible—taking on natural flavours and colours with ease. When made with raspberries, it is the prettiest pink and so tasty. When made with passionfruit, it has a soft glow and a fresh, light passionfruit flavour. When made with white chocolate, it is simply divine.

Buttercream icing can be very rich, but it is one of the best. This icing is based on New York's famous Magnolia Bakery's vanilla buttercream, but I use a thickened milk mixture to reduce the amount of butter. I've played with it a little to suit my needs—a less rich milk, more coconut, lime or raspberry to cut the sweetness and a less refined sugar. All in all, it's delicious and nowhere near as rich.

I like to add a little lemon or lime juice to this to balance out the sweetness.

1 tablespoon cornflour (cornstarch)
60 ml (2 fl oz/¼ cup) rice milk
60 ml (2 fl oz/¼ cup) coconut milk
125 g (4½ oz) unsalted butter, softened
95 g (3¼ oz/½ cup) golden icing (confectioner's) sugar, sifted
2 teaspoons natural vanilla extract or 1 teaspoon vanilla bean paste
2 teaspoons lemon or lime juice

Place the cornflour in a small saucepan, add the rice milk and stir until smooth, then add the coconut milk. Place over medium heat and cook, stirring continuously, until boiling and thickened. Spoon into a small bowl and press some baking paper directly onto the surface to prevent a skin from forming. Cool to room temperature, then refrigerate until cool.

Using electric beaters, beat the butter until it is light and fluffy, then add the icing sugar and beat for a few more minutes or until well combined. Add the cooled milk mixture, vanilla and lime juice and beat for another 2–3 minutes or until the icing is beautifully smooth and fluffy.

Place in the fridge to set just a little before using, but don't leave it too long or the butter will set hard. If the icing has become too firm to use, let it sit at room temperature to soften before using. In winter, the cool air from the beaters may begin to set the butter, so you might need to use a little more coconut milk (about 1 tablespoon) to bring it to a good consistency for spreading or piping.

VARIATIONS

- *Passionfruit buttercream* Scoop the pulp from 2–4 passionfruit, depending on their size, into a sieve placed over a small bowl. Press down with the back of a large spoon to extract as much juice as possible—you will need 2 tablespoons of passionfruit juice. Omit the lime juice from the recipe and use only 1 teaspoon vanilla extract. Stir 1 tablespoon of passionfruit juice, the cooled milk mixture and vanilla into the butter mixture and beat for 2–3 minutes or until smooth and fluffy, adding the remaining passionfruit juice, if necessary, to bring to desired consistency.

- *Raspberry buttercream* Put 90 g (3¼ oz/¾ cup) of raspberries in a fine sieve and place over a bowl. (If using frozen raspberries, thaw them first in a sieve placed over a small bowl and discard the juices.) Using the back of a spoon, push the raspberries through the sieve to make a lovely purée. You will need 3 tablespoons of purée. Discard the seeds and pulp. Omit the lime juice from the recipe. Stir 2 tablespoons of the purée, the cooled milk mixture and vanilla into the butter mixture and beat for 2–3 minutes or until smooth and fluffy, adding the remaining purée, if necessary, for extra flavour or to bring to desired consistency.

- *White chocolate buttercream* Place 100 g (3½ oz) good-quality white chocolate (I use Green & Black's) in a heatproof bowl placed over a saucepan of just-simmering water and melt until smooth. Reduce the quantity of lime juice to 1 teaspoon. When the icing is smooth and fluffy, add the warm melted chocolate. Continue to beat until the chocolate is well incorporated.

Creamy chocolate and coconut frosting

DAIRY FREE

This is a rich and delicious frosting, which can be made ahead of time, as it keeps well and even freezes. It's perfect for spreading and piping. I use Dagoba Chocodrops, which are 73 per cent cocoa solids, are free of soy lecithin, and are made with rapadura sugar. You can soften the taste and intensity of the icing by using a chocolate with less cocoa solids—you may prefer something lighter, around 60 per cent.

150 ml (5 fl oz) coconut milk
1½ teaspoons agar powder
3 teaspoons cornflour (cornstarch)
30 g (1 oz/¼ cup) unsweetened Dutch-processed cocoa powder (see glossary)
185 ml (6 fl oz/¾ cup) maple syrup
½ teaspoon natural vanilla extract
50 g (1¾ oz) dairy-free dark chocolate, roughly chopped

Place 125 ml (4 fl oz/½ cup) of coconut milk in a saucepan and whisk in the agar powder. Place over medium heat and bring to the boil, stirring frequently to prevent the agar sticking to the bottom. When the mixture comes to the boil, reduce the heat to low and simmer, stirring frequently, for 6–7 minutes.

Meanwhile, place the cornflour in a small bowl with the remaining coconut milk and mix to a smooth paste.

Remove the agar mixture from the heat, whisk in the cocoa and maple syrup, then add the cornflour mixture and whisk to combine well. Return the pan to the heat and bring to the boil, stirring constantly. The mixture will thicken and lose its cloudy look when the mixture starts to boil.

Remove from the heat, add the vanilla and chocolate and stir until melted and smooth. Pour into a bowl, leave to cool for 15 minutes, then refrigerate for 1 hour or until set. Process the mixture in a blender or food processor until smooth and silky. Transfer to a bowl, cover and refrigerate until ready to use.

Party food

PLEASE DON'T TURN TO HIGHLY REFINED AND JUNK FOOD to make your celebration special. This doesn't mean it has to be boring—it absolutely shouldn't be boring—it's party time! Let your imagination run away with you, and relax the rules a little. Remember, true deliciousness (and all its gifts) will come from the real and incredibly beautiful colours and flavours of nature.

Popcorn with sea salt

GLUTEN FREE
Makes 4½ cups

Popcorn is so easy to make at home, and gives you a yummy, wholesome snack. Many people ask me if popcorn is similar to a puffed or crispy flaked breakfast cereal, which is subject to extremely high pressure and temperature, and which can be profoundly damaging. It isn't—the temperature used to popcorn is nothing like that used for the puffing and flaking processes. It is, however, high enough to warrant the use of a very stable fat—coconut oil is perfect.

1 tablespoon coconut oil
50 g (1¾ oz/¼ cup) popcorn kernels
butter or coconut oil, melted, to taste

Place the coconut oil in a deep saucepan with 4–5 popcorn kernels. Place over a medium–high heat and when the kernels begin to pop, add the remaining kernels. Cover and shake the pan so all the kernels are coated in the oil, then continue cooking, shaking the pan every now and then until you can't hear anymore popping sounds. Tip into a large bowl and discard any unpopped kernels. Pour the butter over the popped corn and season to taste with sea salt.

For popping corn, you need a large, deep, heavy-based saucepan with a lid, but be wary of cast-iron as it can get too hot. A saucepan with a glass lid is great, because you can see what's happening. The kernels should fit in a single layer in the base of the pan.

Caramel nut popcorn

GLUTEN FREE
Makes 5 cups

Not only for parties, these are perfect for a movie night at home or packed to travel. They store well in an airtight container.

80 ml (2½ fl oz/⅓ cup) rice syrup
2 tablespoons maple syrup
50 g (1¾ oz/⅓ cup) raw peanuts, skins rubbed off
1 quantity popcorn, no added salt (see page 309)

Preheat the oven to 180°C (350°F/Gas 4). Line a baking tray with baking paper.

Warm the rice syrup a little in a saucepan over low heat, so that it just flows, and mix together with the maple syrup and peanuts. Pour the mixture over the popcorn and mix together well until the popcorn is evenly coated. Spread the popcorn mix evenly on the baking tray.

Bake, stirring often, for 10–20 minutes or until lightly golden. Remove from the oven, taking care as the caramel will be very hot. Set aside to cool only until you can touch the popcorn mix—if you leave it too long, it will become too brittle. Spoon the popcorn into a large bowl, breaking it up as you go.

VARIATION

Caramel nut popcorn balls Once the baked popcorn has cooled slightly, pick it up in clumps and gently form it into small balls. Place on a tray lined with baking paper and leave to cool. They will crisp as they cool.

Jelly boats

GLUTEN FREE / DAIRY FREE
Makes 8

These are always popular at a birthday party and easy for children to hold and manage. You could make a couple of different coloured jellies (strawberry or raspberry would be good) to add more colour to the table.

2 small–medium oranges
375 ml (13 fl oz/1½ cups) good-quality fruit juice,
    such as passionfruit, mango or apple
sweetener, such as maple syrup or agave nectar, to taste
1¼ teaspoons agar powder
2–3 sheets edible rice paper
toothpicks

I like to use a mixture of orange and one other juice, such as passionfruit, mango or apple to make the jelly. Alternatively, you can keep the orange juice for drinking and use whatever juice appeals. Agar powder is used to give the jelly a nice firm set which the little boats will need when cut.

Cut the oranges in half, then squeeze the orange halves and strain the juice. Carefully remove the remaining orange pulp from the orange halves, taking care not to make holes in the skin. Place the orange halves upright in a muffin tin.

Pour the juice from the oranges into a measuring cup and add your other juice of choice to make up 500 ml (17 fl oz/2 cups) of liquid. Pour into a saucepan and taste, addding sweetener, as desired. Whisk the agar powder into the juice and bring to the boil over low heat, stirring frequently to prevent the agar sticking to the bottom. When it comes to the boil, reduce the heat to very low and simmer gently, stirring frequently, for another 7–8 minutes or until the agar is dissolved.

Remove from the heat and allow to cool for a few minutes, then pour into the orange halves, filling them as full as possible. Leave to cool until they are beginning to set, then refrigerate until firm.

Remove the orange halves from the muffin tin and cut in half. To make the sails, cut the rice paper into small triangles and pierce with the toothpicks, then stand upright in the jelly boats.

Jelly cakes

Makes 12

Dipped in jelly and coated in coconut, these old-fashioned cakes are always a big hit. Without icing, they are less rich and a great option for younger children. You can make them any shape or size you like—either as a small lamington, mini cupcake or, as I prefer, a small flattish cake baked in a patty cake tin. I make mine with a pure fruit jelly, thick with the fruit itself—it's a bit trickier to handle, but the extra flavour is worth it. When I was a child, Mum used to cut the middle out of these, add a dollop of cream, then cut the little bit in half and set the pieces into the cream as butterfly wings. Yum. I prefer to make these with agar rather than gelatine, as they are sturdier at room temperature, but I have also provided instructions for gelatine (see variation).

> 250–280 g (9–10 oz/2–2¼ cups) raspberries
> ¾ teaspoon agar powder
> 2 teaspoons–1 tablespoon golden caster (superfine) sugar
>   or maple syrup, or to taste
> ½ quantity genoise sponge cake baked into 12 patty cakes (see page 294)
> 135 g (4¾ oz/1½ cups) desiccated coconut

Place the raspberries in a fine sieve and place over a bowl. (If using frozen raspberries, thaw them first.) Using the back of a spoon, push the raspberries through the sieve to make a lovely purée. You will need 375 ml (13 fl oz/1½ cups) of purée so, if necessary, add water to make up the difference. Discard the seeds and pulp.

Place the purée in a small saucepan, whisk in the agar powder, then place over low heat and bring to the boil, stirring frequently to prevent the agar sticking to the bottom. When the mixture comes to the boil, simmer gently, stirring frequently, for another 5–8 minutes or until the agar is dissolved. Add the sweetener to taste—it shouldn't be too strong, as the cake will also add sweetness, then simmer for another 1–2 minutes.

Pour the mixture into a large, shallow dish—I use a 20 cm (8 inch) square baking dish—and allow to stand until the jelly begins to thicken. Agar thickens and sets at room temperature, so the jelly will still be warm when you begin to dip the cakes into the jelly. You do not want the jelly too thick, as it needs to 'soak' into the cake a little.

Place a wire rack over a tray and put the coconut in a large shallow dish beside it. You won't use all the coconut, but you need a good amount to 'bury' the wet cakes and make them easy to coat and handle.

Working with one at a time, dip the cakes into the jelly, turning to coat all over, allowing a little to soak in. Place the cakes in the coconut and cover well, handling them as little as possible—they are still very moist at this stage and the jelly may be displaced with too much handling. Place on the wire rack and leave to stand for 30 minutes before placing on a plate and refrigerating for another 30 minutes or until set. The cakes will keep, covered, for 3–4 days in the fridge.

 VARIATION

Gelatine-based jelly Bring the raspberry purée to the boil, and turn off the heat. Add 3 teaspoons Bernard Jensen gelatine (see page 63) and stir well until dissolved. Pour the mixture into a large, shallow dish— I use a 20 cm (8 inch) square baking dish—and allow it to stand in the fridge until the jelly begins to thicken.

Drinks—true and natural

COMMERCIAL FRUIT JUICES AND BOTTLED DRINKS would have to be one of the best examples of how poor processed foods have become. Made with juice concentrates, large amounts of refined sugar, high-fructose corn syrup (HFCS) and chemicals for colour and flavour, they no longer even taste good. Yet it's very easy to make fabulous drinks using real ingredients, with no need for any chemical additives. Good, ripe fruit will generally provide most of the sweetness required, with a little support from honey, maple syrup or agave nectar. These drinks keep well in the fridge and can be turned into a fizzy drink with the addition of sparkling water.

Bee happy lemonade

GLUTEN FREE / DAIRY FREE
Makes 6½ cups

Honey is such a nourishing food in its own right and a beautiful match with lemon. This is a refreshing drink at any time, especially on hot days.

  60 ml (2 fl oz/¼ cup) honey
  125 ml (4 fl oz/½ cup) strained lemon juice (about 2 lemons)
  10–12 mint leaves
  ice cubes, to serve

Place the honey in a small heatproof bowl with 1 litre (35 fl oz/4 cups) of warm water. Whisk through until the honey is dissolved, then pour into a jug and add another 500 ml (17 fl oz/2 cups) of cold water and the lemon juice. Stir through and add the mint leaves and ice cubes, as desired.

Berry agua fresca

GLUTEN FREE / DAIRY FREE

Makes 750 ml (26 fl oz/3 cups) concentrate

This classic Mexican drink is made up of lightly sweetened fruit and water. Use any type of berry—melons are also great. My preference for sweetening this drink is to use golden caster sugar, as its flavour doesn't overpower the fresh fruit. This is beautiful served with edible flowers sprinkled into the jug and a little rose water.

260 g (9¼ oz/2½ cups) strawberries, hulled and cut into small pieces (if using raspberries, leave whole)
1½–2 tablespoons light agave nectar, honey or golden caster (superfine) sugar, or to taste
sparkling mineral water or water and ice cubes, to serve

The berries are measured as well-packed. If using frozen fruit, thaw before measuring.

Place the strawberries, 1½ teaspoons sweetener and 750 ml (26 fl oz/3 cups) water in a blender and process well. Taste and add a little more sweetener, if desired, then blend again, remembering that this will be diluted further. Strain to catch any pips, if you wish.

To serve, make up a jug with one-third of berry agua fresca and the remaining two-thirds of sparkling mineral water. Add ice cubes, as desired.

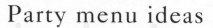

Party menu ideas

GENERALLY, CHILDREN DON'T REALLY EAT MUCH at birthday parties as they are far too busy playing. Regardless of their age, it's best to provide food in small, easy-to-grab and easy-to-eat portions. A well-structured menu for a birthday party would include the following.

SOMETHING FRESH

- *Fruit* Spring and summer bring delicious berries and stone fruit and there would be few children who could resist them. Large fruits, such as melons (of all descriptions), are great when cut into shapes with a cookie cutter.
- *Vegetables* Best served with a dip of some kind. Try the lime and coriander hummus (see page 233) or the funky bright green broad bean dip (see page 164) in a bowl, with sticks of carrot and celery stuck in the dip to mimic a hedgehog and cherry tomatoes for eyes. Small broccoli florets (blanched and lightly cooked) make a great forest when planted in a dip.

SAVOURY FOODS

- Mini sandwiches with egg and olive spread (see page 165); creamy chicken mayonnaise sandwich filling (see page 235); delicious avocado (see page 162) with vegetable and nut pâté (see page 163); or lentil and walnut pâté (see page 234) with goat's cheese. There are many good light breads made from sprouted grain flours and these are perfect for birthday party sandwiches.
- Tombolas (see pages 156 and 226)
- Rustic tray-baked vegetable tart (see page 236)
- Potato and sweet potato pizzettes (see page 253)
- Corn and zucchini fritters (see page 183) with pesto (see pages 230–232)
- Bright and happy quinoa salad (see page 252)

SOMETHING NUTRIENT DENSE

This is what stops them going crazy and helps to give a good foundation to their party eating. Ideally, it will mean protein and/or fat.

- Hard-boiled eggs, served in a variety of ways. Shell the eggs and cut them in half lengthways. Remove the yolk and mash with a little mayonnaise (see page 166) or yoghurt (see page 98) and herbs and place back in. As children get older they may enjoy a little added curry powder and chutney. Or top them with a halved cherry tomato and make them look like little mushrooms by dotting cream cheese on the tomato.
- Vegetable and nut pâté (see page 163), lentil and walnut pâté (see page 234) or liver pâté (see page 138) thickly spread on small bits of toast.
- Chicken fingers (see page 190) with sweet and sour dipping sauce (see page 248)
- Fish fingers with tartare sauce (see page 258)
- As children get older, mini burgers. Buy some good bread rolls and make little mince patties using the meatball recipe (see page 197); shape the mixture into patties and fry. Or use sweet potato patties (see page 180) for a vegetarian version. Spread each roll with butter and fill with a patty, avocado, chopped lettuce, sliced tomato and tomato sauce.

SOMETHING SWEET, BUT NOT TOO SWEET

- Super toddler blueberry and coconut creamy popsicles (see page 207)
- Pure fruit and coconut ice dream (see page 209)
- Jelly cakes (see page 312)
- Oat and spelt crackers (see page 211)
- Jelly boats (see page 311)
- Popcorn with sea salt (see page 309) and caramel nut popcorn (see page 310)

BIRTHDAY CAKE

The birthday cake is the centre of the celebration—this is the place to let your imagination soar. Pages 293–308 offer recipes, ideas and suggestions to help you make delicious, memorable birthday cakes for your child.

GLOSSARY
and
RECOMMENDED READING

*Don't be put off by some of these
ingredients, if you haven't heard of
them before and think that they will be
difficult to find—they're not. All of them
can be found in health food stores,
and many can also be found in the
natural foods section of your local
supermarket. It just might take a little
time to find them when
you're new to it.*

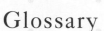

Glossary

ADZUKI BEANS Considered the king of beans in Japan and extremely nourishing for the kidneys, adzuki beans are also much easier to digest than other beans. (See *How to cook beans*, page 84.)

APPLE CIDER VINEGAR Unfiltered apple cider vinegar (a naturally fermented vinegar made from apples) is a health-promoting vinegar, and an extremely rich source of potassium. It is the best choice for making chutneys and pickling.

BARLEY (GLUTEN) Barley is a high-starch grain, wonderful for use in winter soups. As the soup cooks, the starch helps to thicken it while providing flavour, texture and creaminess. For this reason, it is also a good alternative to rice for a winter risotto. The most commonly used barley has two hard inedible husks. Thus, most barley is milled to some degree to make it edible. There are three main types. *Naked barley* is an old variety, no longer popular due to its low yield. It naturally occurs with little husk and is less refined than pearled barley. *Natural barley* is most often a naked barley with the small amount of husk removed, so all of the germ and bran is left intact. Good organic or biodynamic *pearled barley* has had the outer husks removed, with most of the germ and bran left intact, and is brownish in appearance. Supermarket-bought pearled barley removes all but the inner white starch and is highly refined. I prefer organic or biodynamic pearled barley as it is not quite as hefty as the natural or naked, but still has a large amount of goodness. Barley is also available as rolled barley (barley flakes) and barley meal. *Rolled barley* is made from barley that has been steamed and flattened so that it cooks quickly. *Barley meal*, excellent for porridge, is hulled barley that has been broken into small pieces, and requires only a short cooking time. (See also barley flour, page 54.)

BLACK (TURTLE) BEANS Deeply flavoured and delicious, black (turtle) beans are particularly good in Mexican dishes. Be careful when soaking them, as they can stain.

BLACK-EYED PEAS (BLACK-EYED BEANS, COWPEAS) These peas are popular in the United States and are excellent in soups, stews, dips and salads. (See *How to cook lentils and peas*, page 86.)

BORLOTTI (CRANBERRY) BEANS Great for stews and mash well for dips. When fresh, they take about 30 minutes to cook. (See *How to cook beans*, page 84.)

BROWN RICE (GLUTEN FREE) With the bran and germ intact, brown rice comes in long- and short-grain varieties. When buying brown rice, choose a brand that includes some green (unripe) grains, as this is an indication the grains have not been gassed to ripen them. Short-grain rice is generally stickier than long-grain and is the best choice for puddings, sushi and rice balls, where the stickiness is an advantage. Long-grain tends to remain separate and is preferable for savoury dishes, such as fried rice and pilafs, or on its own. Brown rice flour can be used as porridge, and is the essential flour for gluten-free baking. (See also *rice, sticky (glutinous) rice* and *wild rice* and *How to cook grains*, page 89.)

BUCKWHEAT (GLUTEN FREE) Technically not a grain at all, but rather a fruit related to the rhubarb family. Historically, it is a staple peasant food, most notably in the cold climate of Russia. When other crops failed, buckwheat was a grain that could be relied on, able to grow in the poorest soil. It has a distinctive nutty taste and an earthy quality that works well with root vegetables, onions and mushrooms. Buckwheat is high in protein (particularly lysine), is a rich source of B vitamins and a major source of the bioflavonoid rutin, which is good for the heart and circulation. Buckwheat has long been treasured as a health food in Japan, where it is known as soba. Technically, buckwheat is called *groats* when unroasted, and *kasha* when roasted. The unroasted groats are pale, almost light green and tan in colour, with a bland flavour that is enhanced by dry roasting. *Cracked buckwheat* is made from unroasted groats, broken down into smaller pieces. It can be used for porridge. (See also *soba noodles* and buckwheat flour, page 55).

BUTTER (LIMA) BEANS These beans are delicate and delicious. Be careful not to overcook them as they tend to crumble and disintegrate easily. Baby butter beans are also available and are wonderful in salads. (See *How to cook beans*, page 84.)

CANNELLINI (WHITE) BEANS These have a soft, mellow flavour. Be careful not to overcook them as they can lose their shape. (See *How to cook beans*, page 84.)

CHICKPEAS Technically a type of pea, chickpeas are most often categorised as a bean due to their long cooking time. They are excellent for dips, stews and salads, and work well with curry flavours. (See *How to cook beans*, page 84.)

COCOA POWDER This is really concentrated chocolate. It's made from roasted (the temperature for this varies) cocoa nibs which have been ground into a paste, then the fat (cocoa butter) is removed. What remains is cocoa powder. The natural acidity and tartness varies with the variety of bean (similar to coffee) and also increases when the fat is removed. As well as conventional cocoa powder you will come across *Dutch-processed cocoa powder*. Dutching is a process that uses an alkali to remove some of the acidity in cocoa, making it softer, darker and less bitter and acidic. Many Dutch-processed cocoas use harsh chemicals in the alkalising process and some are more processed than others. I use Organic Times, Rapunzel or Green & Blacks. They are all processed in a more wholesome manner, delivering a beautiful, full flavoured end result with much of the aggressive acidity and bitterness removed. I prefer not to use raw cocoa powder and raw chocolate products, for any age. Whilst they may indeed have a higher level of minerals and such, because of the very high level of anti-nutrients, such as phytic acid and oxalic acid, very few of those will actually be bio available and place extra stress on an immature digestive system. Rather, seek out the best quality, fermented and roasted cocoa and chocolate products.

CORN (MAIZE) (GLUTEN FREE) Corn is one of the most loved of grains. 'Corne' was the Old English word for the predominant grain of the land, so when the English first landed in the Americas and saw the abundance of maize they named it 'Indian corne'. There are many varieties of corn products and unfortunately they are often called by different names in different stores. Some varieties to look out for are blue- or red-coloured corn, which is usually ground into flour and used for tortillas in the United States and Mexico. Blue corn is higher in the amino acid, lysine, and has a fabulous flavour. (See also *polenta* and maize flour [golden cornflour], page 55).

GREAT NORTHERN BEANS These are white beans, larger than navy beans, with a beautiful creamy flesh. (See *How to cook beans*, page 84.)

KAMUT (GLUTEN) Like spelt, kamut is a precursor to what we know as wheat today and contains a more digestible form of gluten. Kamut is a deliciously flavoured grain—I especially like to buy pasta and spaghetti made from it. The flour (pharaoh's flour or Egyptian flour) is also lovely in small amounts in a shortcrust pastry, mixed with white spelt, lending it a very nutty and 'short' texture.

LENTILS A large range of lentils (often called dhal) are eaten throughout the world, and they are some of the best things to store in your pantry for a quick meal. *Tiny blue-green lentils* are small, hold their shape well and can be used in place of brown lentils. The best known tiny blue-green lentils are the French Puy lentils. *Brown lentils* are larger than a green lentil, but they both have a strong, deep, astringent taste. They hold their shape well, but can easily be puréed. *Black lentils* (caviar or beluga lentils) are less common than other varieties. They can be interchanged with green or brown lentils in recipes. *Split red lentils* are small and a vibrant orange/red colour and break down easily when cooked. Best used in soups, they can also add flavour and help to thicken dhals and pâtés. *Whole red lentils* are sold with their skins on, and resemble a small brown lentil, but inside are characteristically red. The skins of whole red lentils are quite astringent and need counterbalancing to soften the taste. They take longer to cook than the split red lentil. (See *How to cook lentils and peas*, page 86.)

MILLET (GLUTEN FREE) Millet is vastly underrated, but is a superb, gluten-free grain. It has as much or even more protein than wheat, is high in phosphorus and B vitamins and very high in iron. *Whole millet* has the husk still intact and birds love it. It is difficult for humans to digest, but is good for sprouting. Whole millet should be ground and will take about 1 hour to cook. *Hulled millet* has a lovely sweet, buttery taste. It responds particularly well to dry-roasting before cooking. Hulled millet is easier to digest than whole millet and is my preference when using millet. You can also buy *rolled millet* (millet flakes), which are the flattened whole millet grains. (See also millet flour, page 55, and *How to cook grains*, page 89.)

MIRIN (JAPANESE RICE WINE) This is a sweet and subtle wine, fermented from rice. It has an ability to harmonise harsh or discordant flavours and helps bring ingredients together. It is indispensable in lentil dishes, counterbalancing their astringency beautifully. True (unprocessed) mirin is fermented, producing enzymes and lactic acid bacteria traditionally valued for good health. It does, however, have an alcohol content of approximately 12 per cent—and the content for organic mirin is higher still.

MISO A fermented paste traditionally made from soya beans and salt, often with added grains. Koji (*Aspergillus orzae* culture) is added to cooked soya beans with salt and left to ferment. The longer this fermentation takes place, the stronger the flavour. Miso contains vitamin B12 and is an excellent alkaliniser. Unpasteurised miso is a rich source of live lactobacillus. Miso comes in a wide variety of flavours and colours. Two good misos are *genmai* (brown rice) miso and *shiro* (white rice) miso. Pasteurised genmai is useful for adding flavour and depth to soups and stews, and unpasteurised genmai miso is great as a spread or for miso soup. Shiro miso works well in dressings and dips to soften and bring flavours together.

MUNG (MOONG) BEAN AND DHAL Probably the most widely known of the dhal family, mung beans are small and yellow and cook quickly. They are an easy-to-digest and nourishing legume. When the mung bean is split and the skin is removed you have mung dhal—though in many cases some of the skin is still visible. (See *How to cook lentils and peas*, page 86.)

NAVY BEANS Creamy textured and sweet, these are the classic white bean for baked beans. (See *How to cook beans*, page 84.)

OATS (GLUTEN) Oats are higher in unsaturated fats than other grains and are usually thought of as a winter grain. This higher fat content provides energy for warming—hence their place in many cold-climate cultures, such as Scotland. This grain takes many different forms. Whole oats have the outer husk still intact and are generally sold for sprouting. *Oat groats* (oat kernels) are whole oats from which only the inedible outer hull has been removed. *Steel-cut oats* (sometimes called Scottish oats) are oat groats that have been cut into small pieces. *Rolled oats* (oat flakes) are probably the most common form of oats; they are oat groats that have been flattened. If you see rolled oats referred to as 'stabilised', this means that they have been steamed to make rolling easier. With their high fat content, oatmeal and oat flour are excellent alternatives to wheat and they have a beautiful, mild taste. *Oatmeal* refers to stabilised rolled oats that have been ground to a meal. This is then sifted to remove some of the bran and germ to give you *oat flour*. Thus oatmeal has more bran and germ and is heavier than oat flour.

PINTO BEANS Interchangeable with borlotti (cranberry) beans, pinto beans are excellent for any Mexican dish. They are sweet and lightly flavoured. (See *How to cook beans*, page 84.)

POLENTA (GLUTEN FREE) Made from a hard corn, polenta is available as both a coarsely and finely ground meal, and can come in a variety of colours, but is mostly yellow or white. In many cases the skin and germ are removed to extend shelf life. Search and ask for polenta that is made from corn with the germ intact (this type should be stored in the fridge to avoid spoilage). In many North American cookbooks polenta is often referred to as cornmeal.

QUINOA (GLUTEN FREE) Quinoa is technically not a grain, but a member of the *Chenopodium* plant family. Greatly revered by the ancient Incas, who called it 'the mother grain', quinoa boasts the highest protein content of any grain and is exceptionally high in B vitamins and calcium. It is a rich source of vitamin E and contains the amino acid, lysine. It is coated with saponin, a natural insecticide, and must be well washed before using. It is a wonderfully versatile grain with a delicate flavour and requires only a short cooking time. Traditionally, all quinoa is pre-soaked or at least well rinsed before using and when it is cooked, a tiny, white spiral appears, encircling the grain. Quinoa comes in a variety of colours: white, red and blue. Rolled quinoa (quinoa flakes), pasta and flour are all commercially available. (See *How to cook grains*, page 89.)

RED KIDNEY BEANS One of the harder beans to digest, red kidney beans work best in dishes that cook for a long time. They have a deep, strong flavour. (See *How to cook beans*, page 84.)

RICE (GLUTEN FREE) For many people with allergies, rice is one of the most easily tolerated grains as it is gluten free. Generally speaking, brown rice has a nuttier, stronger flavour than white rice and is more nutritious. *Basmati* and *jasmine* rice are two beautifully flavoured long-grain varieties. Unrefined brown basmati and jasmine rice are also available, but less common. (See also *brown rice, sticky [glutinous] rice* and *wild rice* and *How to cook grains*, page 89.)

SOBA NOODLES (GLUTEN FREE) Made from buckwheat flour, soba noodles are absolutely delicious in Asian-inspired noodle bowls, stir-fries or salads. Be selective when buying, however, as many soba noodles use half wheat flour.

SPLIT PEAS Dried *green split peas* are quite sweet and an excellent addition to vegetable soups, providing flavour and body. *Yellow split peas* are not as sweet, but excellent for soups, dips and dhal. (See *How to cook lentils and peas*, page 86.)

STICKY (GLUTINOUS) RICE (GLUTEN FREE) This rice can be both long- and short-grained, and has a high starch content a little like arborio, a rice used for making risotto. Sticky rice comes in black, white and even red grains; it is the essential ingredient for sticky rice puddings.

TAHINI A paste made from sesame seeds, and can be—but isn't aways—a rich source of calcium. Some people believe *unhulled tahini* is richer in calcium, but the calcium is bound in the oxalic acid in the hull of the seed, and is not readily available. For this reason I prefer to use the softer-flavoured *hulled tahini*, and include other calcium sources in my diet. Take care to buy good-quality tahini—for me this would be organic, since many conventional tahinis are made using seeds that have been hulled using a chemical process.

TAMARI A fermented soy sauce, similar to shoyu, used to enhance flavour. Tamari is widely assumed to be wheat free. This isn't actually so, although you can buy tamaris that are wheat free and salt reduced. Tamari is the soy sauce I most commonly use.

VANILLA Vanilla is enormously popular for flavouring cakes and desserts. Vanilla bean seeds are contained within the *vanilla bean* and impart a subtle flavour. Unlike *vanilla extract*, vanilla seeds do not affect the colour of the finished product, and so are preferable for some dishes. If using a natural vanilla extract, buy a good-quality one. Real vanilla extract will give a truer and more beautiful flavour, and basically just contains vanilla extractives and alcohol, whereas inferior ones contain corn syrup, glycerin, fructose, propylene glycol and preservatives. *Vanilla bean paste* is a paste of vanilla seeds suspended in a liquid—generally a sap such as inulin or tragacanth. One teaspoon of vanilla bean paste is the equivalent of one vanilla bean, and is a great option when you want a lot of vanilla flavour, without the colour that vanilla extract imparts.

VINEGAR True vinegar, traditionally produced, is the product of long fermentation over many months. Unpasteurised and unfiltered, it can be a rich source of many nutrients, and is very different to many instantly produced vinegars on the market today. Buy vinegar in glass—it is a solvent and will break down the polycarbons in plastic. (See also *apple cider vinegar*.)

WHEY When milk sours, lacto-fermentation takes place. The result is that the protein (which contains curds) separates from the watery—and extremely valuable—whey. (You will also end up with whey when making labne, see page 99). Whey is greatly beneficial for soaking grains, nuts and seeds as it helps make them easier to digest.

WILD RICE (GLUTEN FREE) Strictly speaking, this is not actually rice, but an aquatic grass seed. Nutritionally speaking, wild rice has more B vitamins and protein than other rice, and has a very assertive flavour. It is best used in combination with brown rice to soften the taste. Wild rice generally takes 1 hour to cook, with a ratio of 750 ml (26 fl oz/3 cups) of liquid to 190 g (6¾oz/1 cup) of wild rice. After cooking, allow it to sit and steam with the lid on for 10 minutes. (See recipe page 90.)

Recommended reading

Cowan, Thomas S. *The Fourfold Path to Healing: Working with the Laws of Nutrition, Therapeutics, Movement and Meditation in the Art of Medicine.* New Trends Publishing, 2004.

Planck, Nina. *Real Food: What to Eat and Why.* Bloomsbury, 2006.

Planck, Nina. *Real Food for Mother and Baby: The Fertility Diet, Eating for Two, and Baby's First Foods.* Bloomsbury, 2009.

Prentice, Jessica. *Full Moon Feast: Food and the Hunger for Connection.* Chelsea Green, 2006.

Price, Weston A. *Nutrition and Physical Degeneration.* Paul B. Hoeber, 1939.

Schmid, Rod. *The Untold Story of Milk: Green Pastures, Contented Cows and Raw Dairy Foods.* New Trends Publishing, 2003.

Index

This edition published in 2018 by Murdoch Books, an imprint of Allen & Unwin Pty Ltd
Originally published in 2010

Murdoch Books Australia
83 Alexander Street
Crows Nest NSW 2065
Phone: +61 (0) 2 8425 0100
www.murdochbooks.com.au
info@murdochbooks.com.au

Murdoch Books UK
Ormond House
26–27 Boswell Street
London WC1N 3JZ
Phone: +44 (0) 20 8785 5995
murdochbooks.co.uk
info@murdochbooks.co.uk

For Corporate Orders & Custom Publishing
contact our business development team at salesenquiries@murdochbooks.com.au

Publishing Director: Kay Scarlett
Project Editors: Jane Massam and Belinda So
Designer: Yolande Gray
Food Editor: Christine Osmond
Copy Editor: Desney King
Photographer: Natasha Milne
Stylist: Kate Brown
Production: Kita George
Additional photography from Getty Images (page 10) and by Jeff Atkinson (page 294).

ISBN: 978 1 76052 422 7 Australia
ISBN: 978 1 91163 209 2 UK

A cataloguing-in-publication entry is available from the catalogue of the National Library of Australia at nla.gov.au
A catalogue record for this book is available from the British Library

Printed in China by C&C Offset Printing Co. Ltd.

IMPORTANT: Those who might be at risk from the effects of salmonella, *E. coli* and listeria poisoning (the elderly, pregnant women, young children and those suffering from immune deficiency diseases) should consult their doctor with any concerns before consuming raw eggs or raw milk.

OVEN GUIDE: You may find cooking times vary depending on the oven you are using. For fan-forced ovens, as a general rule, set the oven temperature to 20°C (70°F) lower than indicated in the recipe.

The paper in this book is FSC® certified. FSC® promotes environmentally responsible, socially beneficial and economically viable management of the world's forests.